THE CONTACTS OF SHERLOCK HOLMES

...... to speak with to the number of the case you wish to ask about.

Use a '1' for the first case,
"The Final Portrait".

Use a '2' for the second case,
"The Missing Partner".

For example, to speak to John Watson about the first case, go to 31. To consult him regarding the second case, go to 32.

Your contacts are well informed on the details of your cases. If they speak of a person or place you aren't yet familiar with, it would be wise to research that lead.

Madame Hudson 1

Mrs. Hudson is Sherlock's landlord. She'll be able to tell you about the comings and goings at 221B Baker Street, or relay your messages.

John Watson 3

Doctor John Watson is Holmes' friend who has assisted him on many cases. His medical knowledge makes him especially useful in cases where an autopsy or other medical or anatomical expertise is required.

Wiggins 5

Wiggins is a street kid, a newspaper salesman, and the main contact for Holmes' street informants. He can keep you informed on the rumors around town.

Mycroft Holmes 7

Mycroft Holmes is Sherlock's older brother. He holds an important, but incredibly mysterious position in the British government. This affords him a great deal of access to valuable information.

Inspector Lestrade 9

Lestrade is an Inspector for Scotland Yard. He can give you access to certain confidential police information.

SHERLOCK HOLMES

The Challenge of Irene Adler

Author and Illustrator: CED / **Translation**: Adam Marostica
This book is a translation of the original *Sherlock Holmes le défi de Irène Adler* © Makaka Editions

Van Ryder Games and Graphic Novel Adventures are the Trademarks of Van Ryder Games LLC
ISBN : 978-0-9997698-6-7 Library of Congress Control Number: 2019903161

Published by Van Ryder Games and printed in China by Avenue 4. First Edition

English Layout: Evan Derrick and Shaun Varsos

Find printable investigation sheets and other Graphic Novel Adventures at www.vanrydergames.com

Character
Rules

Dear reader, the only accessory you need is a sheet of paper to note anything interesting or suspicious you find along the way. During this adventure, you may choose to embody either one of these two characters, each with their own abilities and allies at their disposal.

According to Holmes, Irene Adler is THE woman. During a previous investigation, she proved that she was just as discerning as he is.

She can pose four questions during each interrogation, and consult two of her contacts during each investigation.

If you are playing with two players, it is Irene that begins.

Sherlock Holmes is the most celebrated detective-consultant in London.

He can only pose three questions during each interrogation, but may consult three of his contacts during each investigation.

Certain questions may offend the people you interrogate, which in turn could cause them to refuse answering further questions.

> Note: When you present an object or a document to a suspect, you are not considered to be asking a question.

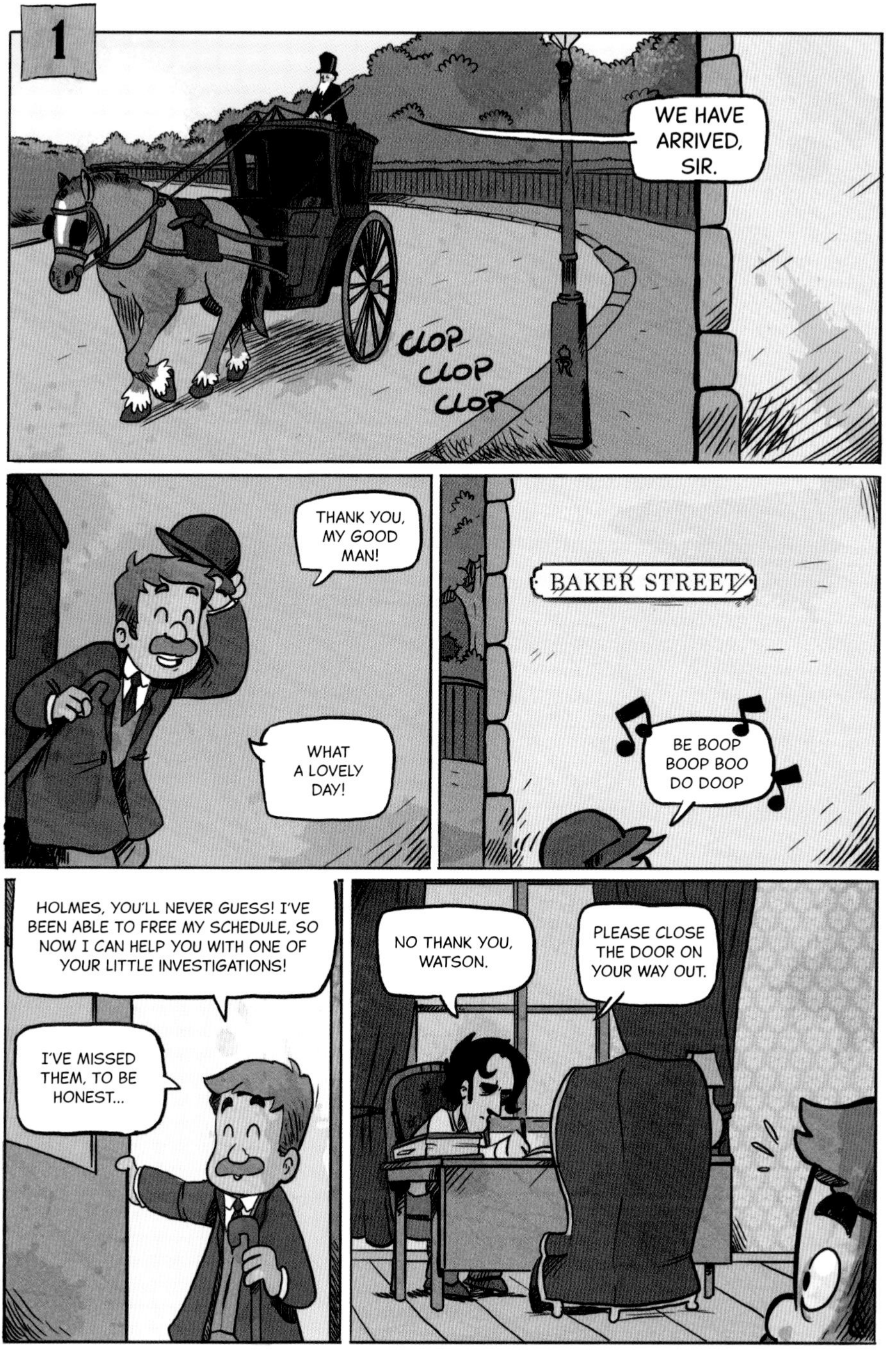
1
WE HAVE ARRIVED, SIR.
CLOP CLOP CLOP
THANK YOU, MY GOOD MAN!
WHAT A LOVELY DAY!
BAKER STREET
BE BOOP BOOP BOO DO DOOP
HOLMES, YOU'LL NEVER GUESS! I'VE BEEN ABLE TO FREE MY SCHEDULE, SO NOW I CAN HELP YOU WITH ONE OF YOUR LITTLE INVESTIGATIONS!
I'VE MISSED THEM, TO BE HONEST...
NO THANK YOU, WATSON.
PLEASE CLOSE THE DOOR ON YOUR WAY OUT.

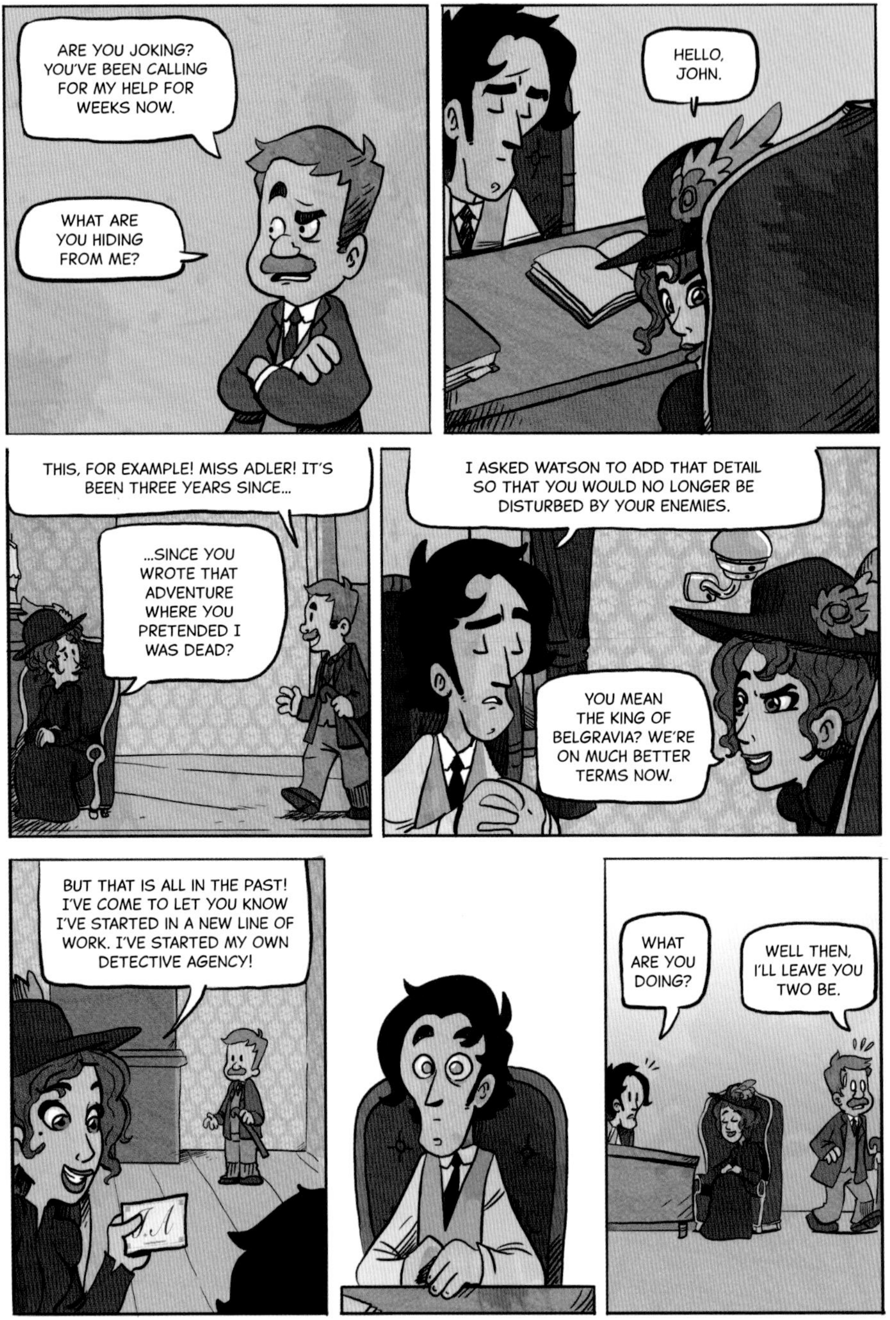
ARE YOU JOKING? YOU'VE BEEN CALLING FOR MY HELP FOR WEEKS NOW.
WHAT ARE YOU HIDING FROM ME?
HELLO, JOHN.
THIS, FOR EXAMPLE! MISS ADLER! IT'S BEEN THREE YEARS SINCE...
...SINCE YOU WROTE THAT ADVENTURE WHERE YOU PRETENDED I WAS DEAD?
I ASKED WATSON TO ADD THAT DETAIL SO THAT YOU WOULD NO LONGER BE DISTURBED BY YOUR ENEMIES.
YOU MEAN THE KING OF BELGRAVIA? WE'RE ON MUCH BETTER TERMS NOW.
BUT THAT IS ALL IN THE PAST! I'VE COME TO LET YOU KNOW I'VE STARTED IN A NEW LINE OF WORK. I'VE STARTED MY OWN DETECTIVE AGENCY!
I.A
WHAT ARE YOU DOING?
WELL THEN, I'LL LEAVE YOU TWO BE.

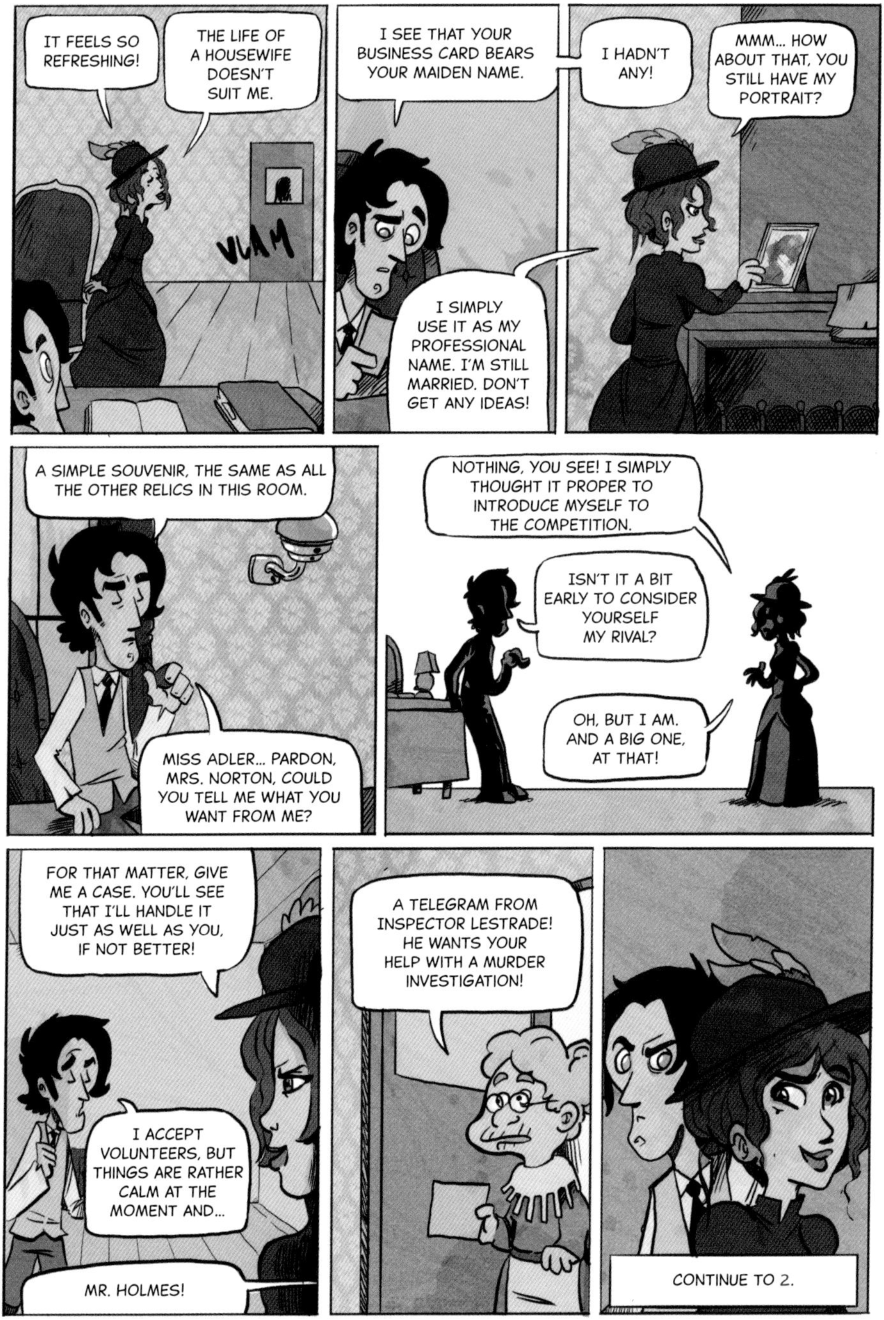
IT FEELS SO REFRESHING!
THE LIFE OF A HOUSEWIFE DOESN'T SUIT ME.
VLAM
I SEE THAT YOUR BUSINESS CARD BEARS YOUR MAIDEN NAME.
I SIMPLY USE IT AS MY PROFESSIONAL NAME. I'M STILL MARRIED. DON'T GET ANY IDEAS!
I HADN'T ANY!
MMM... HOW ABOUT THAT, YOU STILL HAVE MY PORTRAIT?
A SIMPLE SOUVENIR, THE SAME AS ALL THE OTHER RELICS IN THIS ROOM.
MISS ADLER... PARDON, MRS. NORTON, COULD YOU TELL ME WHAT YOU WANT FROM ME?
NOTHING, YOU SEE! I SIMPLY THOUGHT IT PROPER TO INTRODUCE MYSELF TO THE COMPETITION.
ISN'T IT A BIT EARLY TO CONSIDER YOURSELF MY RIVAL?
OH, BUT I AM. AND A BIG ONE, AT THAT!
FOR THAT MATTER, GIVE ME A CASE. YOU'LL SEE THAT I'LL HANDLE IT JUST AS WELL AS YOU, IF NOT BETTER!
I ACCEPT VOLUNTEERS, BUT THINGS ARE RATHER CALM AT THE MOMENT AND...
MR. HOLMES!
A TELEGRAM FROM INSPECTOR LESTRADE! HE WANTS YOUR HELP WITH A MURDER INVESTIGATION!
CONTINUE TO 2.

2

Rules
of Play

GAME RULES

Who is the better detective? Sherlock Holmes or Irene Adler? You can choose to play solo, or, like our two protagonists, you can challenge another reader.

If there is one player:

Choose the character you wish to be, then read the instructions below.

If there are two players:

Determine who will play as Holmes and who as Adler. If you should disagree, flip a gold sovereign to decide. If you don't have one, any coin will do.

All set? You will each conduct two investigations, one after the other. Irene Adler begins. After the first investigation, she'll pass the book to Holmes, then compare your results before proceeding to the second investigation.

The strengths of each character are on page 0. Irene Adler's investigation sheet and contacts are at the beginning of the book, and Sherlock's investigation sheet and contacts are at the end.

Extra challenge: Irene entrusted some street children to distribute her business cards. Between those that were given away and those that were lost, they're bound to be all over the place! Count them during your adventure and record them on your investigation sheet!

Now, go to 3.

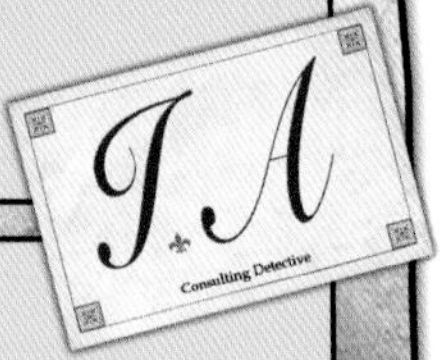
I.A
Consulting Detective

Investigation start reminders
Investigation 1: 3
Investigation 2: 172

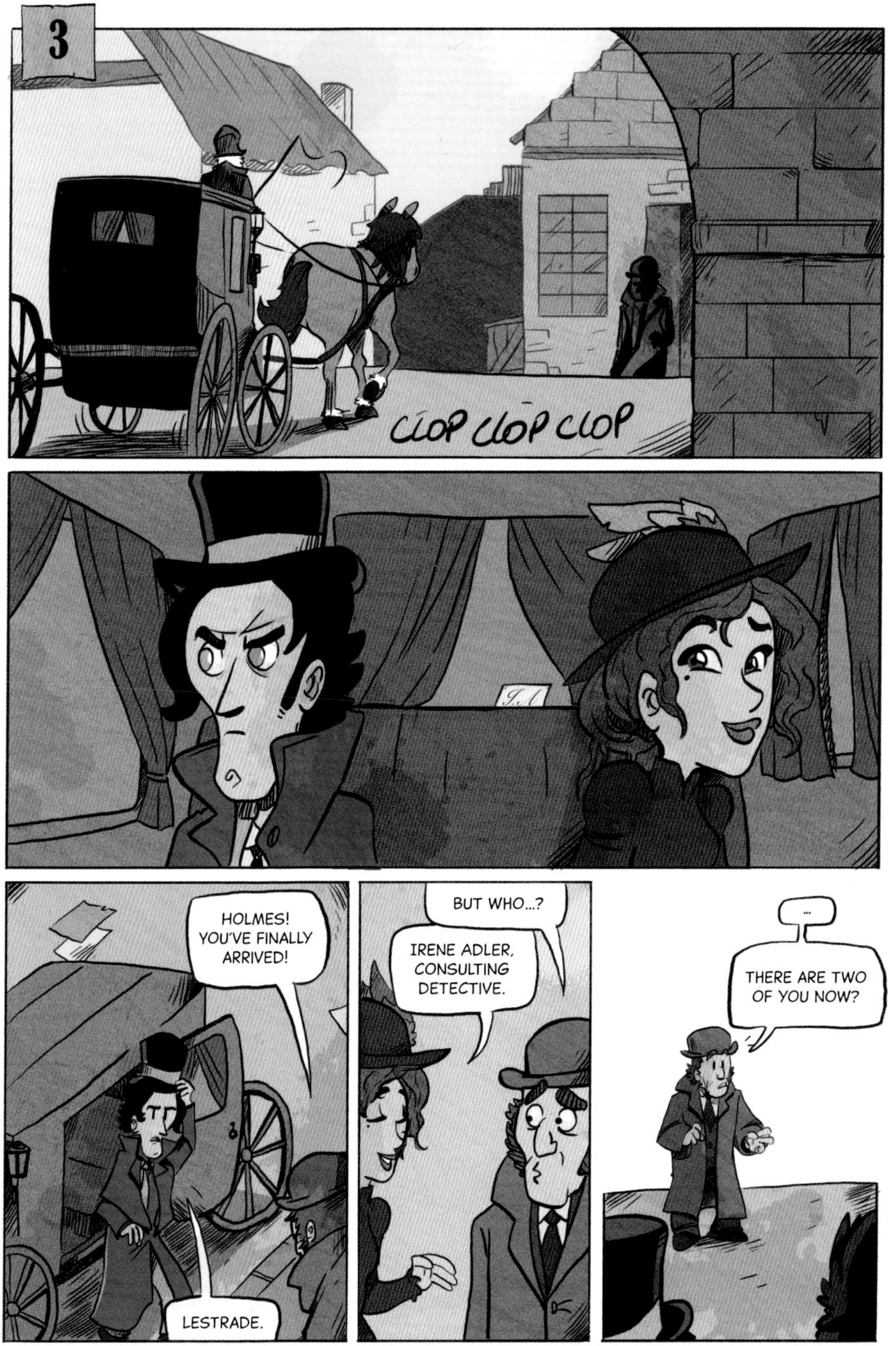
3
CLOP CLOP CLOP
HOLMES! YOU'VE FINALLY ARRIVED!
LESTRADE.
BUT WHO...?
IRENE ADLER, CONSULTING DETECTIVE.
...
THERE ARE TWO OF YOU NOW?

AM I DREAMING OR HAS DR. WATSON CHANGED HIS LOOK?

THE MURDER, LESTRADE...

ALRIGHT. ALRIGHT. THE VICTIM'S NAME IS JOHN GABRIEL HURT.

HE WAS KILLED THIS MORNING, HERE, IN HIS PAINTING STUDIO. WE'RE THINKING IT'S A BURGLARY GONE WRONG.

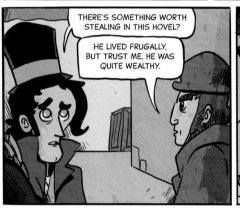

THERE'S SOMETHING WORTH STEALING IN THIS HOVEL?

HE LIVED FRUGALLY, BUT TRUST ME, HE WAS QUITE WEALTHY.

HURT WAS THE OFFICIAL PAINTER OF ROYALTY. HE WAS WELL LOVED AT BUCKINGHAM PALACE.

IT WAS THE QUEEN HERSELF WHO WAS RATHER INSISTENT WE CALL YOU.

OOOH...

IT WOULD SEEM RATHER FORTUITOUS I STOPPED BY.

WE GET TO THE STUDIO THROUGH THIS HALLWAY.

HOWEVER, THE KILLER BROKE A WINDOW TO GET IN.

DID THE NEIGHBORS HEAR ANYTHING?

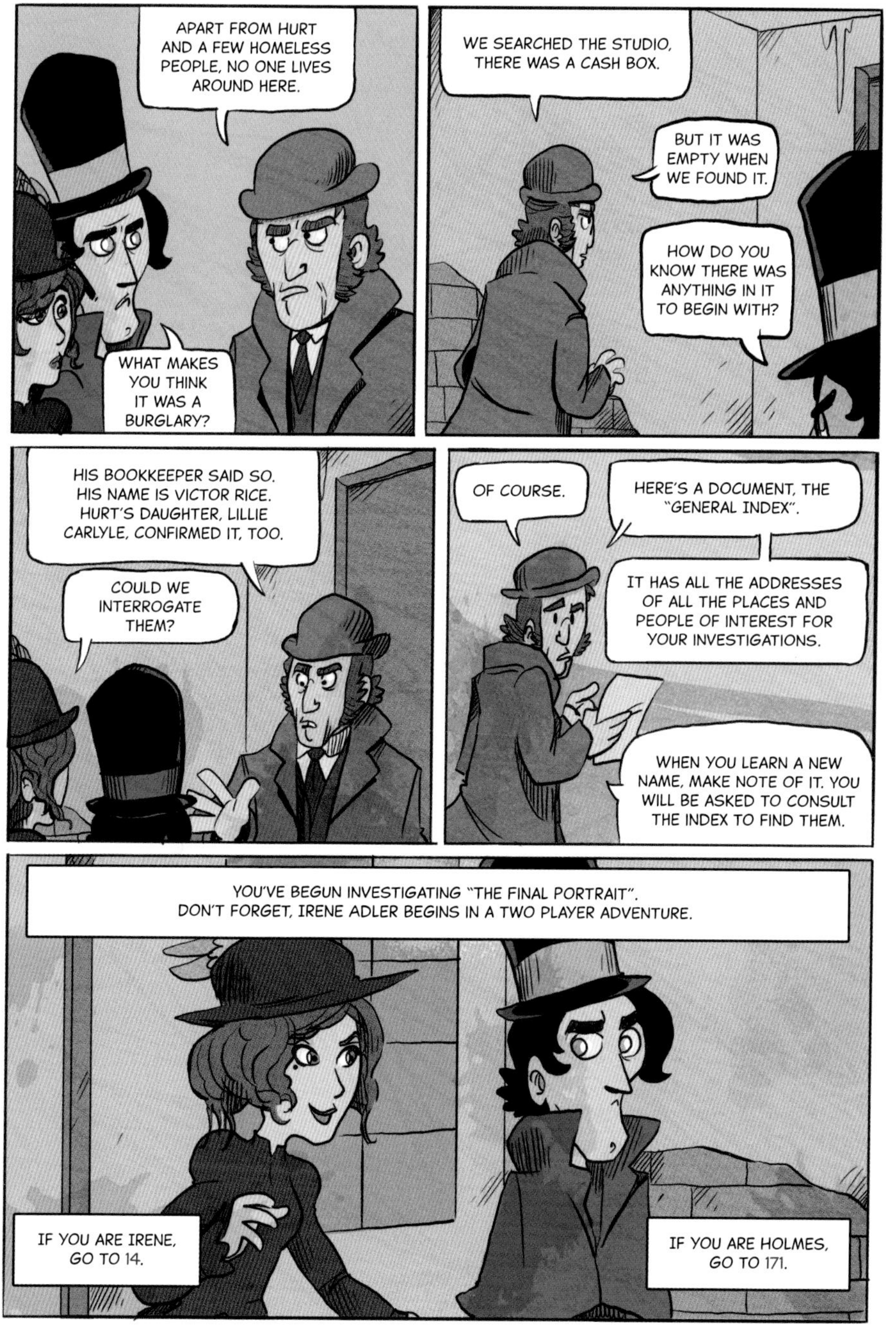
APART FROM HURT AND A FEW HOMELESS PEOPLE, NO ONE LIVES AROUND HERE.
WHAT MAKES YOU THINK IT WAS A BURGLARY?
WE SEARCHED THE STUDIO, THERE WAS A CASH BOX.
BUT IT WAS EMPTY WHEN WE FOUND IT.
HOW DO YOU KNOW THERE WAS ANYTHING IN IT TO BEGIN WITH?
HIS BOOKKEEPER SAID SO. HIS NAME IS VICTOR RICE. HURT'S DAUGHTER, LILLIE CARLYLE, CONFIRMED IT, TOO.
COULD WE INTERROGATE THEM?
OF COURSE.
HERE'S A DOCUMENT, THE "GENERAL INDEX".
IT HAS ALL THE ADDRESSES OF ALL THE PLACES AND PEOPLE OF INTEREST FOR YOUR INVESTIGATIONS.
WHEN YOU LEARN A NEW NAME, MAKE NOTE OF IT. YOU WILL BE ASKED TO CONSULT THE INDEX TO FIND THEM.
YOU'VE BEGUN INVESTIGATING "THE FINAL PORTRAIT".
DON'T FORGET, IRENE ADLER BEGINS IN A TWO PLAYER ADVENTURE.
IF YOU ARE IRENE, GO TO 14.
IF YOU ARE HOLMES, GO TO 171.

ALL THAT FOR THIS? NOTHING TO SEE HERE, GO TO 162.

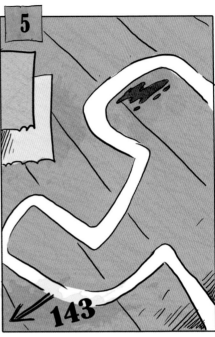

143

IT'S A DEAD END. WE HAVE NO SUSPECTS.

RETURN TO 66.

WHAT NOW?

Return to the crime scene 98

Consult the General Index 194

Consult your contacts (start of the book for Irène, end of the book for Sherlock)

I understand and I want to solve the case! 68

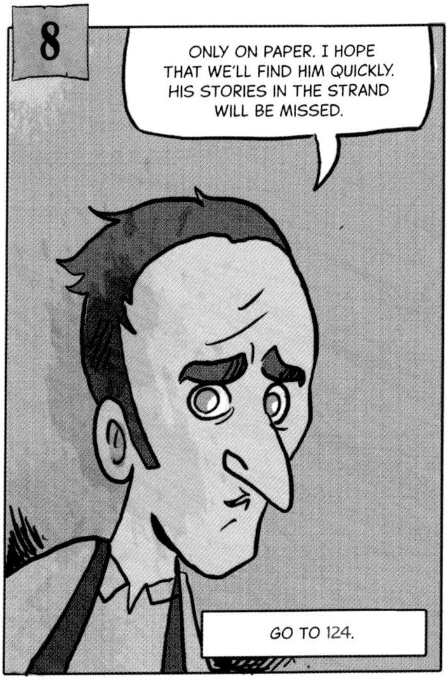
8
ONLY ON PAPER. I HOPE THAT WE'LL FIND HIM QUICKLY. HIS STORIES IN THE STRAND WILL BE MISSED.
GO TO 124.

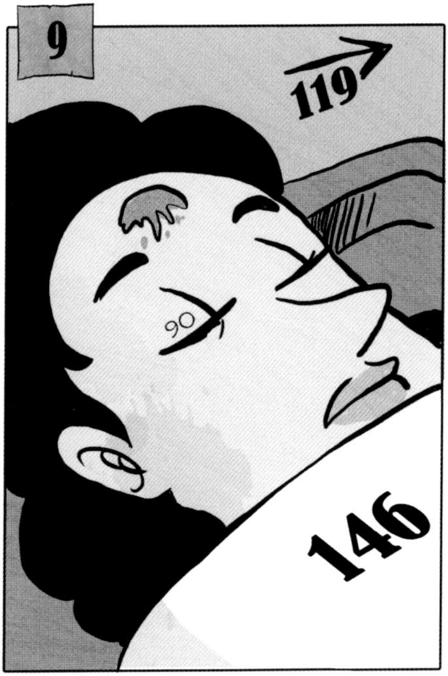
9
119
90
146

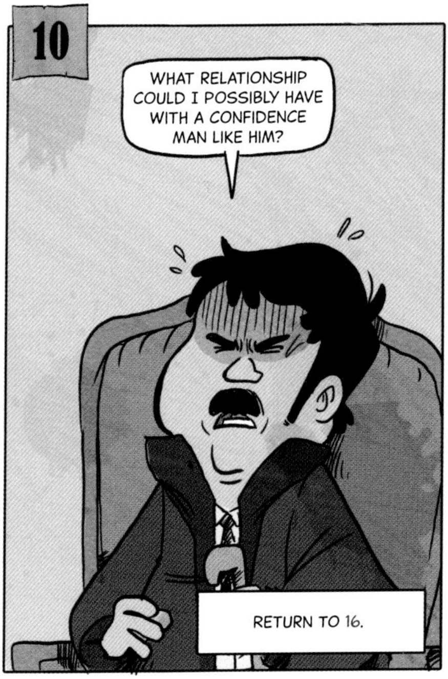
10
WHAT RELATIONSHIP COULD I POSSIBLY HAVE WITH A CONFIDENCE MAN LIKE HIM?
RETURN TO 16.

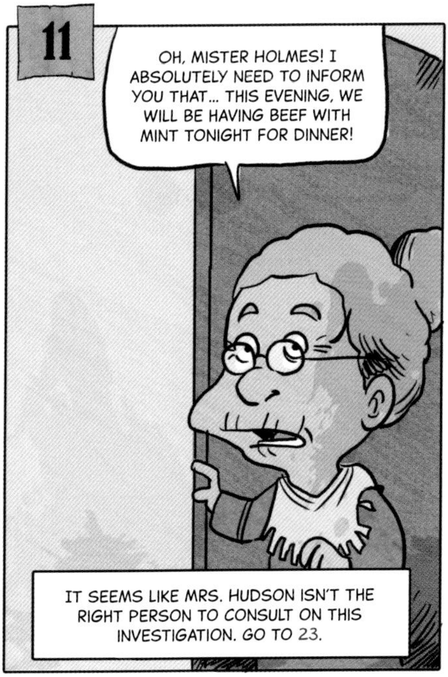
11
OH, MISTER HOLMES! I ABSOLUTELY NEED TO INFORM YOU THAT... THIS EVENING, WE WILL BE HAVING BEEF WITH MINT TONIGHT FOR DINNER!
IT SEEMS LIKE MRS. HUDSON ISN'T THE RIGHT PERSON TO CONSULT ON THIS INVESTIGATION. GO TO 23.

12

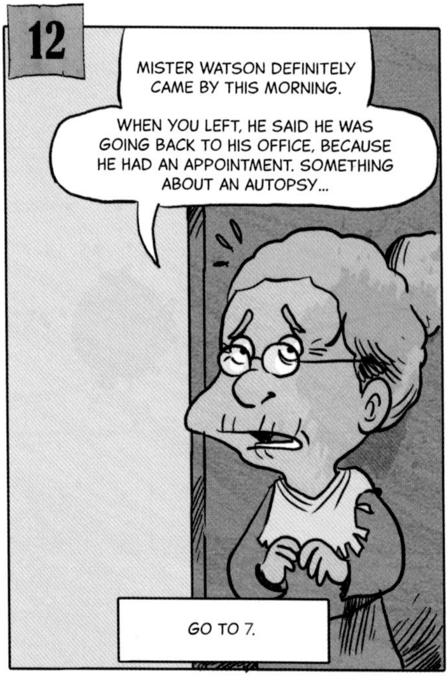
MISTER WATSON DEFINITELY CAME BY THIS MORNING.
WHEN YOU LEFT, HE SAID HE WAS GOING BACK TO HIS OFFICE, BECAUSE HE HAD AN APPOINTMENT. SOMETHING ABOUT AN AUTOPSY...
GO TO 7.

13

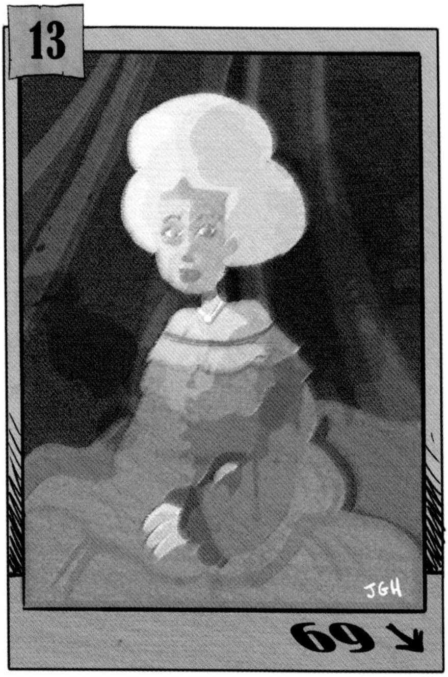
JGH
69

14

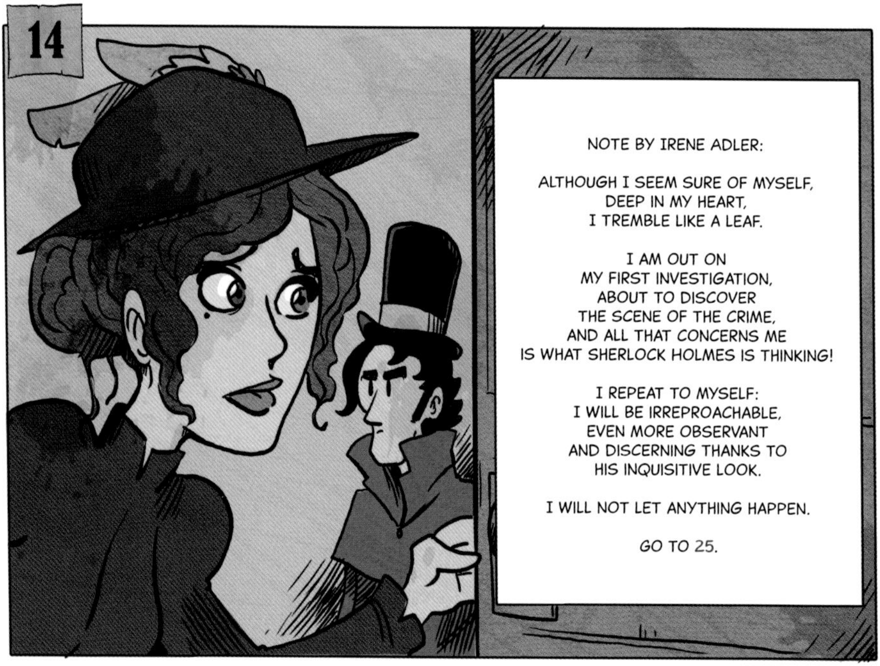
NOTE BY IRENE ADLER:
ALTHOUGH I SEEM SURE OF MYSELF, DEEP IN MY HEART, I TREMBLE LIKE A LEAF.
I AM OUT ON MY FIRST INVESTIGATION, ABOUT TO DISCOVER THE SCENE OF THE CRIME, AND ALL THAT CONCERNS ME IS WHAT SHERLOCK HOLMES IS THINKING!
I REPEAT TO MYSELF: I WILL BE IRREPROACHABLE, EVEN MORE OBSERVANT AND DISCERNING THANKS TO HIS INQUISITIVE LOOK.
I WILL NOT LET ANYTHING HAPPEN.
GO TO 25.

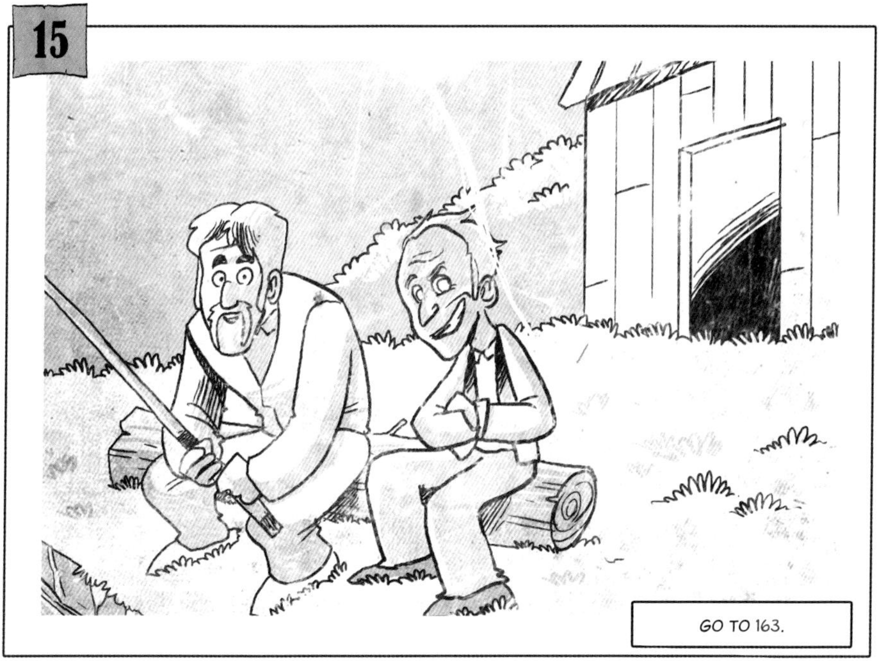
15
GO TO 163.

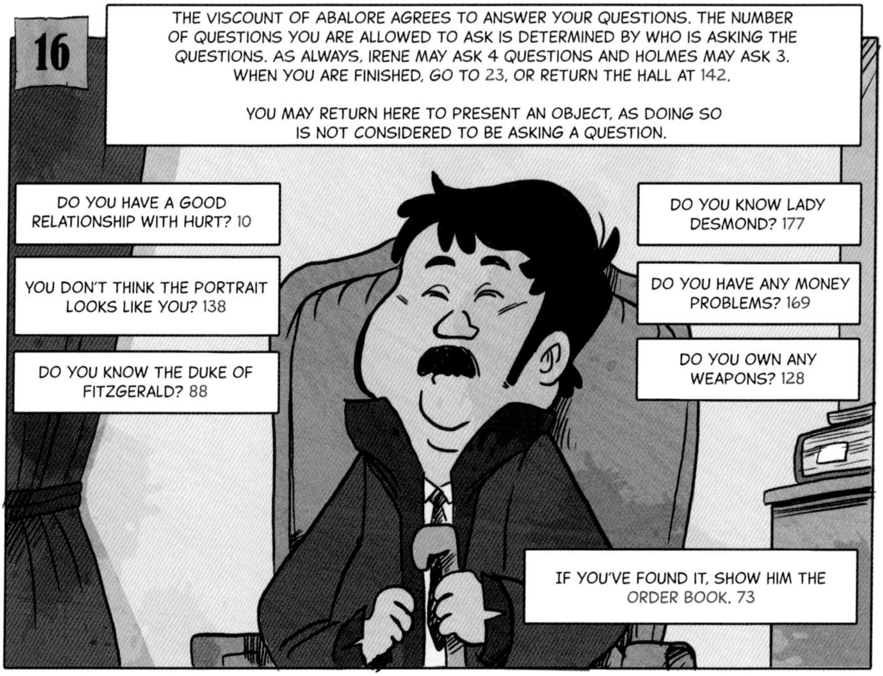
16
THE VISCOUNT OF ABALORE AGREES TO ANSWER YOUR QUESTIONS. THE NUMBER OF QUESTIONS YOU ARE ALLOWED TO ASK IS DETERMINED BY WHO IS ASKING THE QUESTIONS. AS ALWAYS, IRENE MAY ASK 4 QUESTIONS AND HOLMES MAY ASK 3. WHEN YOU ARE FINISHED, GO TO 23, OR RETURN THE HALL AT 142.
YOU MAY RETURN HERE TO PRESENT AN OBJECT, AS DOING SO IS NOT CONSIDERED TO BE ASKING A QUESTION.
DO YOU HAVE A GOOD RELATIONSHIP WITH HURT? 10
YOU DON'T THINK THE PORTRAIT LOOKS LIKE YOU? 138
DO YOU KNOW THE DUKE OF FITZGERALD? 88
DO YOU KNOW LADY DESMOND? 177
DO YOU HAVE ANY MONEY PROBLEMS? 169
DO YOU OWN ANY WEAPONS? 128
IF YOU'VE FOUND IT, SHOW HIM THE ORDER BOOK. 73

17

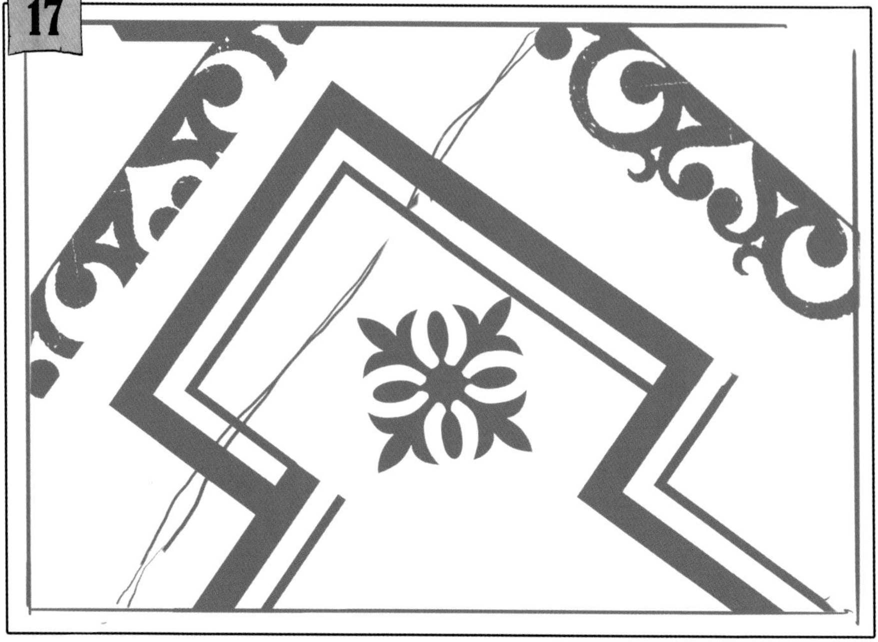

18

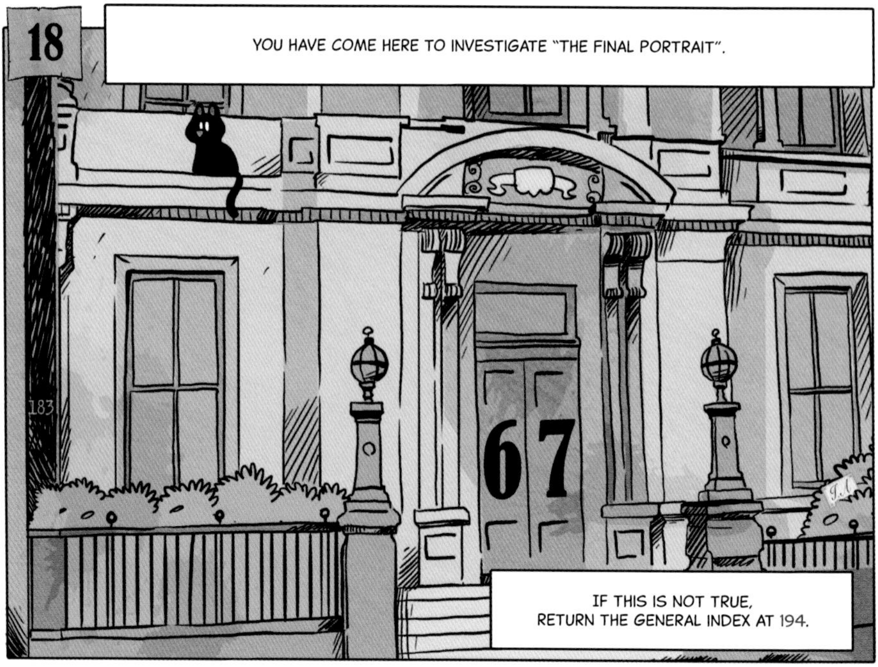
YOU HAVE COME HERE TO INVESTIGATE "THE FINAL PORTRAIT".
183
67
IF THIS IS NOT TRUE,
RETURN THE GENERAL INDEX AT 194.

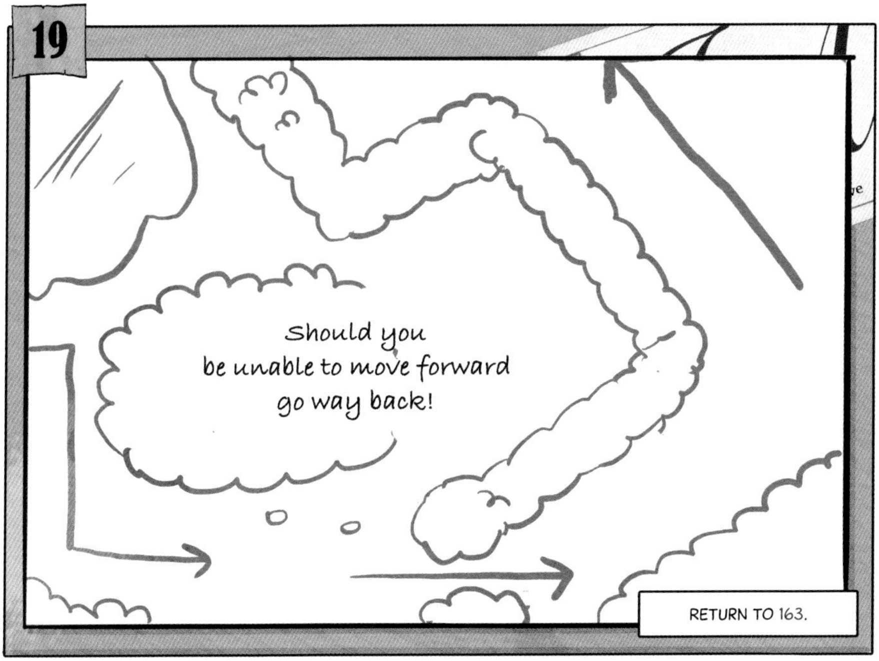
19
Should you be unable to move forward go way back!
RETURN TO 163.

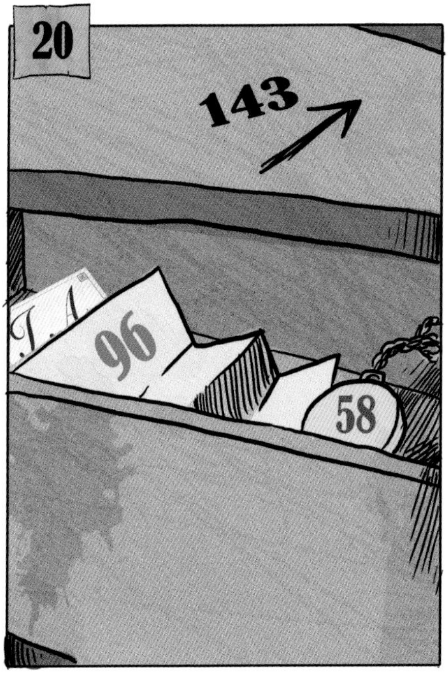
20
143
96
58

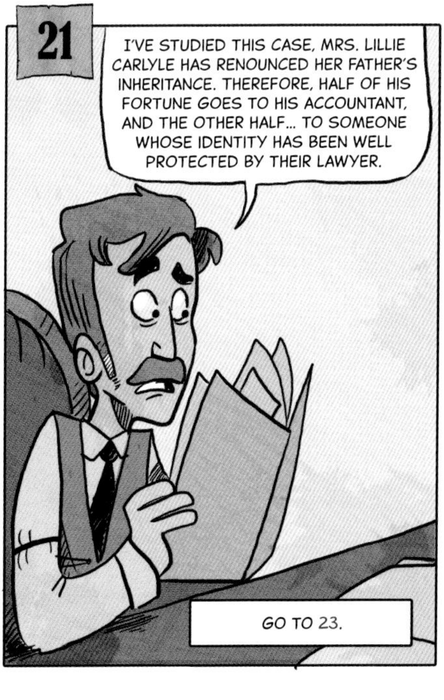
21
I'VE STUDIED THIS CASE, MRS. LILLIE CARLYLE HAS RENOUNCED HER FATHER'S INHERITANCE. THEREFORE, HALF OF HIS FORTUNE GOES TO HIS ACCOUNTANT, AND THE OTHER HALF... TO SOMEONE WHOSE IDENTITY HAS BEEN WELL PROTECTED BY THEIR LAWYER.
GO TO 23.

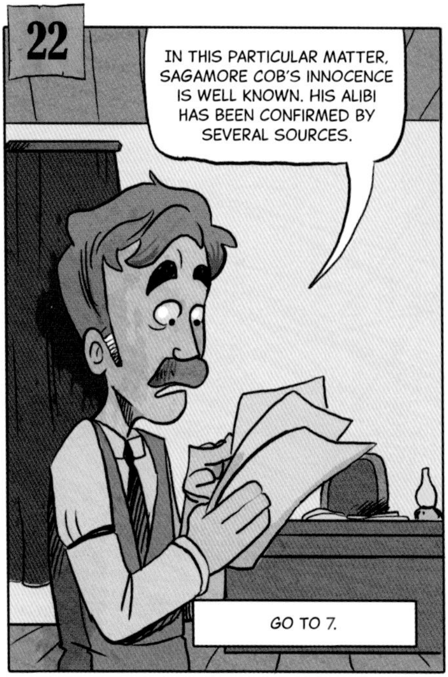
22
IN THIS PARTICULAR MATTER, SAGAMORE COB'S INNOCENCE IS WELL KNOWN. HIS ALIBI HAS BEEN CONFIRMED BY SEVERAL SOURCES.
GO TO 7.

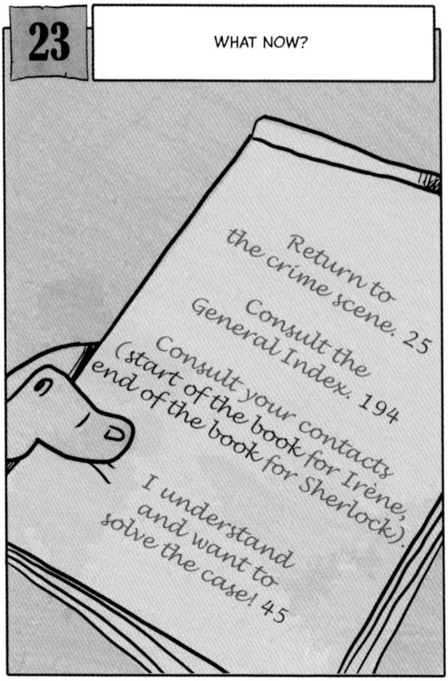
23
WHAT NOW?
Return to the crime scene. 25
Consult the General Index. 194
Consult your contacts (start of the book for Irène, end of the book for Sherlock).
I understand and want to solve the case! 45

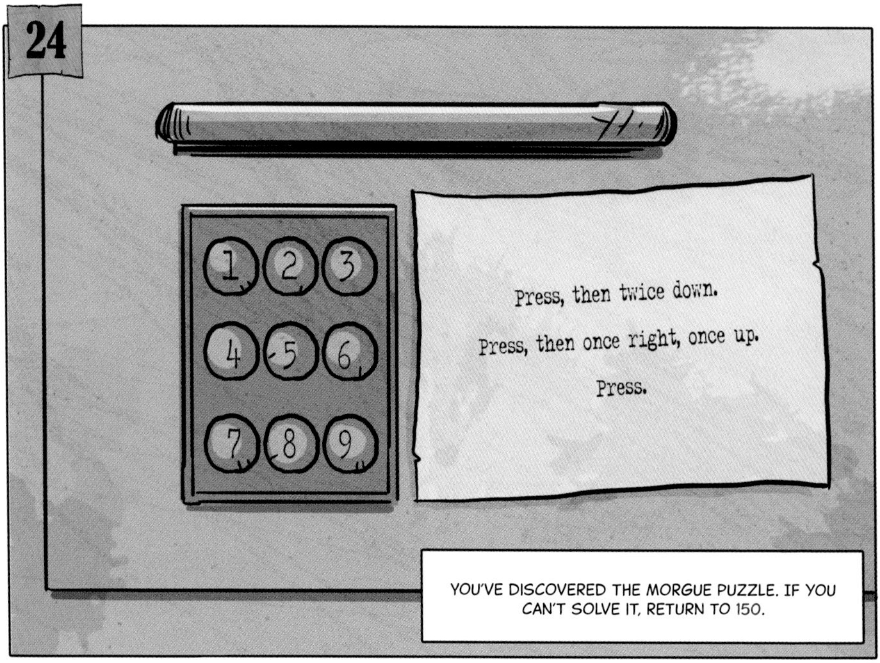
24
1 2 3
4 5 6
7 8 9
Press, then twice down.
Press, then once right, once up.
Press.
YOU'VE DISCOVERED THE MORGUE PUZZLE. IF YOU CAN'T SOLVE IT, RETURN TO 150.

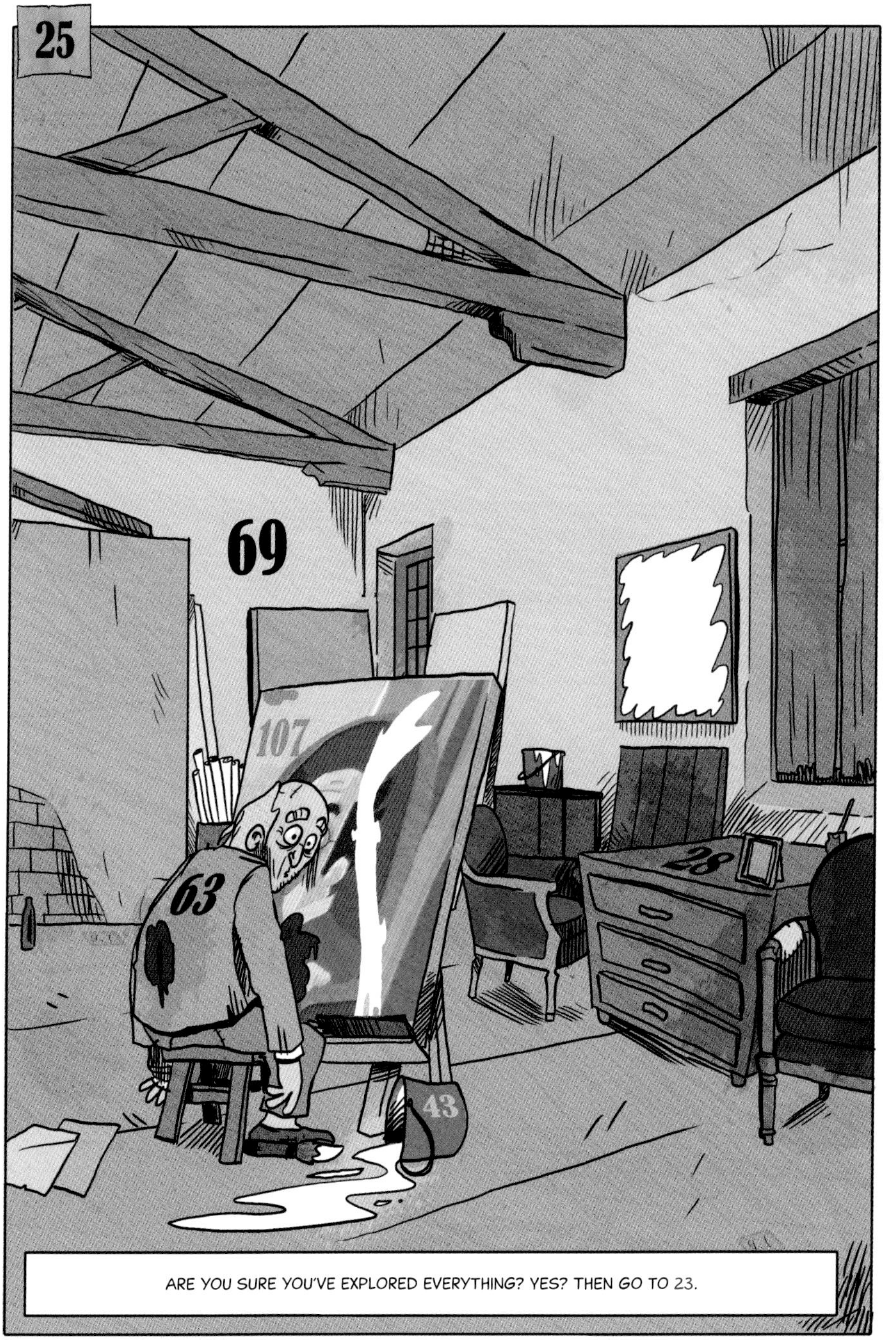
25
69
107
63
28
43
ARE YOU SURE YOU'VE EXPLORED EVERYTHING? YES? THEN GO TO 23.

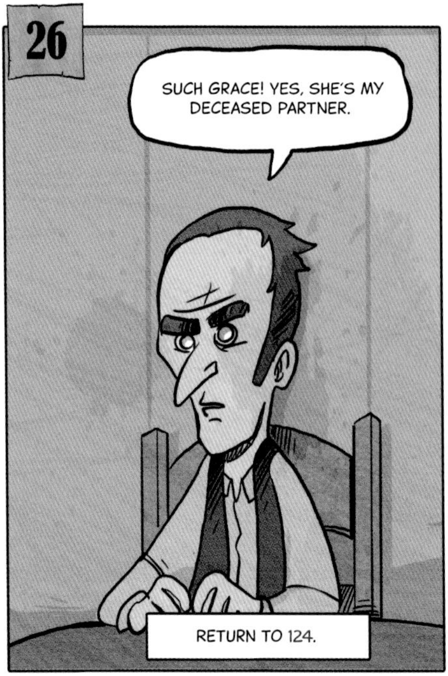
26
SUCH GRACE! YES, SHE'S MY DECEASED PARTNER.
RETURN TO 124.

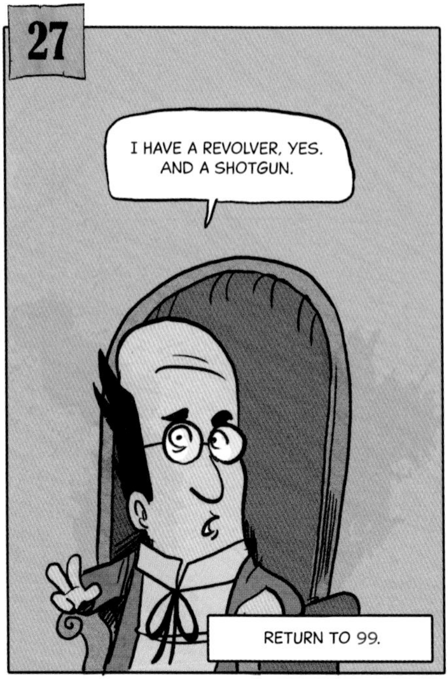
27
I HAVE A REVOLVER, YES. AND A SHOTGUN.
RETURN TO 99.

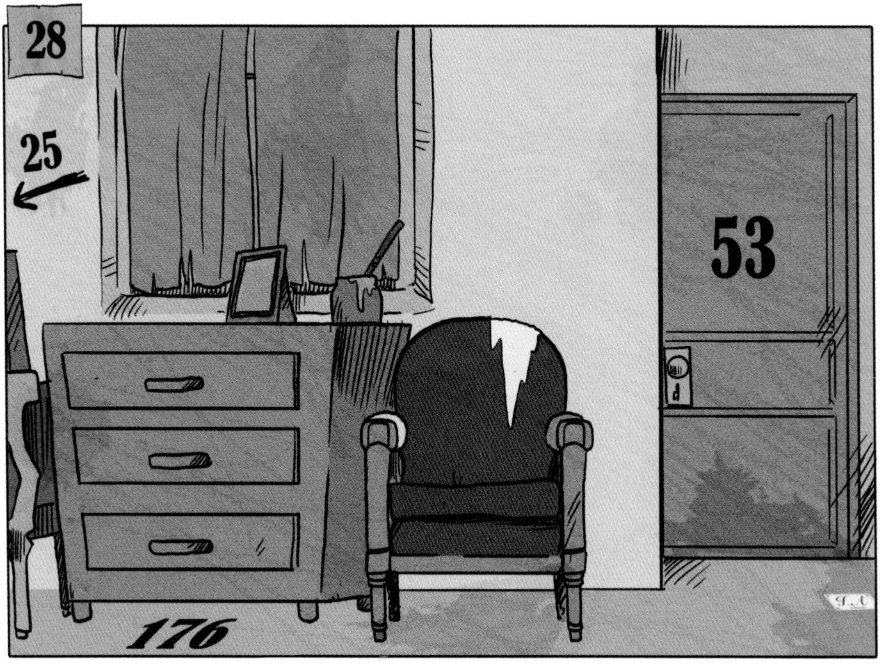
28
25
53
176

29

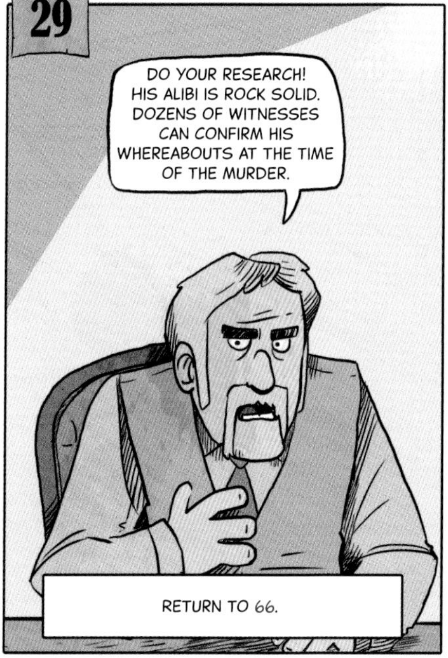
DO YOUR RESEARCH! HIS ALIBI IS ROCK SOLID. DOZENS OF WITNESSES CAN CONFIRM HIS WHEREABOUTS AT THE TIME OF THE MURDER.
RETURN TO 66.

30

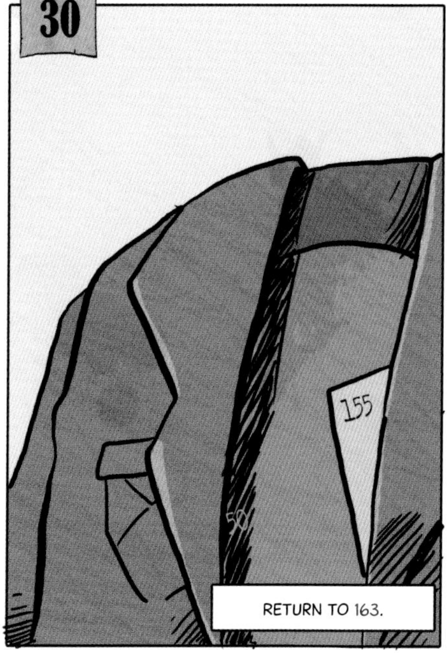
155
RETURN TO 163.

31

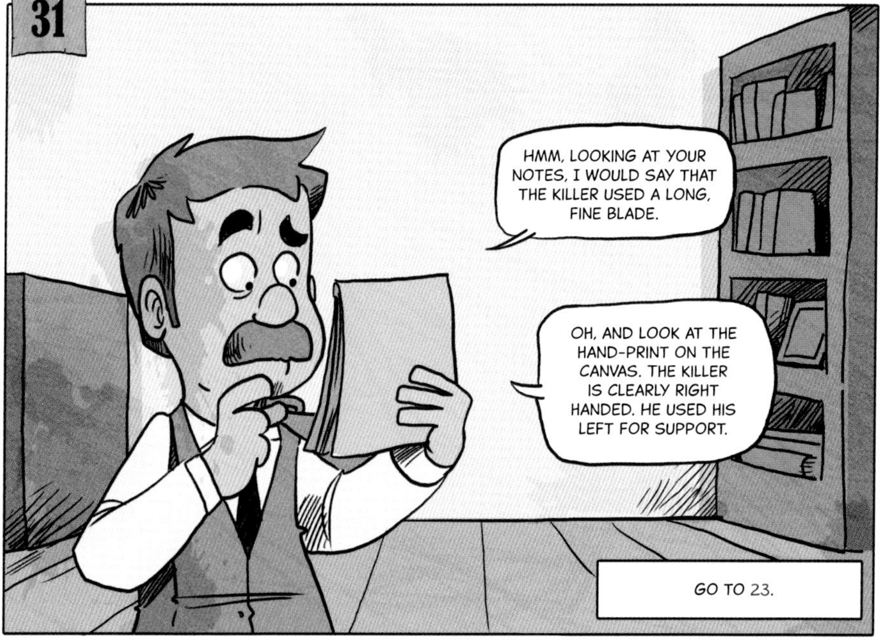
HMM, LOOKING AT YOUR NOTES, I WOULD SAY THAT THE KILLER USED A LONG, FINE BLADE.
OH, AND LOOK AT THE HAND-PRINT ON THE CANVAS. THE KILLER IS CLEARLY RIGHT HANDED. HE USED HIS LEFT FOR SUPPORT.
GO TO 23.

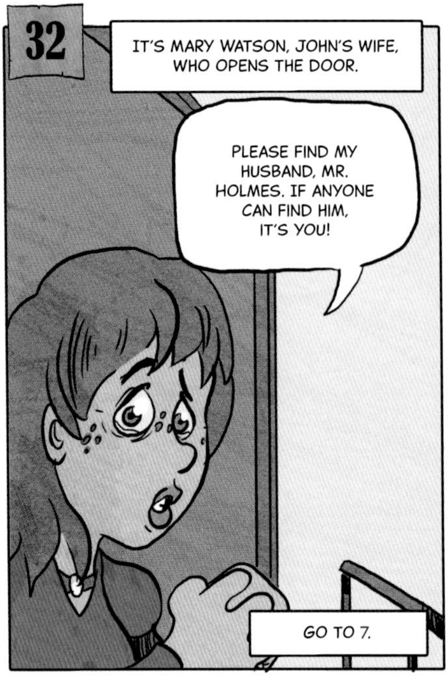
32
IT'S MARY WATSON, JOHN'S WIFE, WHO OPENS THE DOOR.
PLEASE FIND MY HUSBAND, MR. HOLMES. IF ANYONE CAN FIND HIM, IT'S YOU!
GO TO 7.

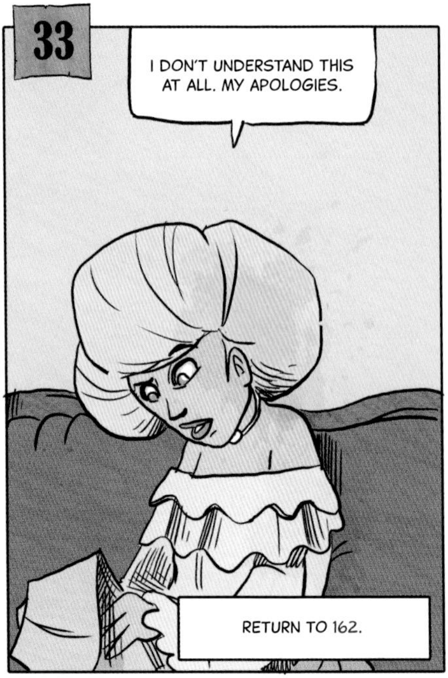
33
I DON'T UNDERSTAND THIS AT ALL. MY APOLOGIES.
RETURN TO 162.

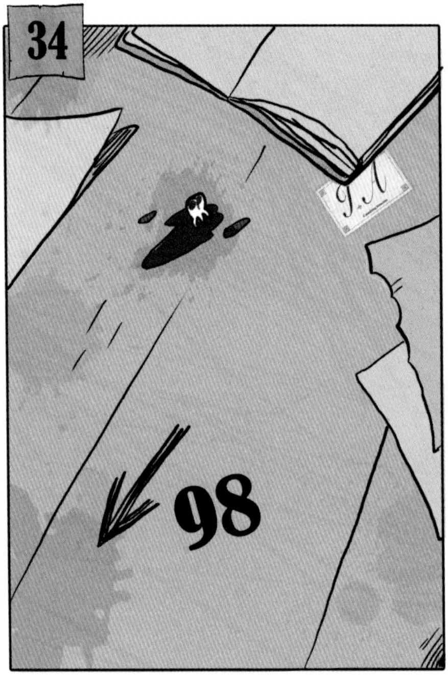
34
98

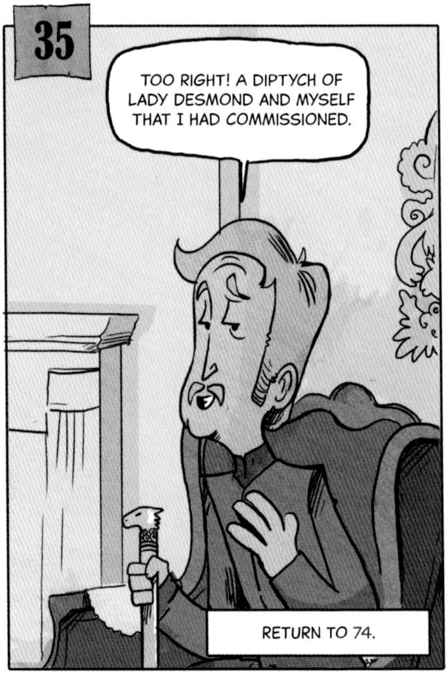
35
TOO RIGHT! A DIPTYCH OF LADY DESMOND AND MYSELF THAT I HAD COMMISSIONED.
RETURN TO 74.

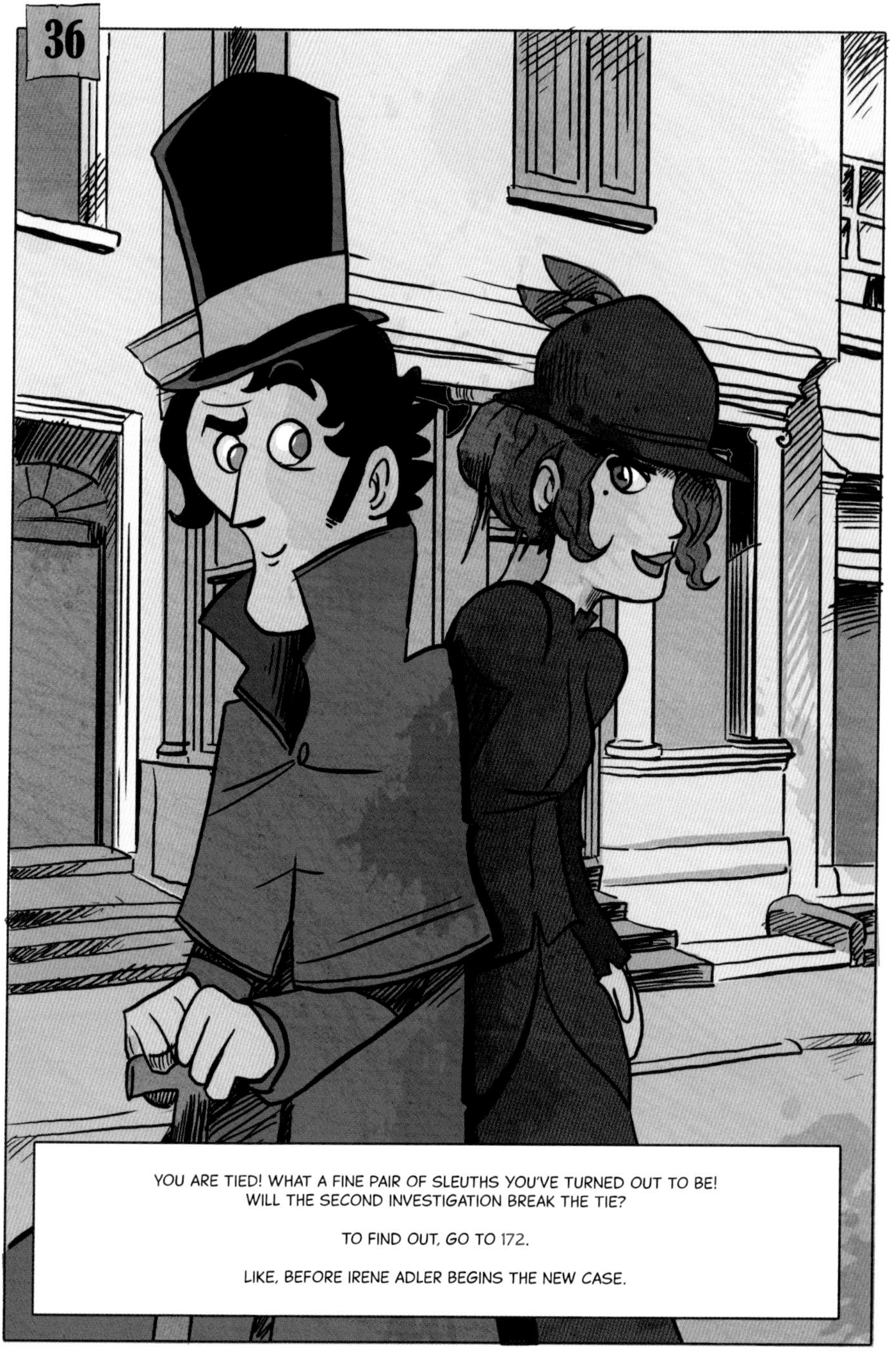
36
YOU ARE TIED! WHAT A FINE PAIR OF SLEUTHS YOU'VE TURNED OUT TO BE!
WILL THE SECOND INVESTIGATION BREAK THE TIE?
TO FIND OUT, GO TO 172.
LIKE, BEFORE IRENE ADLER BEGINS THE NEW CASE.

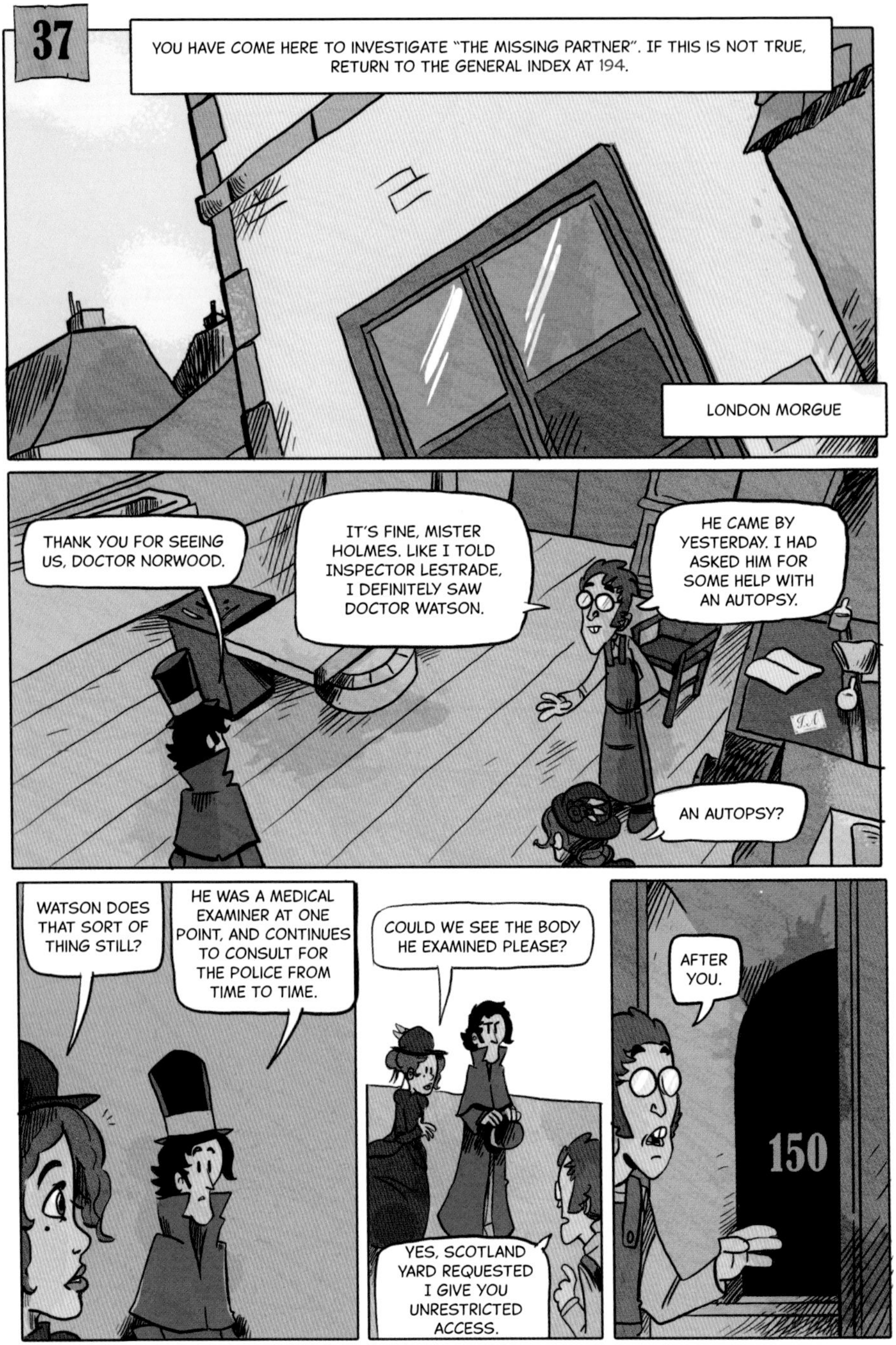
37
YOU HAVE COME HERE TO INVESTIGATE "THE MISSING PARTNER". IF THIS IS NOT TRUE, RETURN TO THE GENERAL INDEX AT 194.
LONDON MORGUE
THANK YOU FOR SEEING US, DOCTOR NORWOOD.
IT'S FINE, MISTER HOLMES. LIKE I TOLD INSPECTOR LESTRADE, I DEFINITELY SAW DOCTOR WATSON.
HE CAME BY YESTERDAY. I HAD ASKED HIM FOR SOME HELP WITH AN AUTOPSY.
AN AUTOPSY?
WATSON DOES THAT SORT OF THING STILL?
HE WAS A MEDICAL EXAMINER AT ONE POINT, AND CONTINUES TO CONSULT FOR THE POLICE FROM TIME TO TIME.
COULD WE SEE THE BODY HE EXAMINED PLEASE?
YES, SCOTLAND YARD REQUESTED I GIVE YOU UNRESTRICTED ACCESS.
AFTER YOU.
150

38

I'M MARRIED. SIMPLE AS THAT. DENIS CARLYLE IS MY HUSBAND. HE'S A NOTARY.

RETURN TO 67.

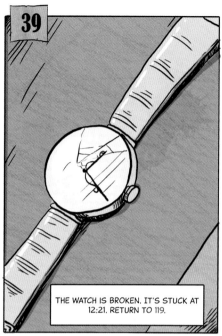

39

THE WATCH IS BROKEN. IT'S STUCK AT 12:21. RETURN TO 119.

40

A FEW DAYS AGO NOW. WE WERE IN A RELATIONSHIP, BUT, UNFORTUNATELY, IT WASN'T GOING VERY WELL BETWEEN US.

GO TO 124.

41

THE ONLY THING I HAVE TO SAY ON THE MATTER IS THAT IF JOHN GABRIEL HURT OFFERS YOU A PORTRAIT...

IT'S BECAUSE HE HOLDS YOU IN HIGH ESTEEM...

GO TO 23.

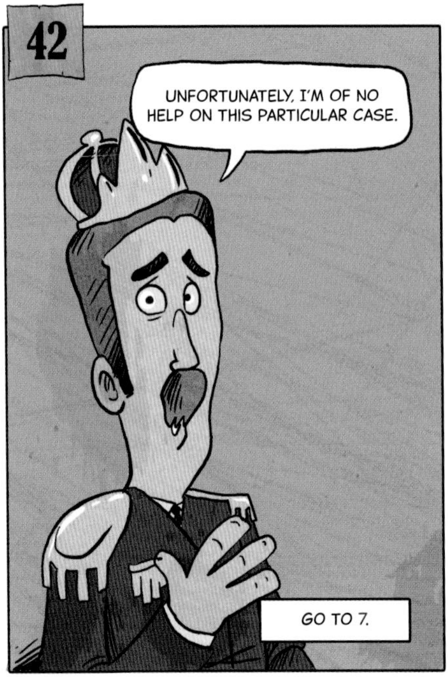
42
UNFORTUNATELY, I'M OF NO HELP ON THIS PARTICULAR CASE.
GO TO 7.

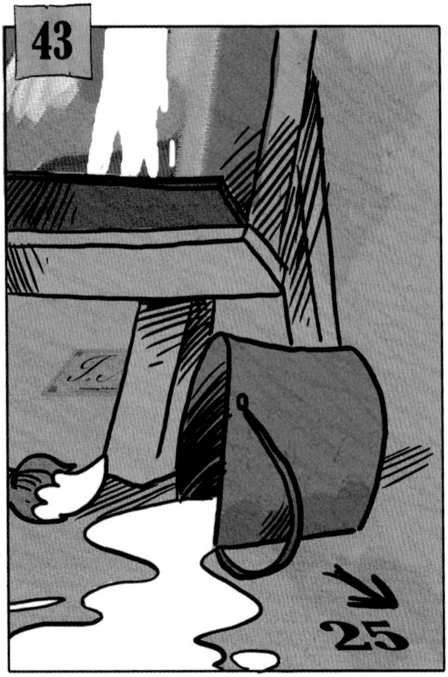
43
25

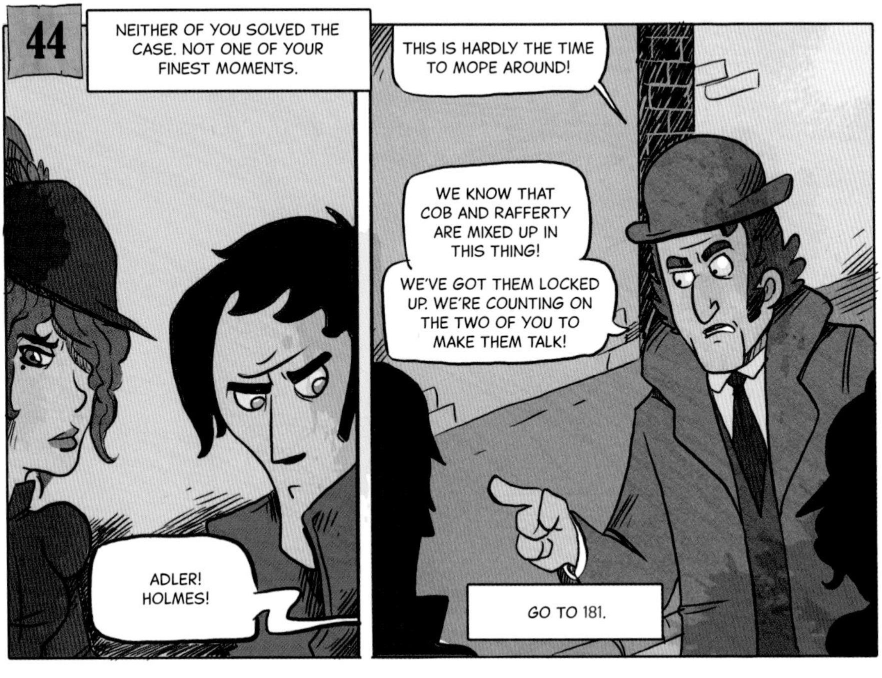
44
NEITHER OF YOU SOLVED THE CASE. NOT ONE OF YOUR FINEST MOMENTS.
ADLER! HOLMES!
THIS IS HARDLY THE TIME TO MOPE AROUND!
WE KNOW THAT COB AND RAFFERTY ARE MIXED UP IN THIS THING!
WE'VE GOT THEM LOCKED UP. WE'RE COUNTING ON THE TWO OF YOU TO MAKE THEM TALK!
GO TO 181.

45

IT'S TIME TO SOLVE THE CASE!
ANSWER THE QUESTIONS FOUND BELOW ON YOUR INVESTIGATION SHEET.
TO DO SO, WRITE THE NUMBERS CORRESPONDING TO THE CORRECT ANSWERS.
(NOTE: THE NUMBERS DO NOT INDICATE FRAMES.)

Case 1: The Final Portrait

- Question 1: Who Killed John Gabriel Hurt?

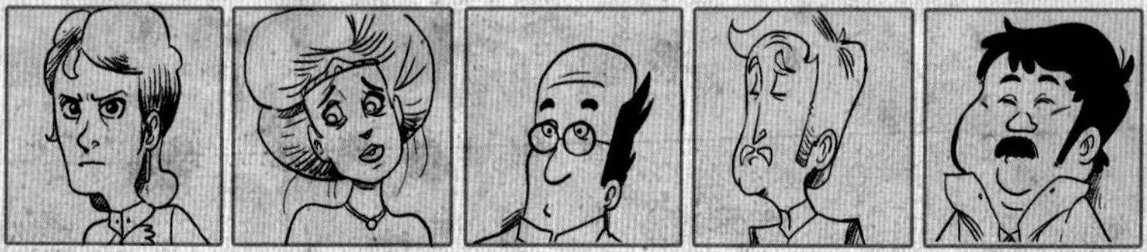

Lillie Carlyle, his daughter.	Lady Desmond.	Victor Rice, his accountant.	The Duke of Fitzgerald.	The Viscount of Abalore.
400	100	300	500	200

- Question 2: What was their motive?

Greed	30
Jealousy	20
He had compromising information	40

- Question 3: What was the murder weapon?

A cane sword	2
A sabre	5
A pistol	8

ADD YOUR ANSWERS TOGETHER AND NOTE THE SUM ON YOUR INVESTIGATION SHEET.

IF YOU'RE PLAYING SOLO, GO TO 158. IF THERE ARE TWO OF YOU, IT'S SHERLOCK'S TURN TO INVESTIGATE. OH, HE'S DONE? THEN, GO TOGETHER TO 158.

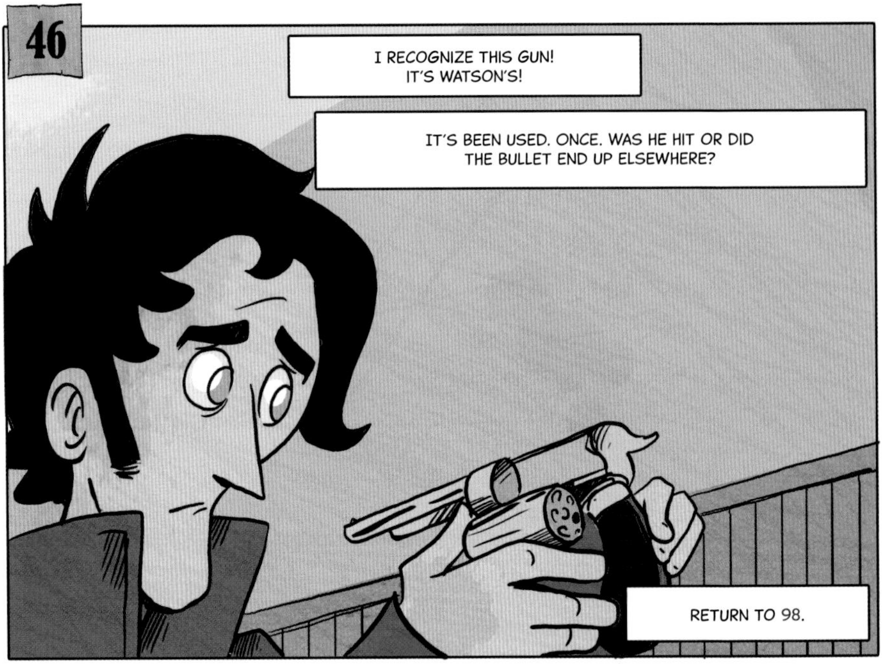
46
I RECOGNIZE THIS GUN!
IT'S WATSON'S!
IT'S BEEN USED. ONCE. WAS HE HIT OR DID
THE BULLET END UP ELSEWHERE?
RETURN TO 98.

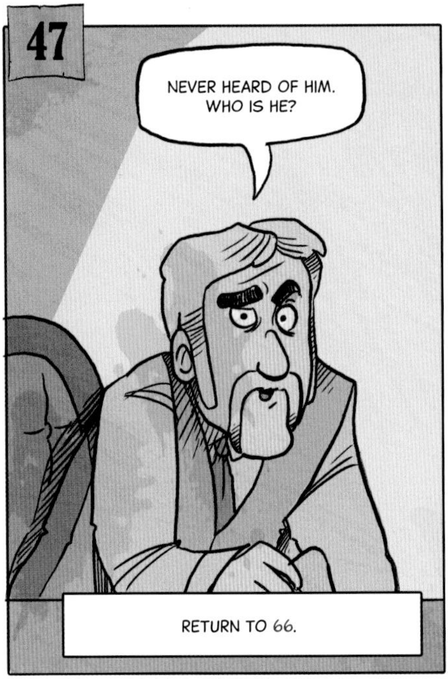
47
NEVER HEARD OF HIM.
WHO IS HE?
RETURN TO 66.

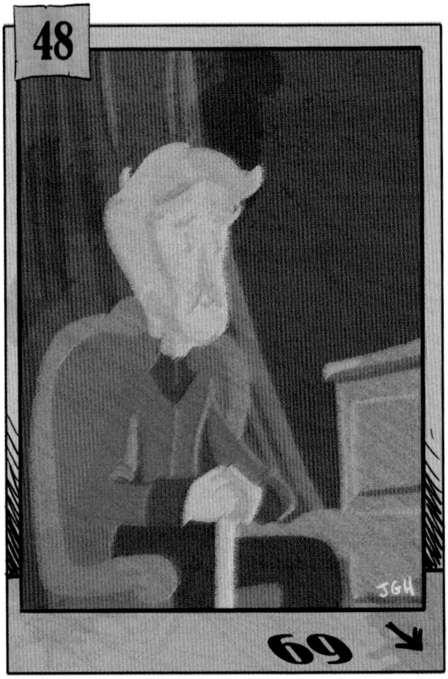
48
JGH
69

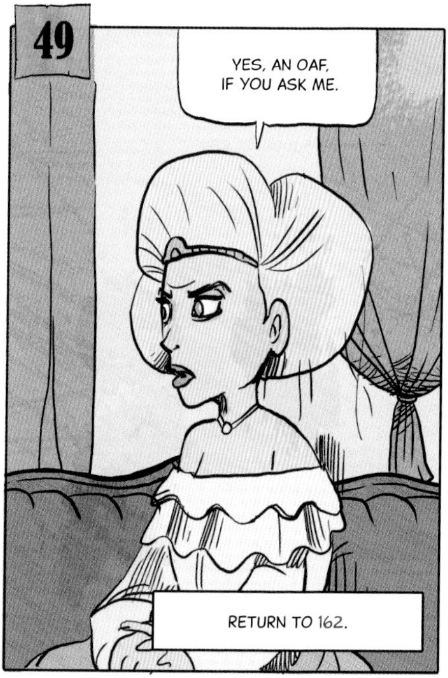
49
YES, AN OAF, IF YOU ASK ME.
RETURN TO 162.

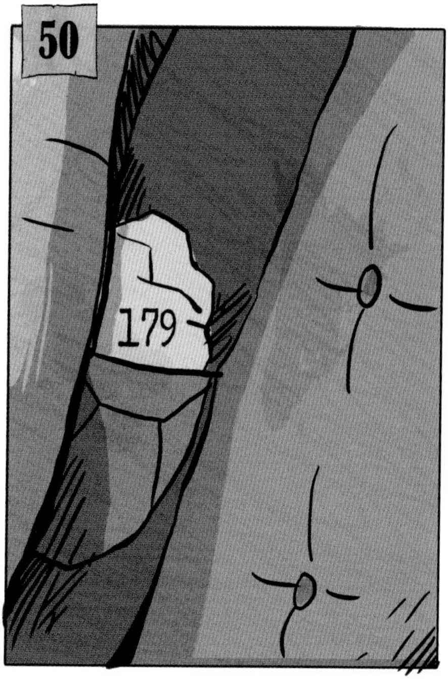
50
179

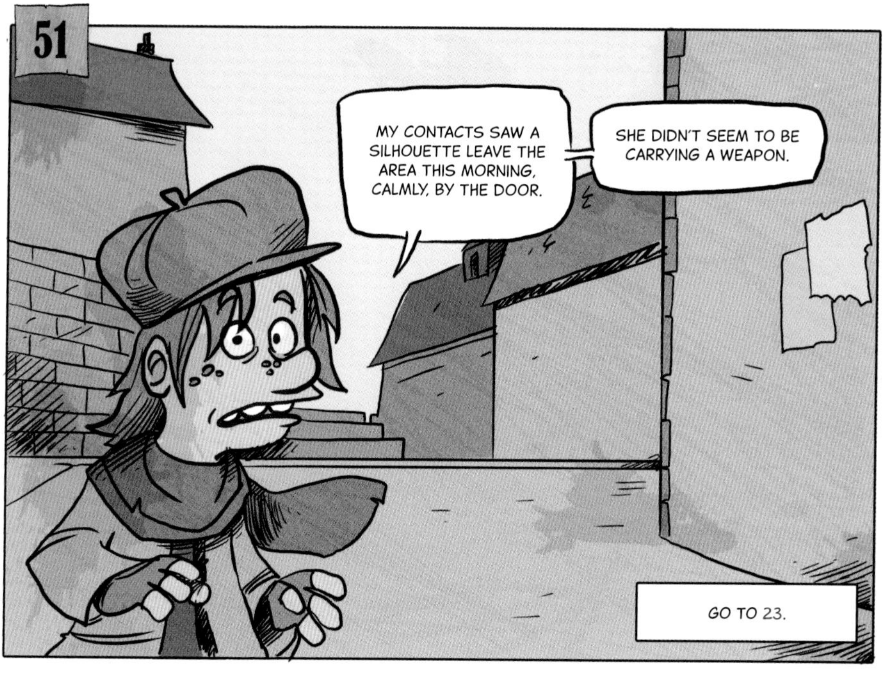
51
MY CONTACTS SAW A SILHOUETTE LEAVE THE AREA THIS MORNING, CALMLY, BY THE DOOR.
SHE DIDN'T SEEM TO BE CARRYING A WEAPON.
GO TO 23.

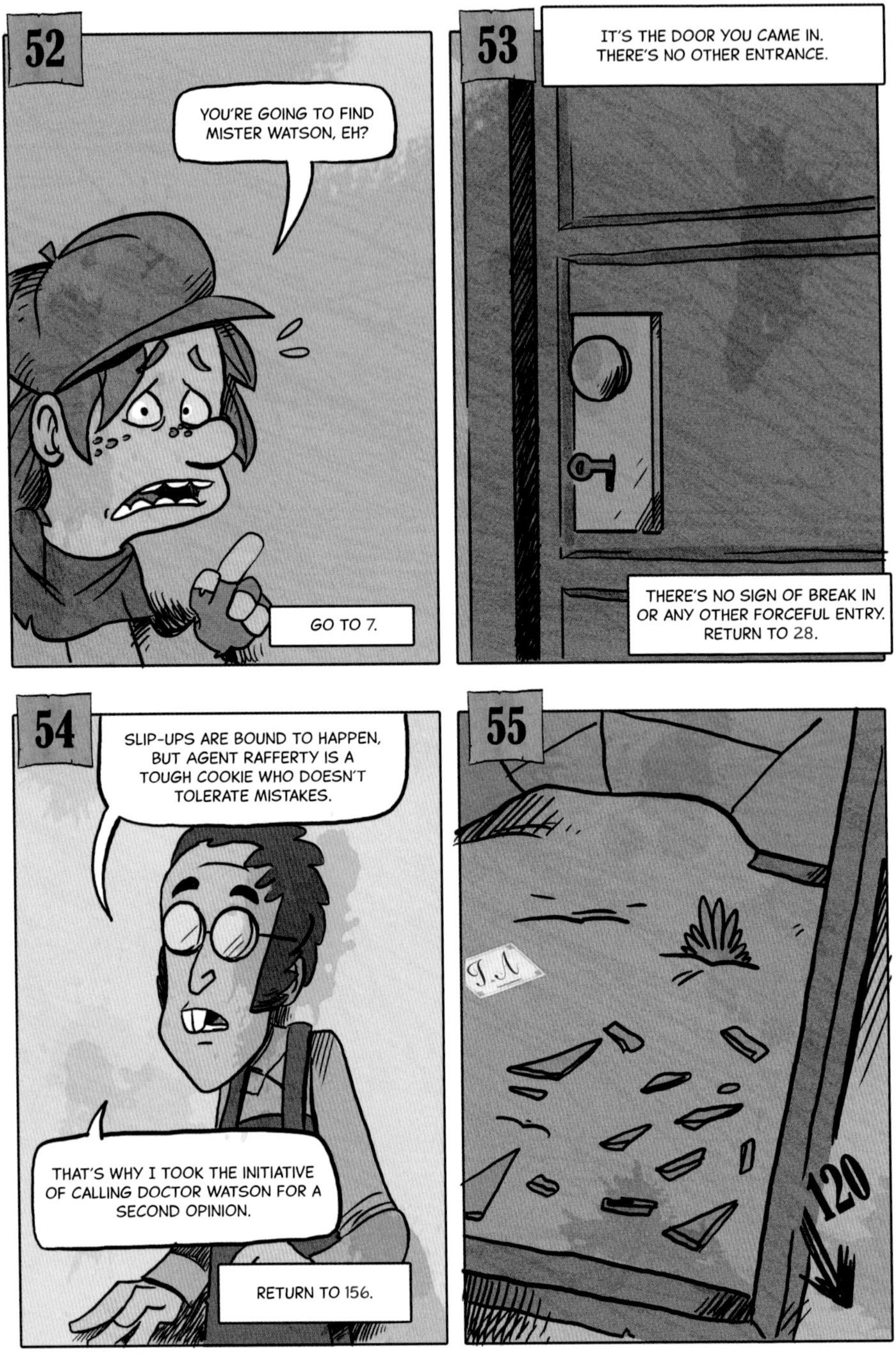
52
YOU'RE GOING TO FIND MISTER WATSON, EH?
GO TO 7.
53
IT'S THE DOOR YOU CAME IN. THERE'S NO OTHER ENTRANCE.
THERE'S NO SIGN OF BREAK IN OR ANY OTHER FORCEFUL ENTRY. RETURN TO 28.
54
SLIP-UPS ARE BOUND TO HAPPEN, BUT AGENT RAFFERTY IS A TOUGH COOKIE WHO DOESN'T TOLERATE MISTAKES.
THAT'S WHY I TOOK THE INITIATIVE OF CALLING DOCTOR WATSON FOR A SECOND OPINION.
RETURN TO 156.
55
120

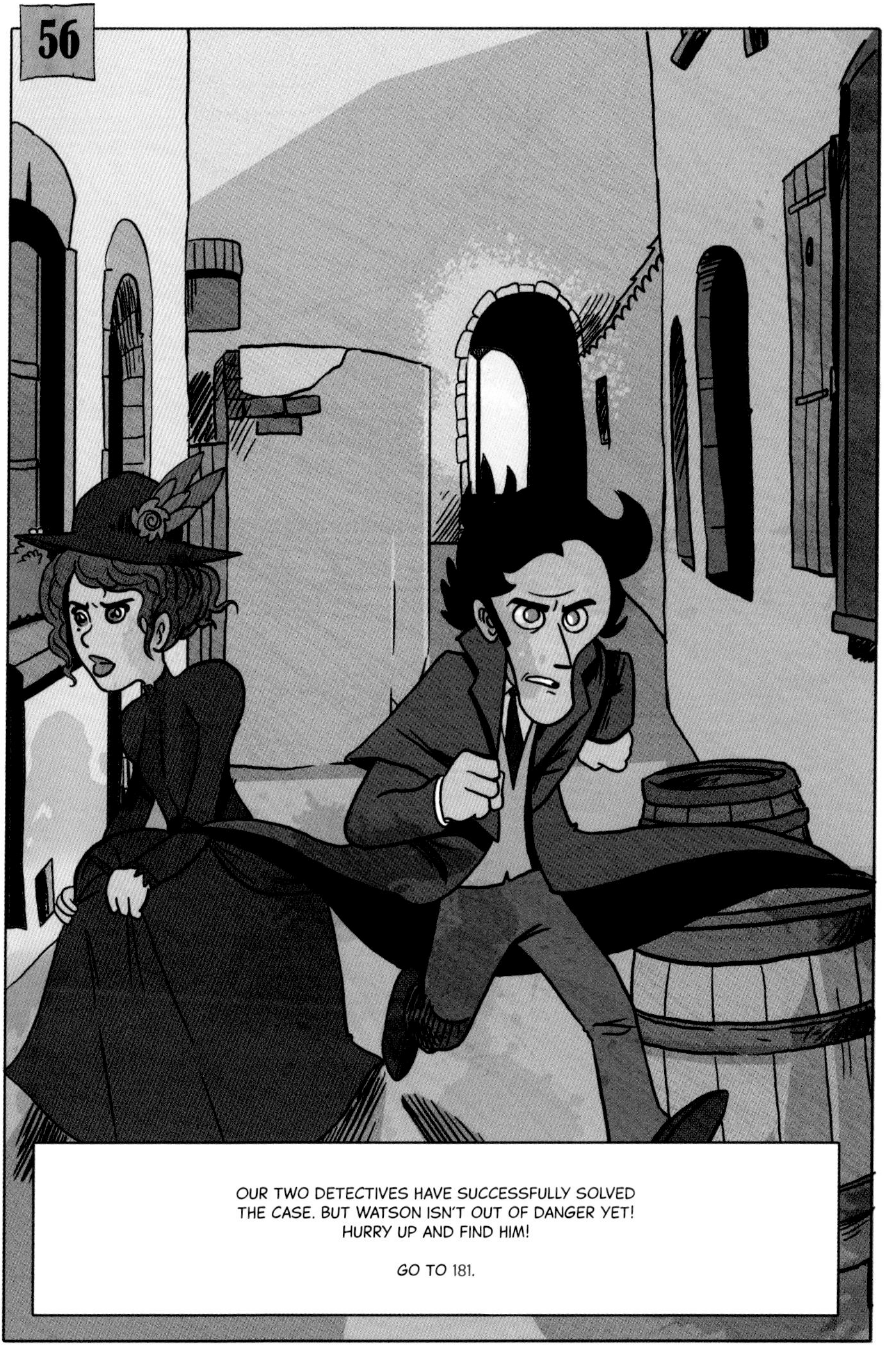
56
OUR TWO DETECTIVES HAVE SUCCESSFULLY SOLVED THE CASE. BUT WATSON ISN'T OUT OF DANGER YET! HURRY UP AND FIND HIM!
GO TO 181.

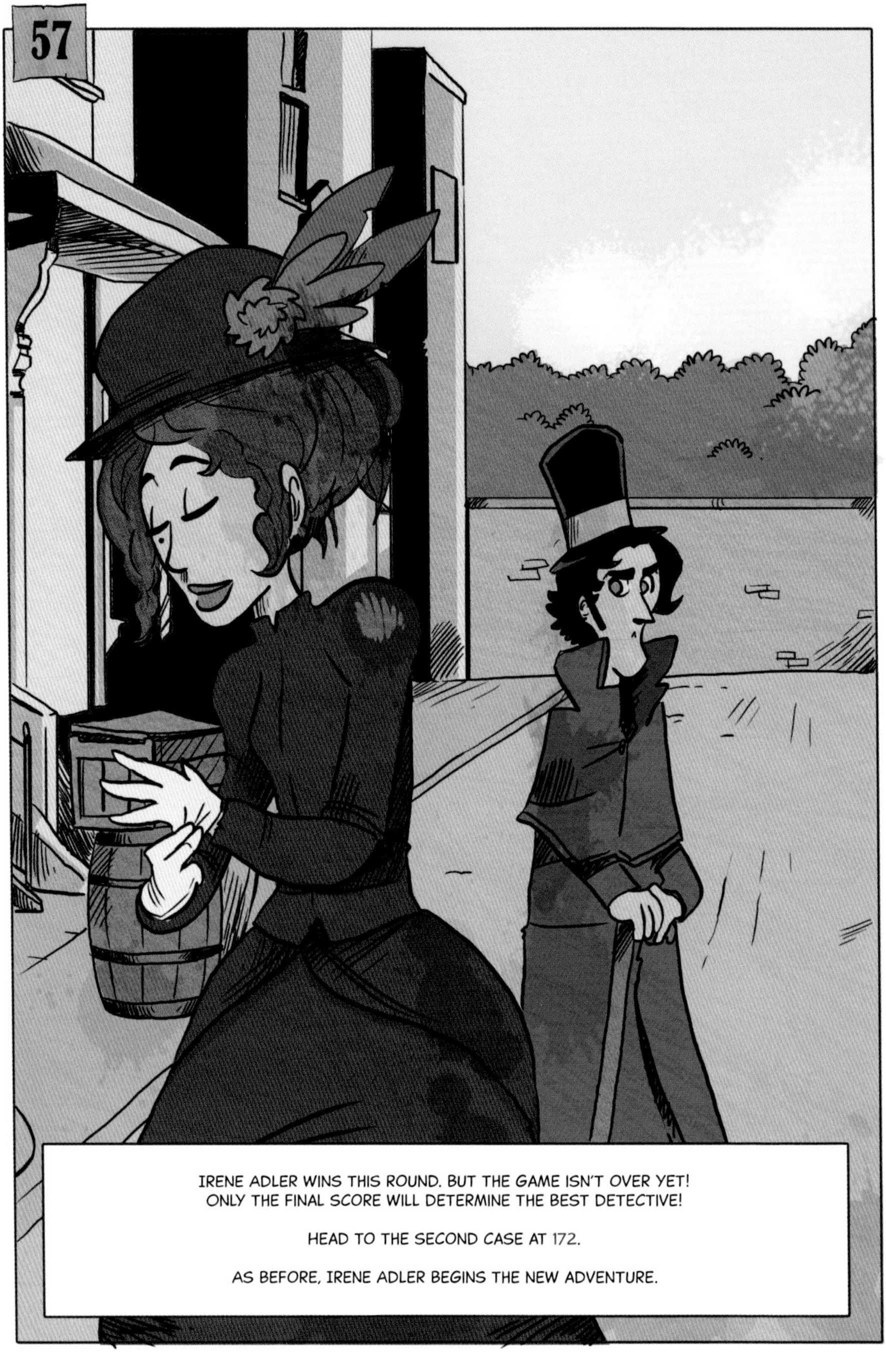
57
IRENE ADLER WINS THIS ROUND. BUT THE GAME ISN'T OVER YET! ONLY THE FINAL SCORE WILL DETERMINE THE BEST DETECTIVE!
HEAD TO THE SECOND CASE AT 172.
AS BEFORE, IRENE ADLER BEGINS THE NEW ADVENTURE.

58

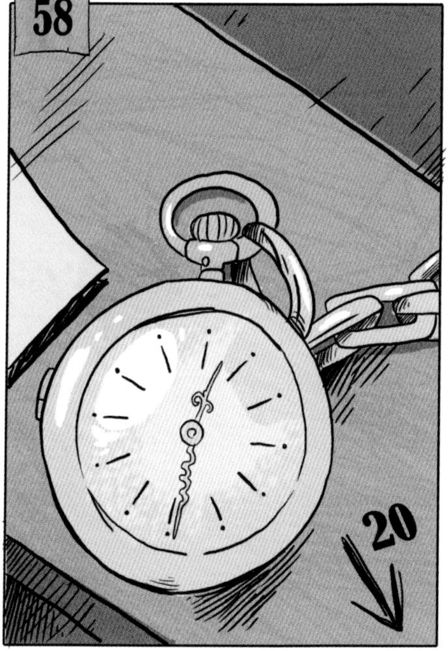
20

59

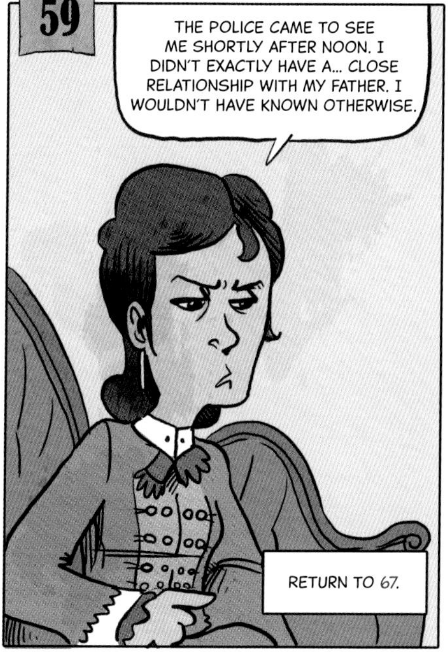
THE POLICE CAME TO SEE ME SHORTLY AFTER NOON. I DIDN'T EXACTLY HAVE A... CLOSE RELATIONSHIP WITH MY FATHER. I WOULDN'T HAVE KNOWN OTHERWISE.
RETURN TO 67.

60

The result you're looking for is one hundred and forty-three.

One Player:
If you succeeded with Holmes, go to 135, otherwise go to 105.

If you succeeded with Adler, go to 105, otherwise go to 135.

Two Players:
Only Holmes succeeded: 135
Only Adler succeeded: 105
Both Succeeded: 56
Neither Succeeded: 44

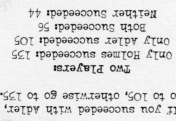

61

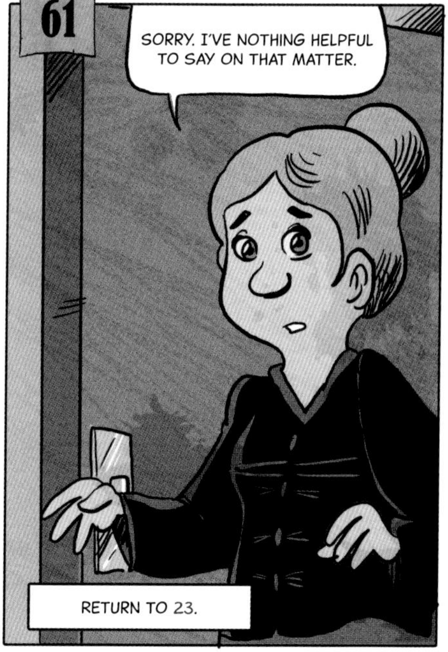
SORRY. I'VE NOTHING HELPFUL TO SAY ON THAT MATTER.
RETURN TO 23.

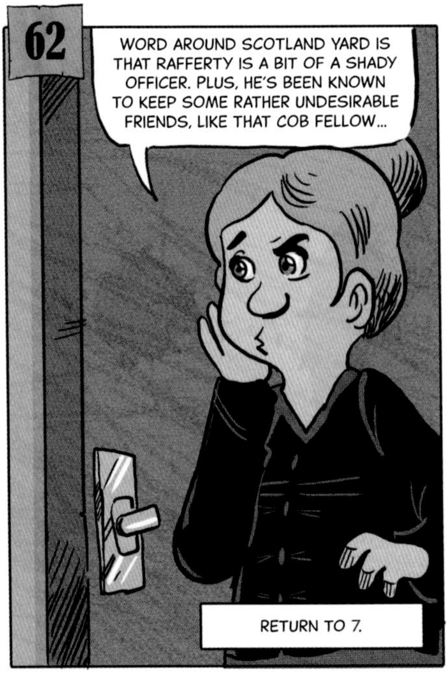
62
WORD AROUND SCOTLAND YARD IS THAT RAFFERTY IS A BIT OF A SHADY OFFICER. PLUS, HE'S BEEN KNOWN TO KEEP SOME RATHER UNDESIRABLE FRIENDS, LIKE THAT COB FELLOW...
RETURN TO 7.

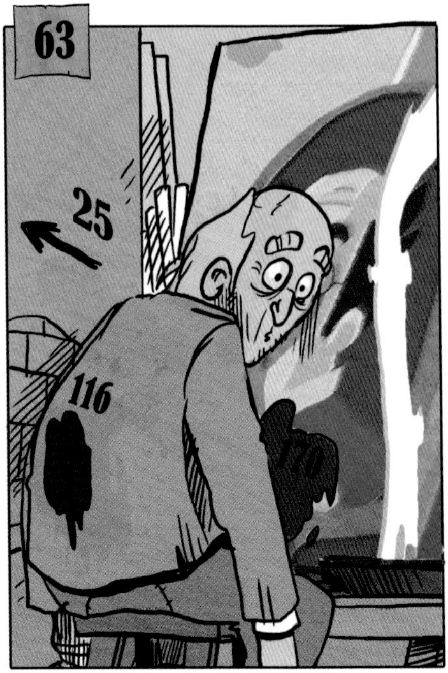
63
25
116
170

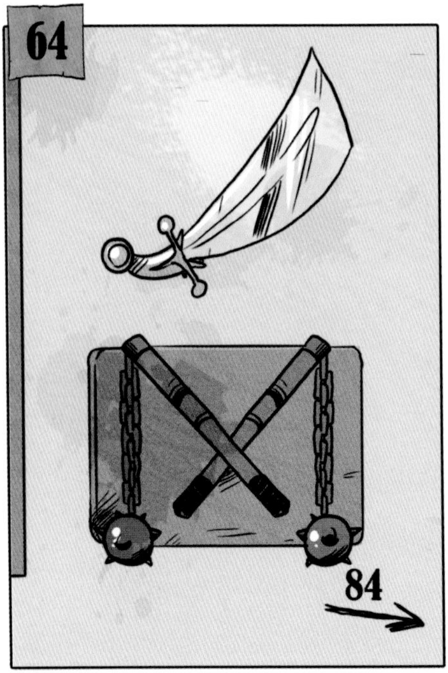
64
84

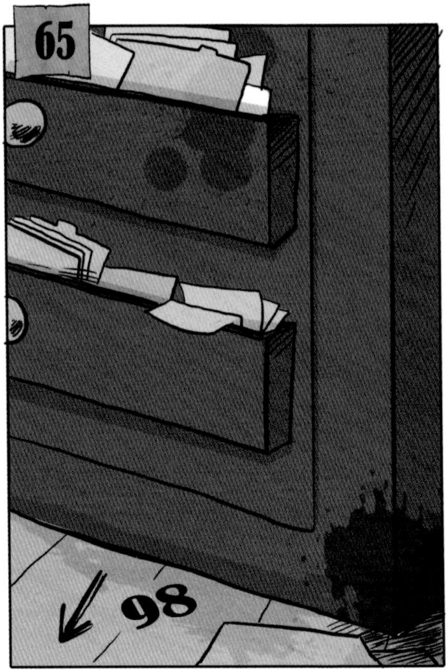
65
98

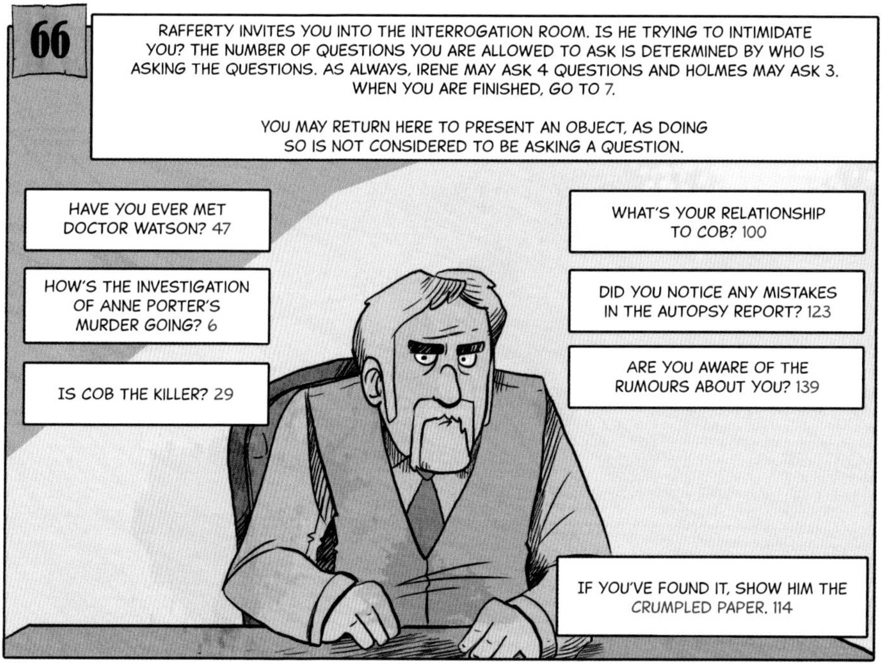
66
RAFFERTY INVITES YOU INTO THE INTERROGATION ROOM. IS HE TRYING TO INTIMIDATE YOU? THE NUMBER OF QUESTIONS YOU ARE ALLOWED TO ASK IS DETERMINED BY WHO IS ASKING THE QUESTIONS. AS ALWAYS, IRENE MAY ASK 4 QUESTIONS AND HOLMES MAY ASK 3. WHEN YOU ARE FINISHED, GO TO 7.
YOU MAY RETURN HERE TO PRESENT AN OBJECT, AS DOING SO IS NOT CONSIDERED TO BE ASKING A QUESTION.
HAVE YOU EVER MET DOCTOR WATSON? 47
HOW'S THE INVESTIGATION OF ANNE PORTER'S MURDER GOING? 6
IS COB THE KILLER? 29
WHAT'S YOUR RELATIONSHIP TO COB? 100
DID YOU NOTICE ANY MISTAKES IN THE AUTOPSY REPORT? 123
ARE YOU AWARE OF THE RUMOURS ABOUT YOU? 139
IF YOU'VE FOUND IT, SHOW HIM THE CRUMPLED PAPER. 114

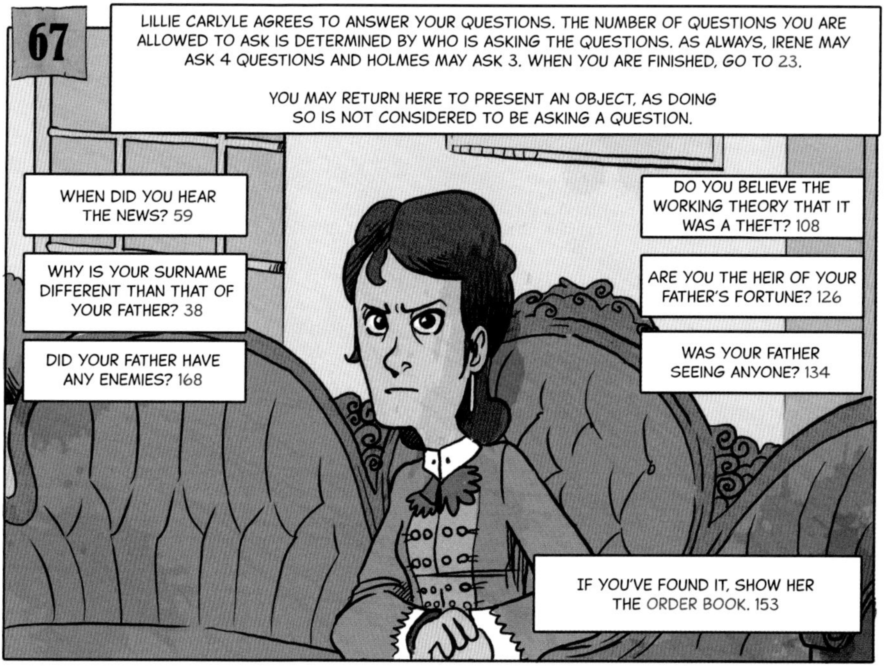
67
LILLIE CARLYLE AGREES TO ANSWER YOUR QUESTIONS. THE NUMBER OF QUESTIONS YOU ARE ALLOWED TO ASK IS DETERMINED BY WHO IS ASKING THE QUESTIONS. AS ALWAYS, IRENE MAY ASK 4 QUESTIONS AND HOLMES MAY ASK 3. WHEN YOU ARE FINISHED, GO TO 23.
YOU MAY RETURN HERE TO PRESENT AN OBJECT, AS DOING SO IS NOT CONSIDERED TO BE ASKING A QUESTION.
WHEN DID YOU HEAR THE NEWS? 59
WHY IS YOUR SURNAME DIFFERENT THAN THAT OF YOUR FATHER? 38
DID YOUR FATHER HAVE ANY ENEMIES? 168
DO YOU BELIEVE THE WORKING THEORY THAT IT WAS A THEFT? 108
ARE YOU THE HEIR OF YOUR FATHER'S FORTUNE? 126
WAS YOUR FATHER SEEING ANYONE? 134
IF YOU'VE FOUND IT, SHOW HER THE ORDER BOOK. 153

68

IT'S TIME TO SOLVE THE CASE!
ANSWER THE QUESTIONS FOUND BELOW ON YOUR INVESTIGATION SHEET.
TO DO SO, WRITE THE NUMBERS CORRESPONDING TO THE CORRECT ANSWERS.
(NOTE: THE NUMBERS DO NOT INDICATE FRAMES.)

Case 2: The Missing Partner

- Question 1: Who abducted Doctor Watson?

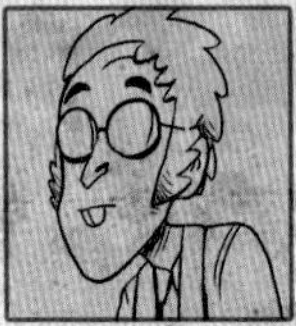
Frank Norwood.
300

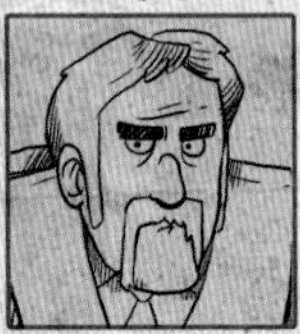
Mickey Rafferty.
100

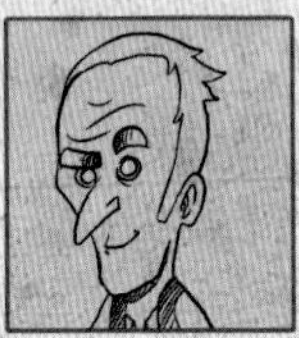
Sagamore Cob.
200

- Question 2: What was their motive?

Watson was going to take his job	20
To keep him quiet	40
To demand a ransom	30

- Question 3: Who was actually detaining him?

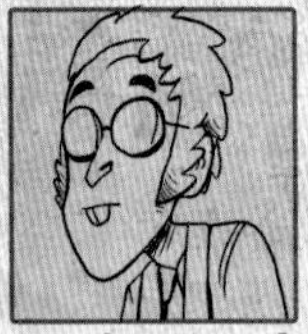
Frank Norwood.
2

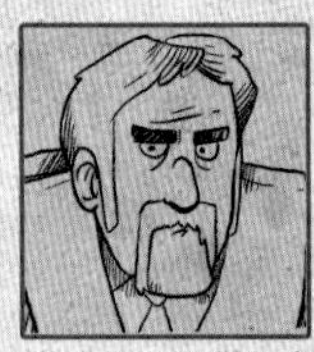
Mickey Rafferty.
4

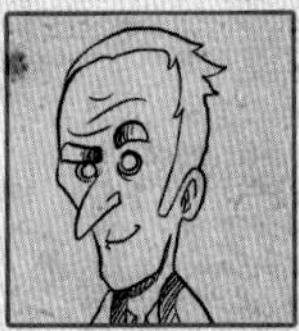
Sagamore Cob.
3

ADD YOUR ANSWERS TOGETHER AND NOTE THE SUM ON YOUR INVESTIGATION SHEET.

IF YOU'RE PLAYING SOLO, GO TO 60. IF THERE ARE TWO OF YOU, IT'S SHERLOCK'S TURN TO INVESTIGATE. OH, HE'S DONE? THEN, GO TOGETHER TO 60.

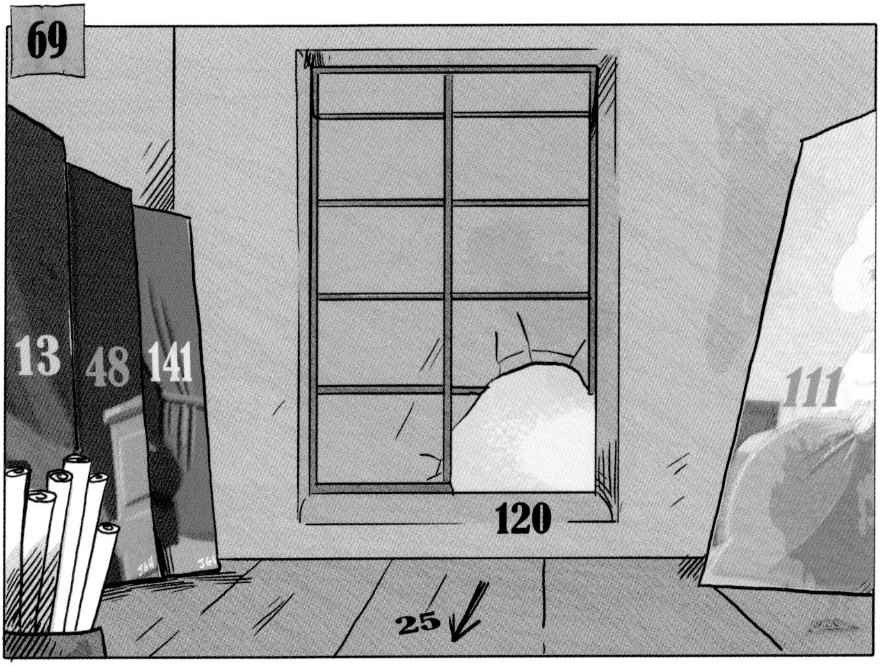
69
13
48
141
120
111
25

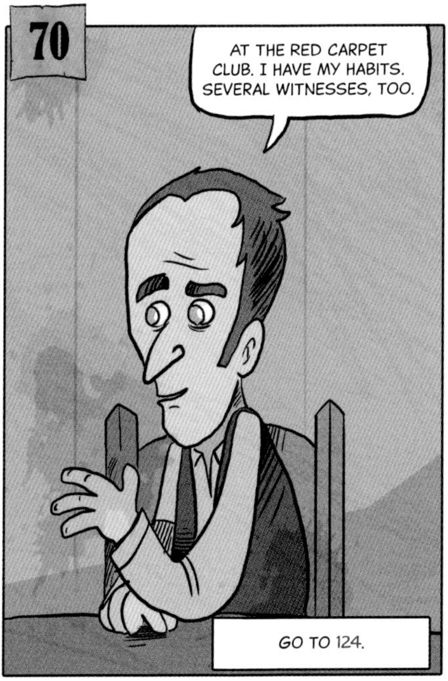
70
AT THE RED CARPET CLUB. I HAVE MY HABITS. SEVERAL WITNESSES, TOO.
GO TO 124.

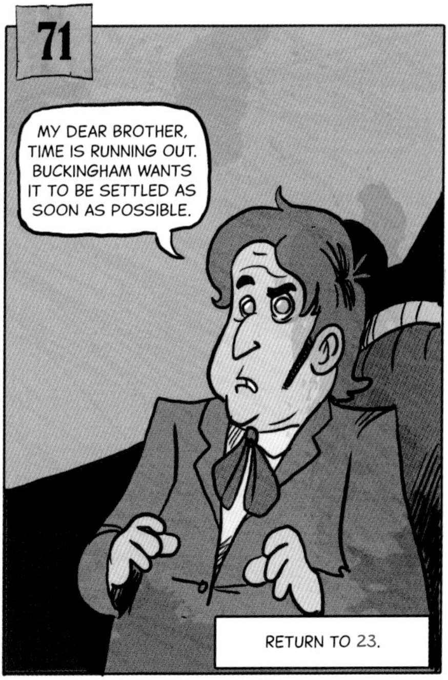
71
MY DEAR BROTHER, TIME IS RUNNING OUT. BUCKINGHAM WANTS IT TO BE SETTLED AS SOON AS POSSIBLE.
RETURN TO 23.

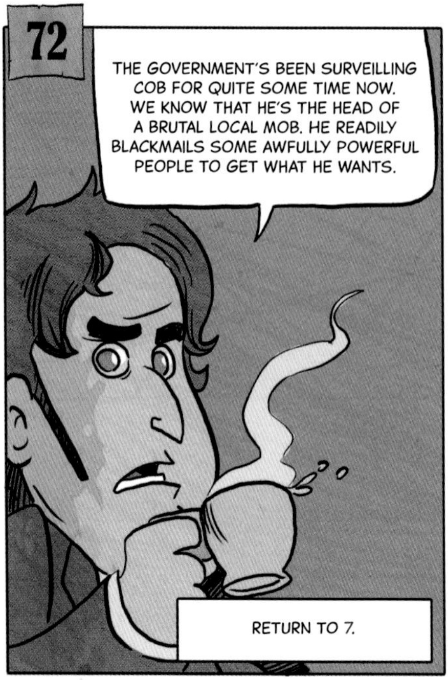
72
THE GOVERNMENT'S BEEN SURVEILLING COB FOR QUITE SOME TIME NOW. WE KNOW THAT HE'S THE HEAD OF A BRUTAL LOCAL MOB. HE READILY BLACKMAILS SOME AWFULLY POWERFUL PEOPLE TO GET WHAT HE WANTS.
RETURN TO 7.

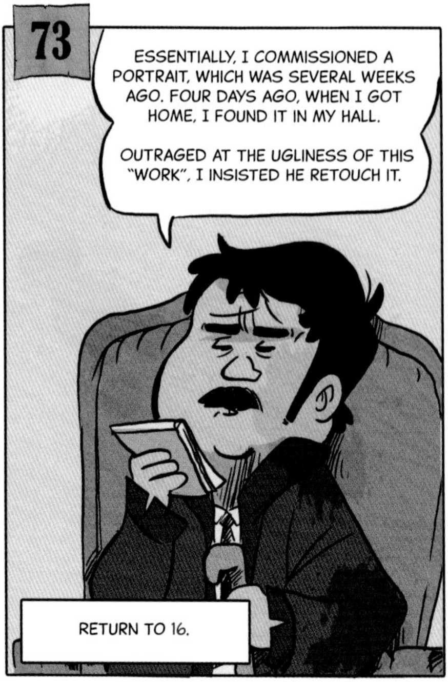
73
ESSENTIALLY, I COMMISSIONED A PORTRAIT, WHICH WAS SEVERAL WEEKS AGO. FOUR DAYS AGO, WHEN I GOT HOME, I FOUND IT IN MY HALL.
OUTRAGED AT THE UGLINESS OF THIS "WORK", I INSISTED HE RETOUCH IT.
RETURN TO 16.

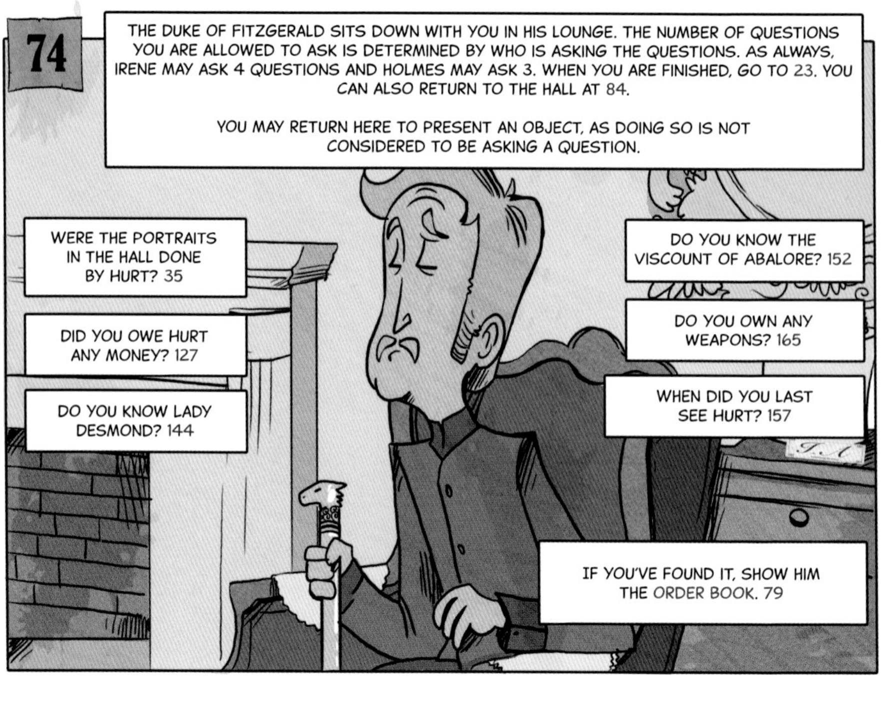
74
THE DUKE OF FITZGERALD SITS DOWN WITH YOU IN HIS LOUNGE. THE NUMBER OF QUESTIONS YOU ARE ALLOWED TO ASK IS DETERMINED BY WHO IS ASKING THE QUESTIONS. AS ALWAYS, IRENE MAY ASK 4 QUESTIONS AND HOLMES MAY ASK 3. WHEN YOU ARE FINISHED, GO TO 23. YOU CAN ALSO RETURN TO THE HALL AT 84.
YOU MAY RETURN HERE TO PRESENT AN OBJECT, AS DOING SO IS NOT CONSIDERED TO BE ASKING A QUESTION.
WERE THE PORTRAITS IN THE HALL DONE BY HURT? 35
DID YOU OWE HURT ANY MONEY? 127
DO YOU KNOW LADY DESMOND? 144
DO YOU KNOW THE VISCOUNT OF ABALORE? 152
DO YOU OWN ANY WEAPONS? 165
WHEN DID YOU LAST SEE HURT? 157
IF YOU'VE FOUND IT, SHOW HIM THE ORDER BOOK. 79

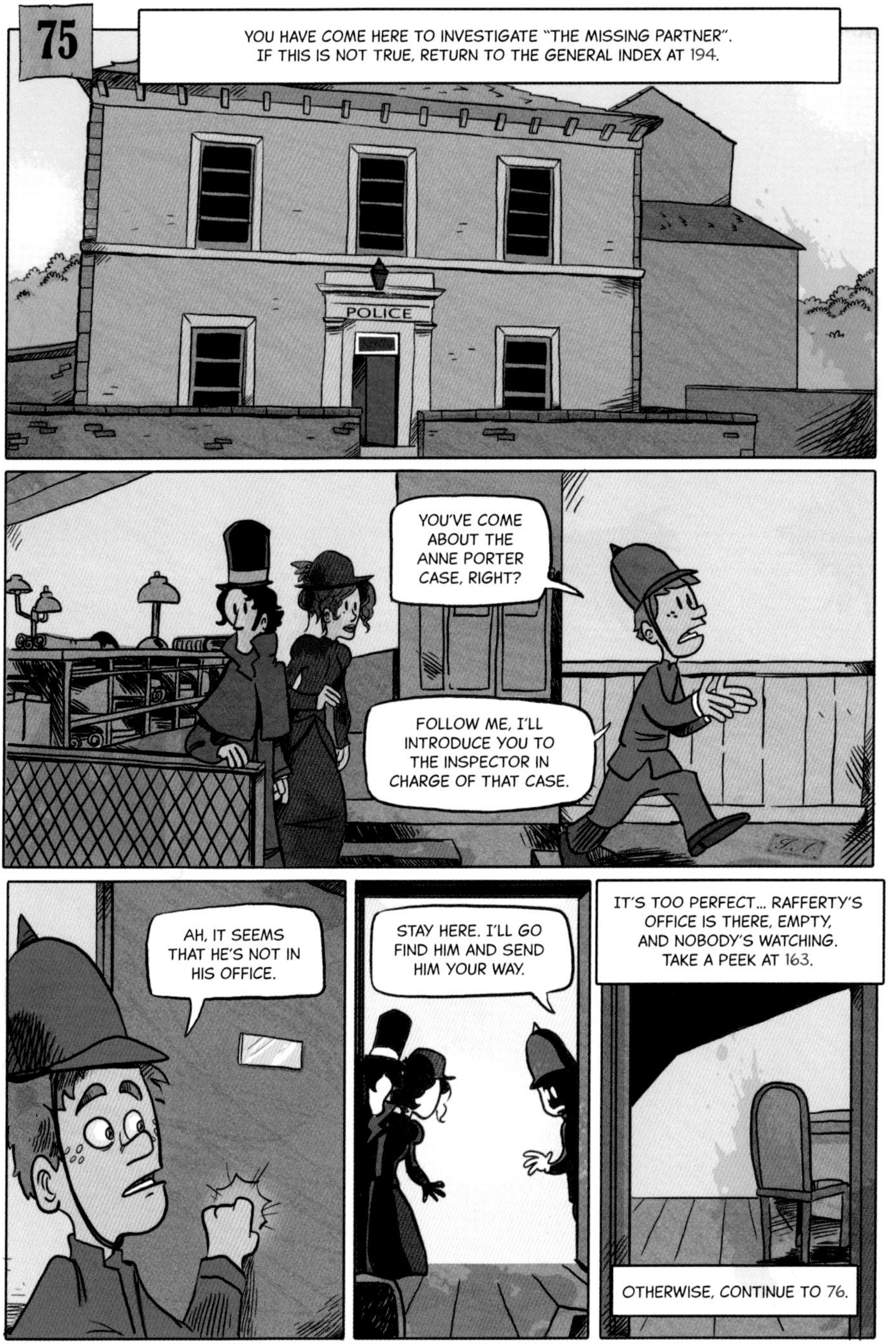
75
YOU HAVE COME HERE TO INVESTIGATE "THE MISSING PARTNER". IF THIS IS NOT TRUE, RETURN TO THE GENERAL INDEX AT 194.
POLICE
YOU'VE COME ABOUT THE ANNE PORTER CASE, RIGHT?
FOLLOW ME, I'LL INTRODUCE YOU TO THE INSPECTOR IN CHARGE OF THAT CASE.
AH, IT SEEMS THAT HE'S NOT IN HIS OFFICE.
STAY HERE. I'LL GO FIND HIM AND SEND HIM YOUR WAY.
IT'S TOO PERFECT... RAFFERTY'S OFFICE IS THERE, EMPTY, AND NOBODY'S WATCHING. TAKE A PEEK AT 163.
OTHERWISE, CONTINUE TO 76.

76

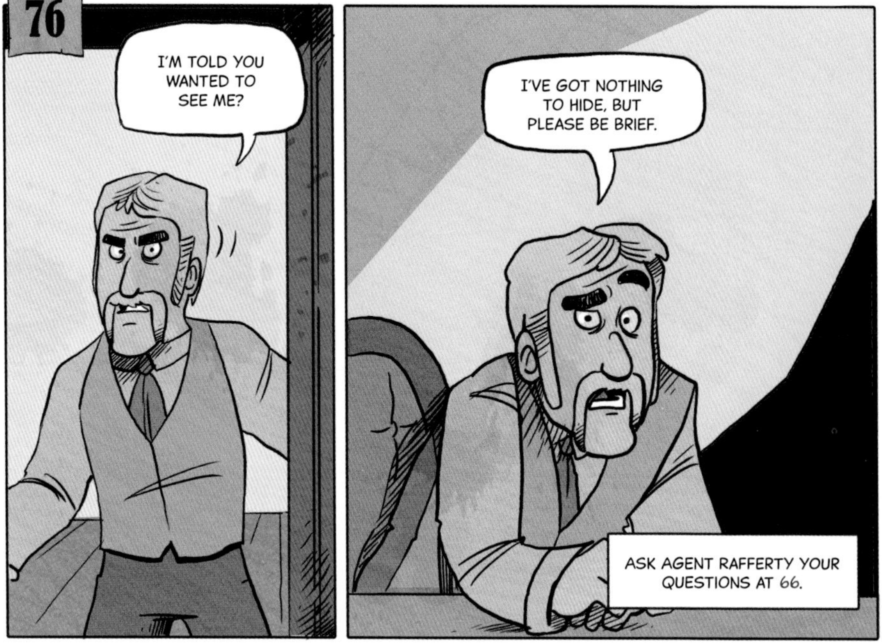
I'M TOLD YOU WANTED TO SEE ME?
I'VE GOT NOTHING TO HIDE, BUT PLEASE BE BRIEF.
ASK AGENT RAFFERTY YOUR QUESTIONS AT 66.

77

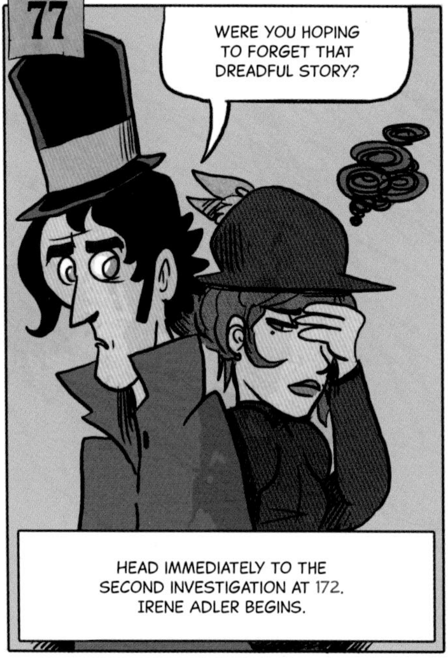
WERE YOU HOPING TO FORGET THAT DREADFUL STORY?
HEAD IMMEDIATELY TO THE SECOND INVESTIGATION AT 172. IRENE ADLER BEGINS.

78

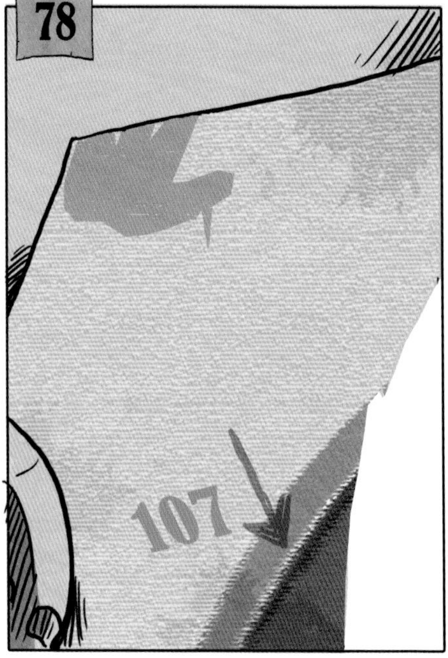
107

79

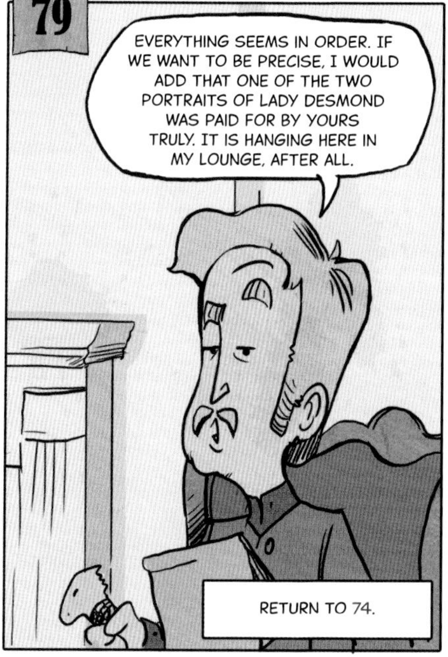
EVERYTHING SEEMS IN ORDER. IF WE WANT TO BE PRECISE, I WOULD ADD THAT ONE OF THE TWO PORTRAITS OF LADY DESMOND WAS PAID FOR BY YOURS TRULY. IT IS HANGING HERE IN MY LOUNGE, AFTER ALL.
RETURN TO 74.

80

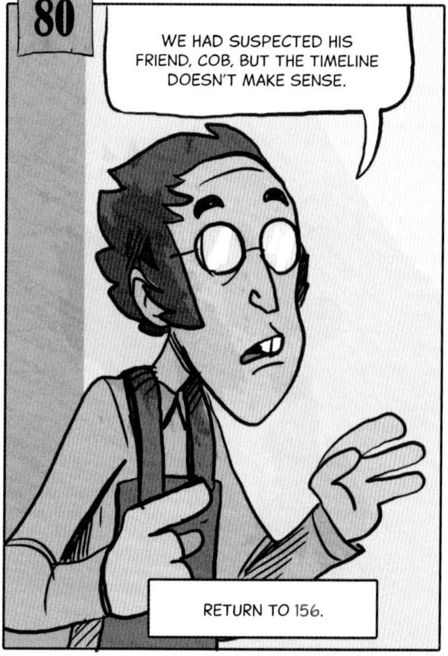
WE HAD SUSPECTED HIS FRIEND, COB, BUT THE TIMELINE DOESN'T MAKE SENSE.
RETURN TO 156.

81

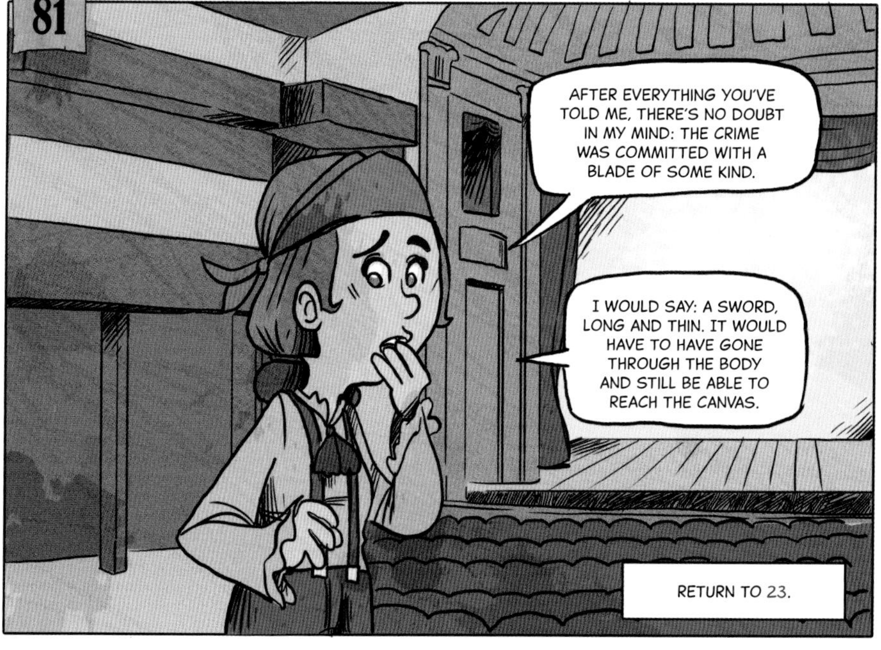
AFTER EVERYTHING YOU'VE TOLD ME, THERE'S NO DOUBT IN MY MIND: THE CRIME WAS COMMITTED WITH A BLADE OF SOME KIND.
I WOULD SAY: A SWORD, LONG AND THIN. IT WOULD HAVE TO HAVE GONE THROUGH THE BODY AND STILL BE ABLE TO REACH THE CANVAS.
RETURN TO 23.

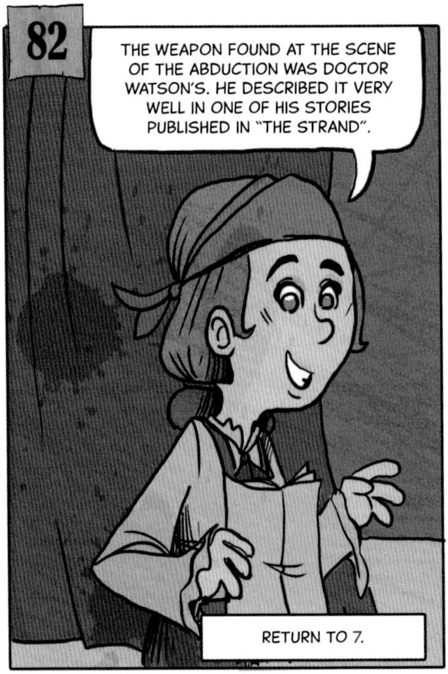
82
THE WEAPON FOUND AT THE SCENE OF THE ABDUCTION WAS DOCTOR WATSON'S. HE DESCRIBED IT VERY WELL IN ONE OF HIS STORIES PUBLISHED IN "THE STRAND".
RETURN TO 7.

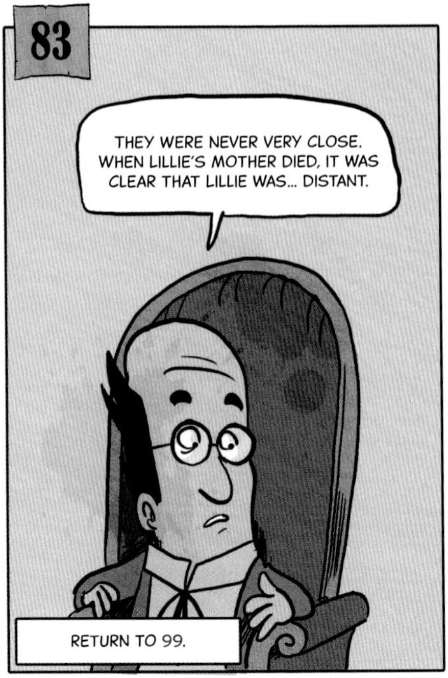
83
THEY WERE NEVER VERY CLOSE. WHEN LILLIE'S MOTHER DIED, IT WAS CLEAR THAT LILLIE WAS... DISTANT.
RETURN TO 99.

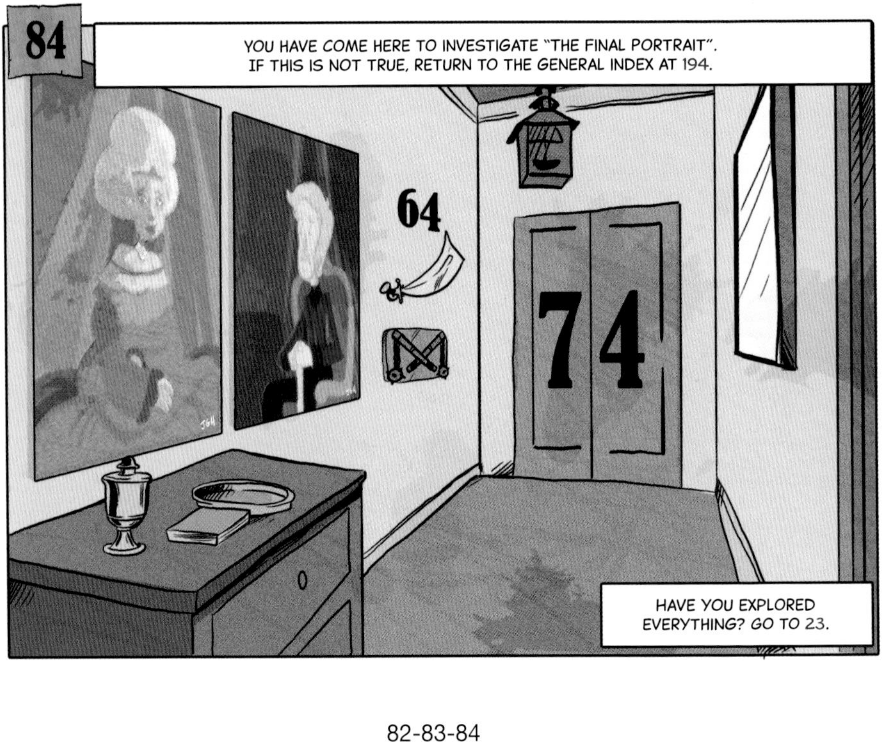
84
YOU HAVE COME HERE TO INVESTIGATE "THE FINAL PORTRAIT". IF THIS IS NOT TRUE, RETURN TO THE GENERAL INDEX AT 194.
64
74
HAVE YOU EXPLORED EVERYTHING? GO TO 23.

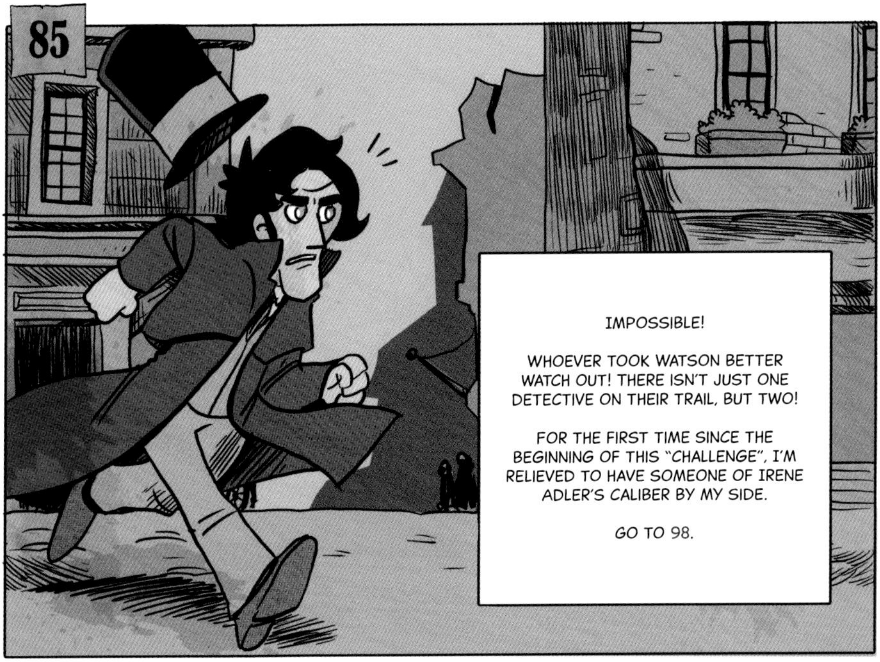
85
IMPOSSIBLE!
WHOEVER TOOK WATSON BETTER WATCH OUT! THERE ISN'T JUST ONE DETECTIVE ON THEIR TRAIL, BUT TWO!
FOR THE FIRST TIME SINCE THE BEGINNING OF THIS "CHALLENGE", I'M RELIEVED TO HAVE SOMEONE OF IRENE ADLER'S CALIBER BY MY SIDE.
GO TO 98.

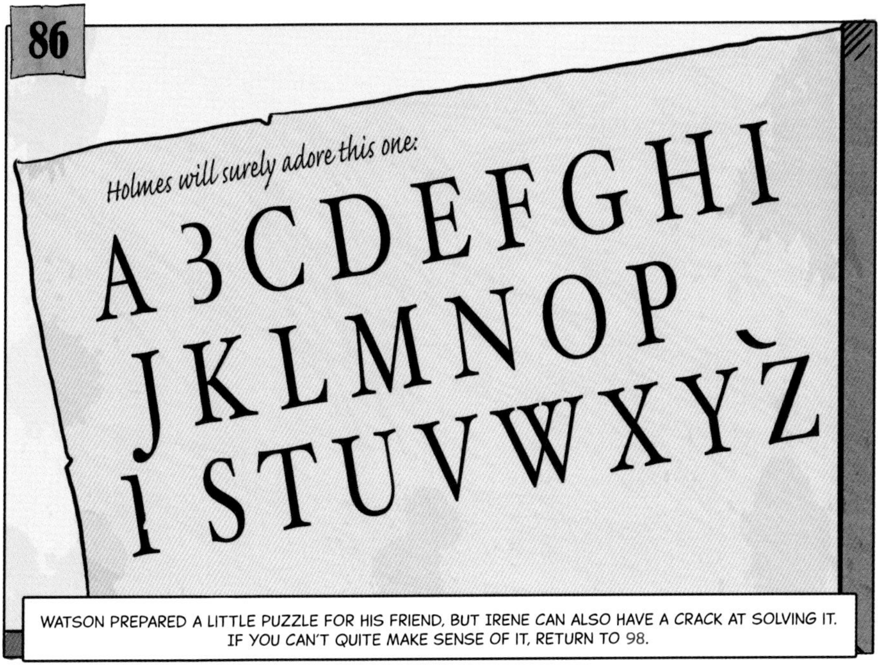
86
Holmes will surely adore this one:
A 3 C D E F G H I
J K L M N O P
İ S T U V W X Y Z̀
WATSON PREPARED A LITTLE PUZZLE FOR HIS FRIEND, BUT IRENE CAN ALSO HAVE A CRACK AT SOLVING IT. IF YOU CAN'T QUITE MAKE SENSE OF IT, RETURN TO 98.

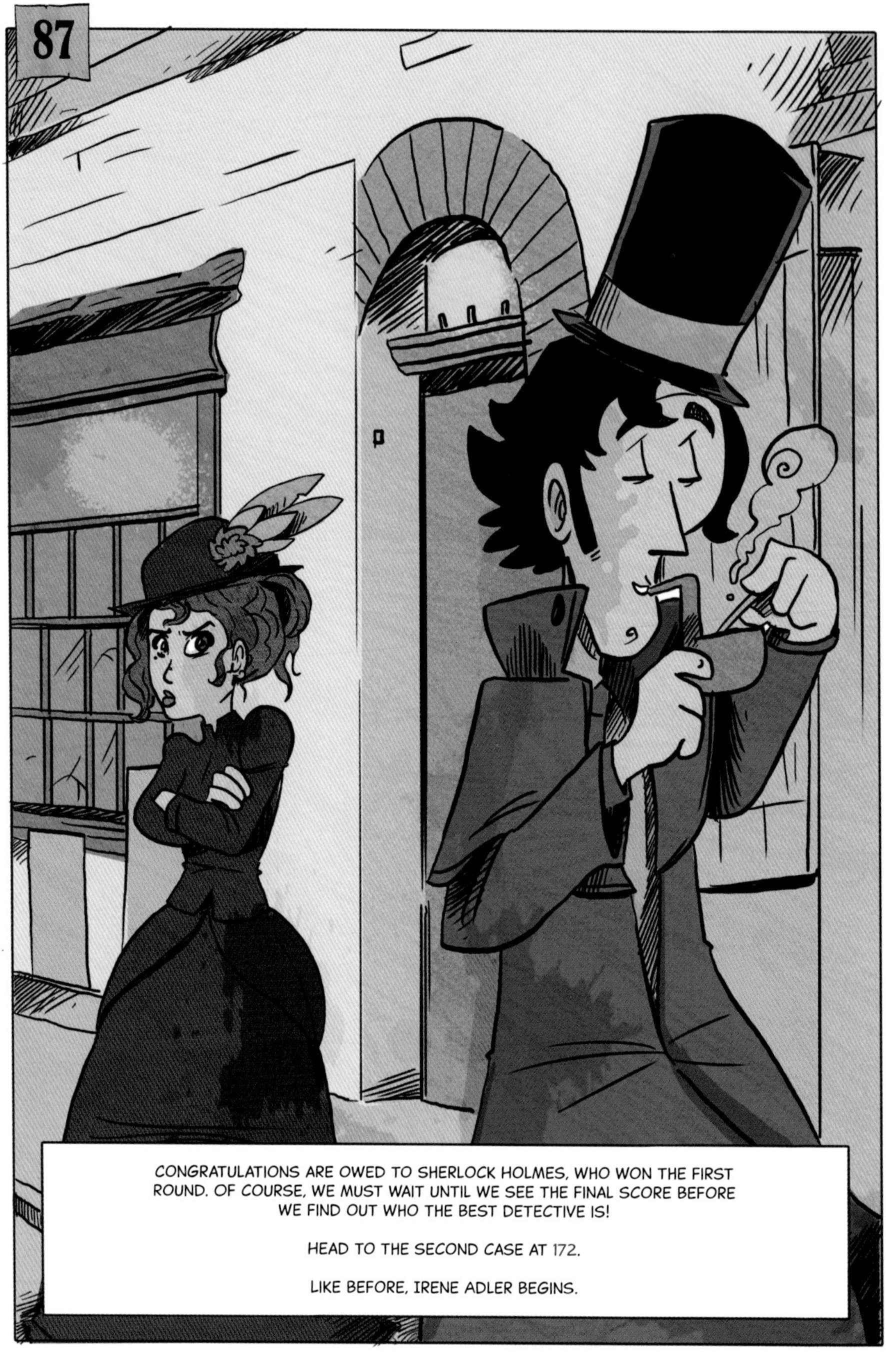
87
CONGRATULATIONS ARE OWED TO SHERLOCK HOLMES, WHO WON THE FIRST ROUND. OF COURSE, WE MUST WAIT UNTIL WE SEE THE FINAL SCORE BEFORE WE FIND OUT WHO THE BEST DETECTIVE IS!
HEAD TO THE SECOND CASE AT 172.
LIKE BEFORE, IRENE ADLER BEGINS.

88

YES, VAGUELY.
NOT ENOUGH TO
COMMENT, THOUGH.

RETURN TO 16.

89

Victor,
I hid some money,
just in case.

Just solve the equation:

DIX - 394.

J.G.H.

WHAT A FUNNY LITTLE PUZZLE!
IF *YOU* GIVE UP, RETURN TO 147.

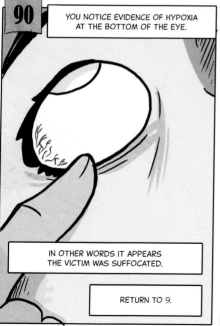

90

YOU NOTICE EVIDENCE OF HYPOXIA
AT THE BOTTOM OF THE EYE.

IN OTHER WORDS IT APPEARS
THE VICTIM WAS SUFFOCATED.

RETURN TO 9.

91

I JUST NOTICED... THERE'S AN
INCONSISTENCY, ISN'T THERE?
WITH THE BROKEN WINDOW!

RETURN TO 23.

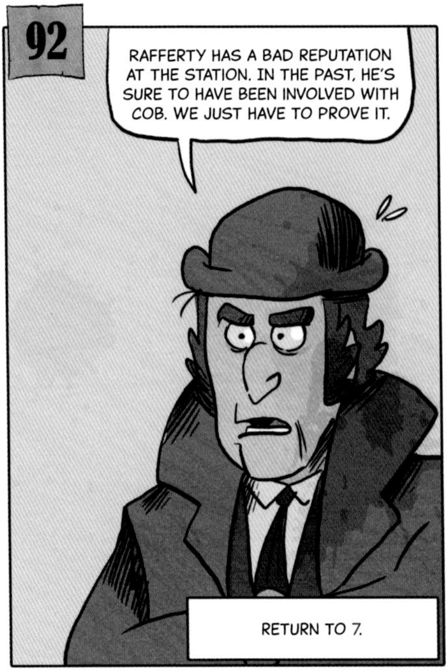
92
RAFFERTY HAS A BAD REPUTATION AT THE STATION. IN THE PAST, HE'S SURE TO HAVE BEEN INVOLVED WITH COB. WE JUST HAVE TO PROVE IT.
RETURN TO 7.

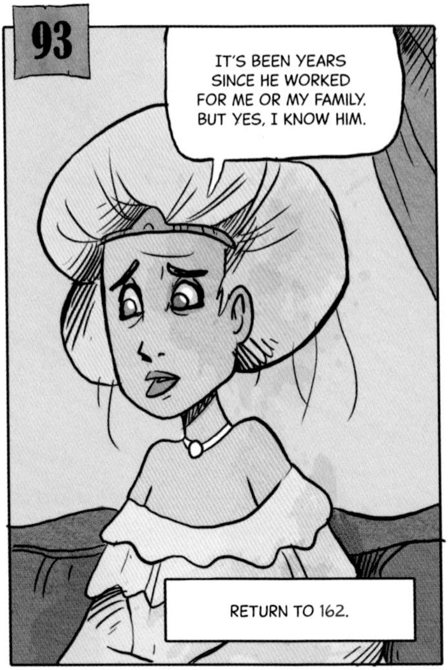
93
IT'S BEEN YEARS SINCE HE WORKED FOR ME OR MY FAMILY. BUT YES, I KNOW HIM.
RETURN TO 162.

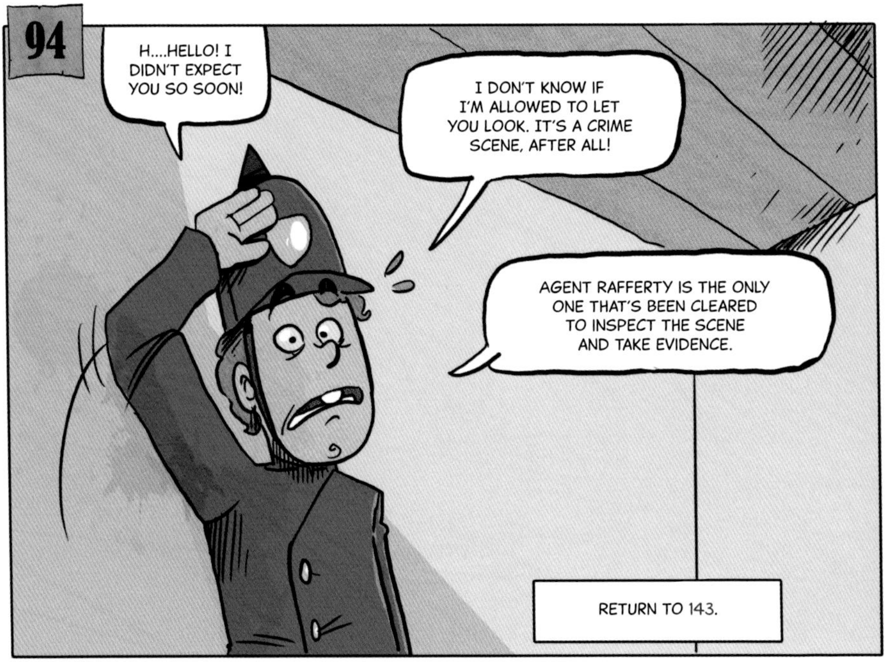
94
H....HELLO! I DIDN'T EXPECT YOU SO SOON!
I DON'T KNOW IF I'M ALLOWED TO LET YOU LOOK. IT'S A CRIME SCENE, AFTER ALL!
AGENT RAFFERTY IS THE ONLY ONE THAT'S BEEN CLEARED TO INSPECT THE SCENE AND TAKE EVIDENCE.
RETURN TO 143.

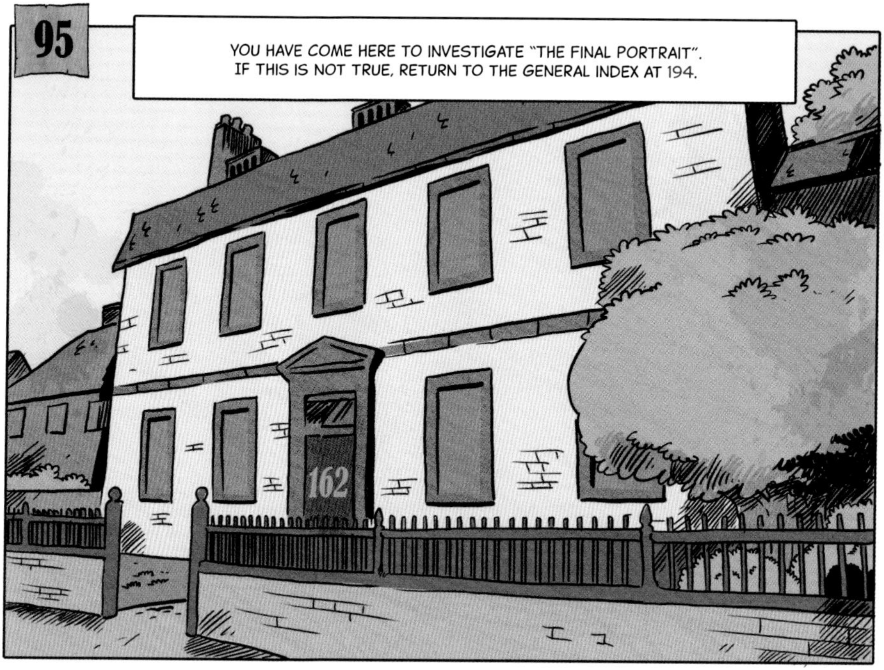
95
YOU HAVE COME HERE TO INVESTIGATE "THE FINAL PORTRAIT".
IF THIS IS NOT TRUE, RETURN TO THE GENERAL INDEX AT 194.
162

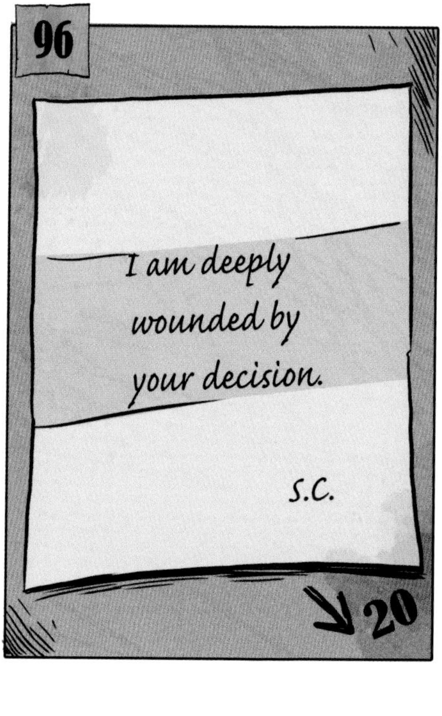
96
I am deeply wounded by your decision.
S.C.
20

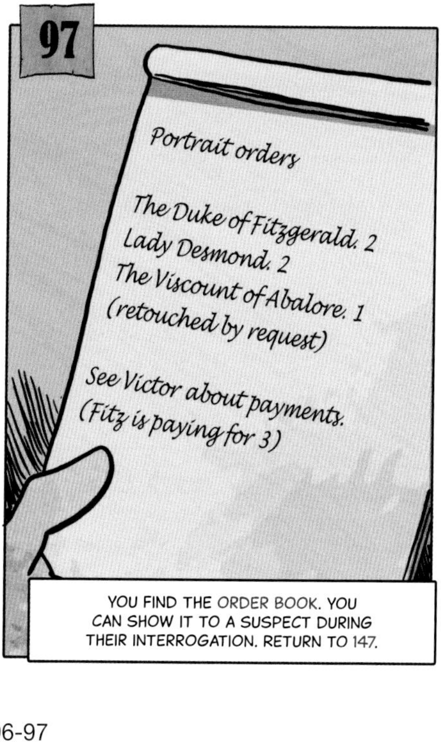
97
Portrait orders
The Duke of Fitzgerald. 2
Lady Desmond. 2
The Viscount of Abalore. 1
(retouched by request)
See Victor about payments.
(Fitz is paying for 3)
YOU FIND THE ORDER BOOK. YOU CAN SHOW IT TO A SUSPECT DURING THEIR INTERROGATION. RETURN TO 147.

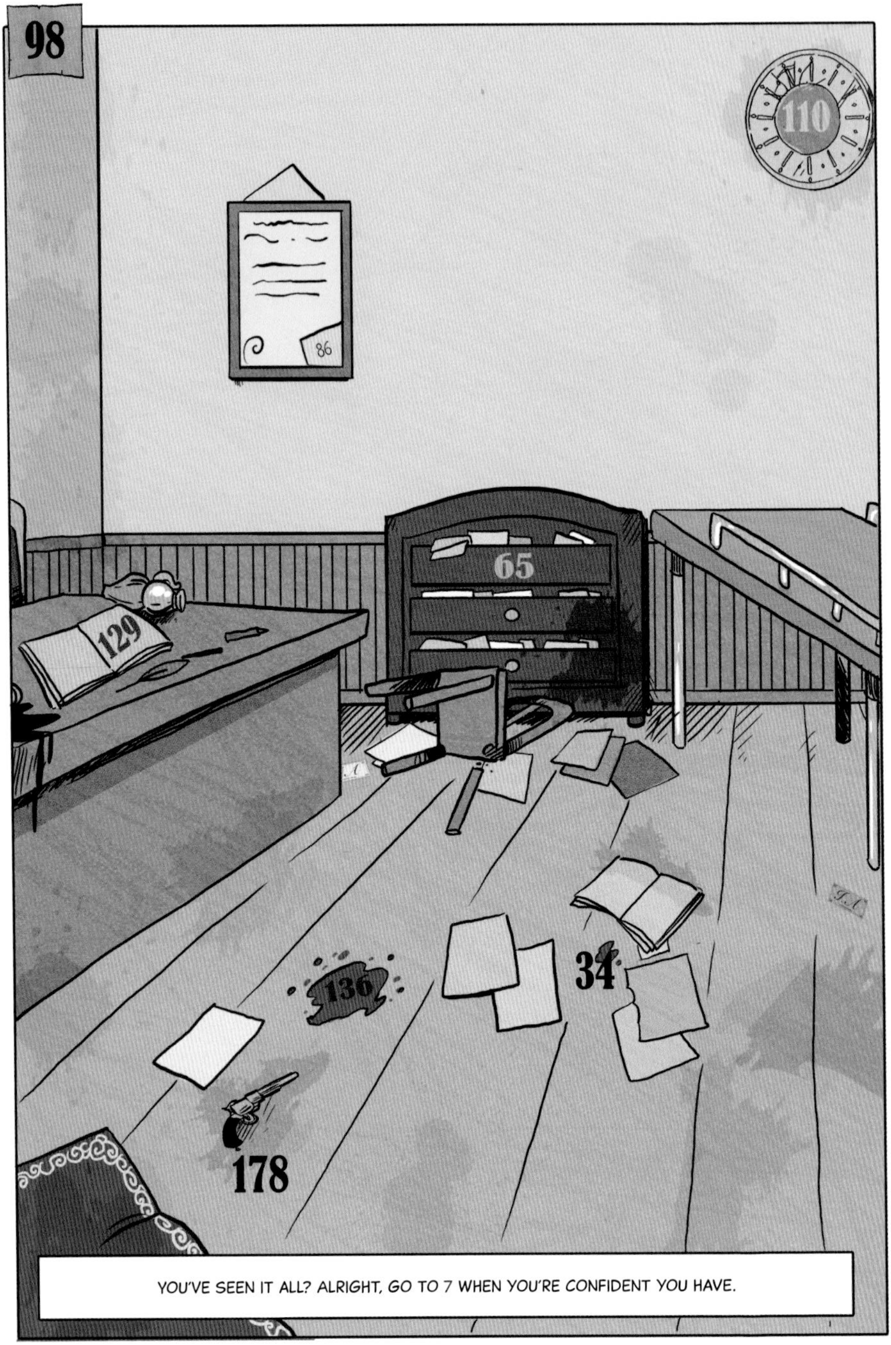
98
110
86
65
129
136
34
178
YOU'VE SEEN IT ALL? ALRIGHT, GO TO 7 WHEN YOU'RE CONFIDENT YOU HAVE.

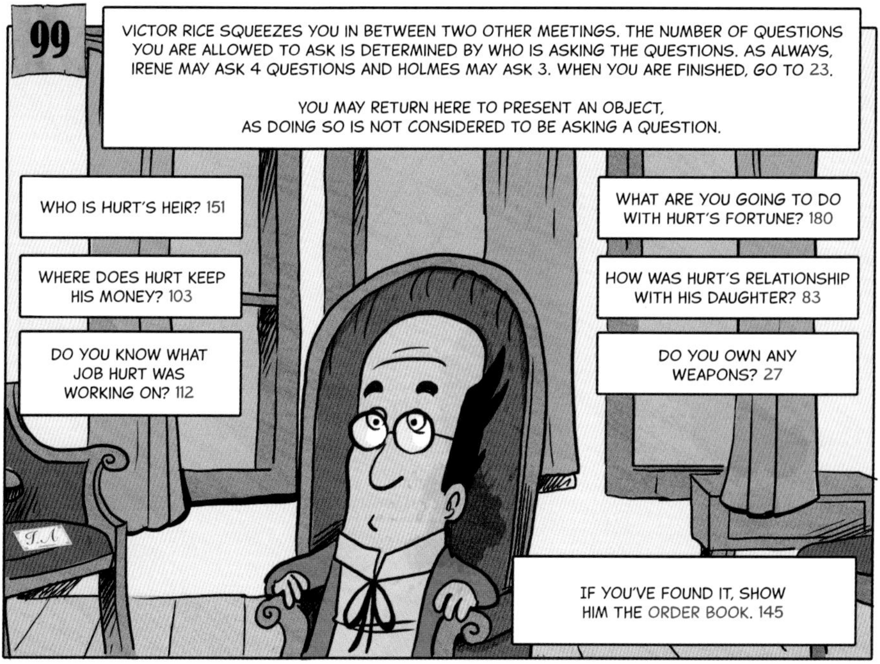
99
VICTOR RICE SQUEEZES YOU IN BETWEEN TWO OTHER MEETINGS. THE NUMBER OF QUESTIONS YOU ARE ALLOWED TO ASK IS DETERMINED BY WHO IS ASKING THE QUESTIONS. AS ALWAYS, IRENE MAY ASK 4 QUESTIONS AND HOLMES MAY ASK 3. WHEN YOU ARE FINISHED, GO TO 23.
YOU MAY RETURN HERE TO PRESENT AN OBJECT, AS DOING SO IS NOT CONSIDERED TO BE ASKING A QUESTION.
WHO IS HURT'S HEIR? 151
WHERE DOES HURT KEEP HIS MONEY? 103
DO YOU KNOW WHAT JOB HURT WAS WORKING ON? 112
WHAT ARE YOU GOING TO DO WITH HURT'S FORTUNE? 180
HOW WAS HURT'S RELATIONSHIP WITH HIS DAUGHTER? 83
DO YOU OWN ANY WEAPONS? 27
I.A.
IF YOU'VE FOUND IT, SHOW HIM THE ORDER BOOK. 145

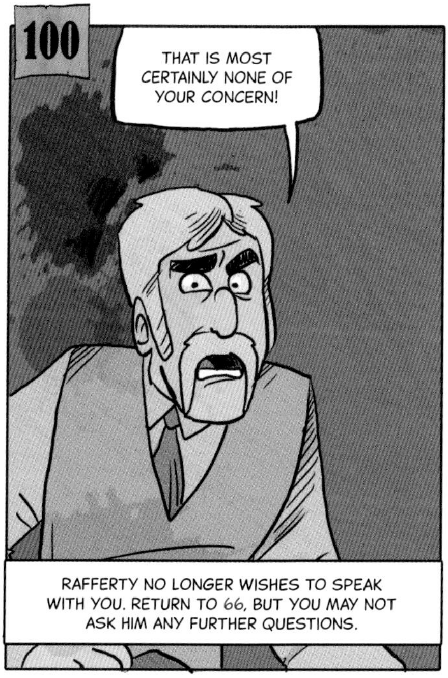
100
THAT IS MOST CERTAINLY NONE OF YOUR CONCERN!
RAFFERTY NO LONGER WISHES TO SPEAK WITH YOU. RETURN TO 66, BUT YOU MAY NOT ASK HIM ANY FURTHER QUESTIONS.

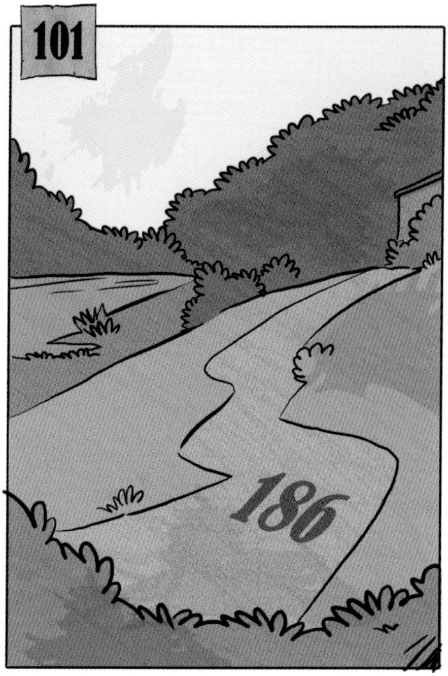
101
186

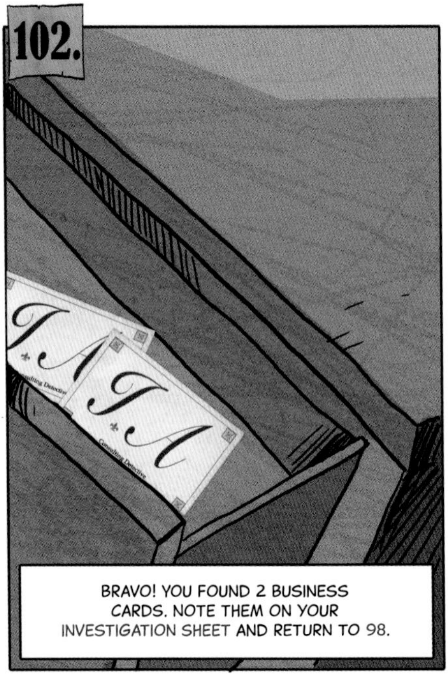
102.
BRAVO! YOU FOUND 2 BUSINESS CARDS. NOTE THEM ON YOUR INVESTIGATION SHEET AND RETURN TO 98.

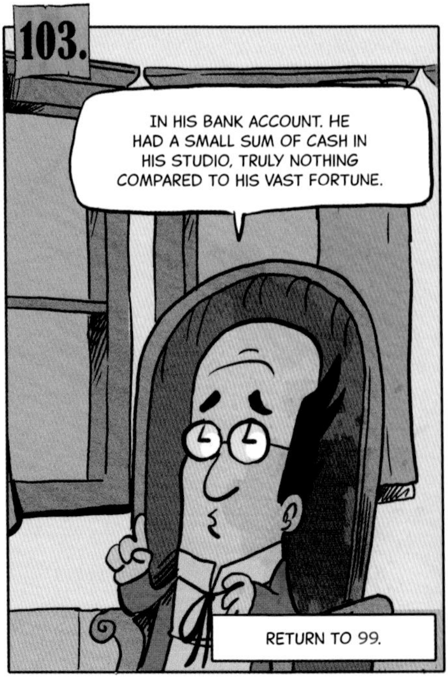
103.
IN HIS BANK ACCOUNT. HE HAD A SMALL SUM OF CASH IN HIS STUDIO, TRULY NOTHING COMPARED TO HIS VAST FORTUNE.
RETURN TO 99.

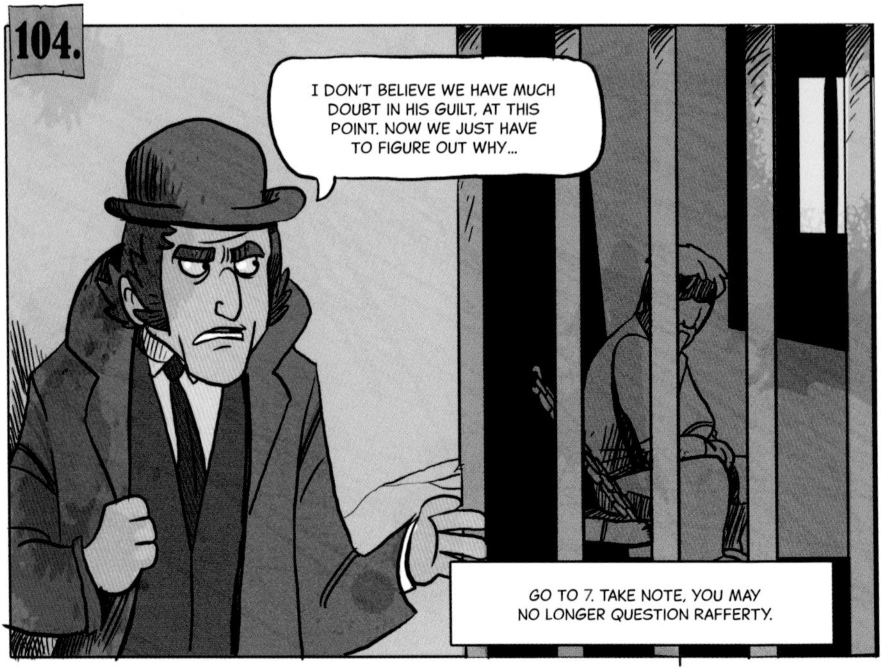
104.
I DON'T BELIEVE WE HAVE MUCH DOUBT IN HIS GUILT, AT THIS POINT. NOW WE JUST HAVE TO FIGURE OUT WHY...
GO TO 7. TAKE NOTE, YOU MAY NO LONGER QUESTION RAFFERTY.

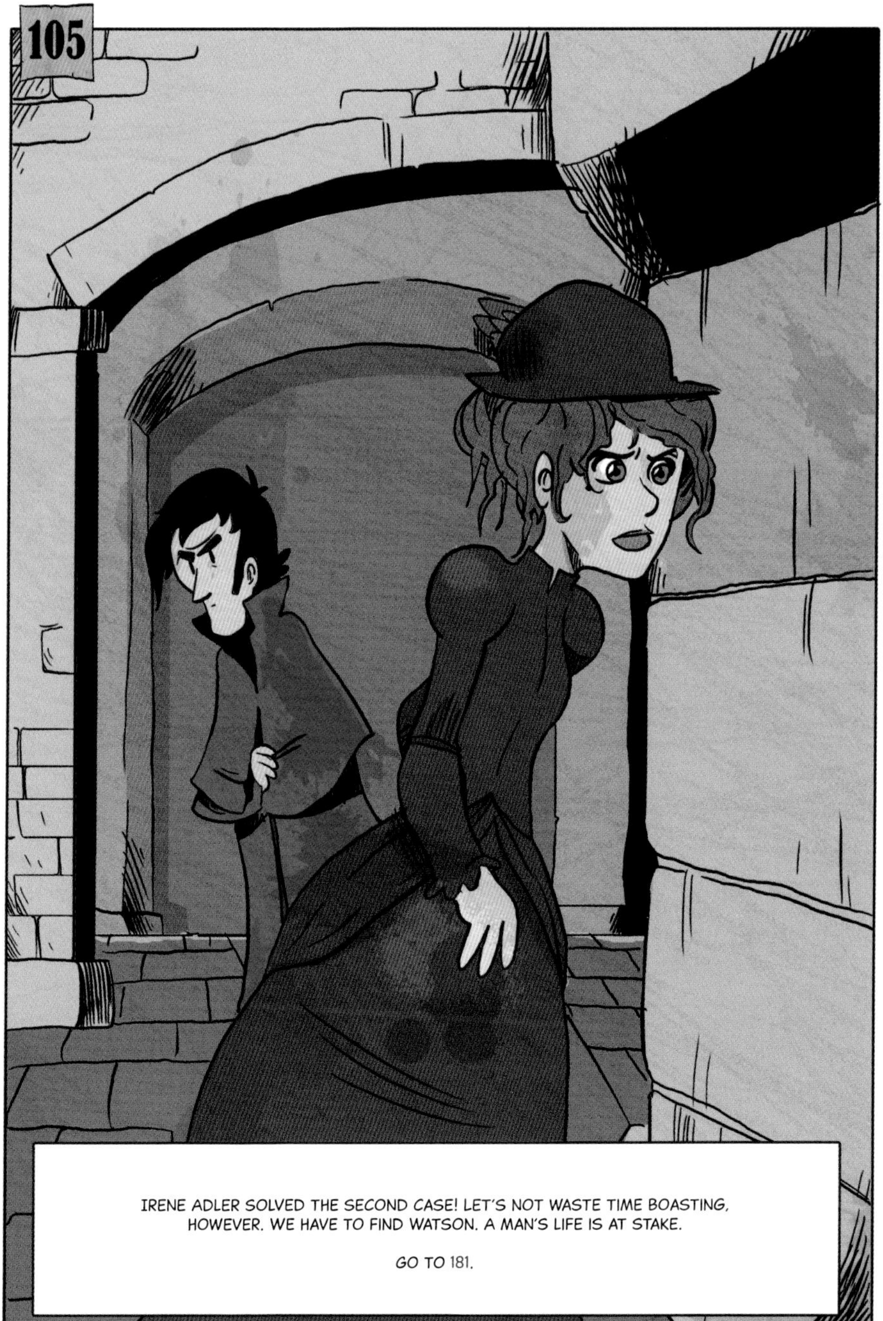
105
IRENE ADLER SOLVED THE SECOND CASE! LET'S NOT WASTE TIME BOASTING, HOWEVER. WE HAVE TO FIND WATSON. A MAN'S LIFE IS AT STAKE.
GO TO 181.

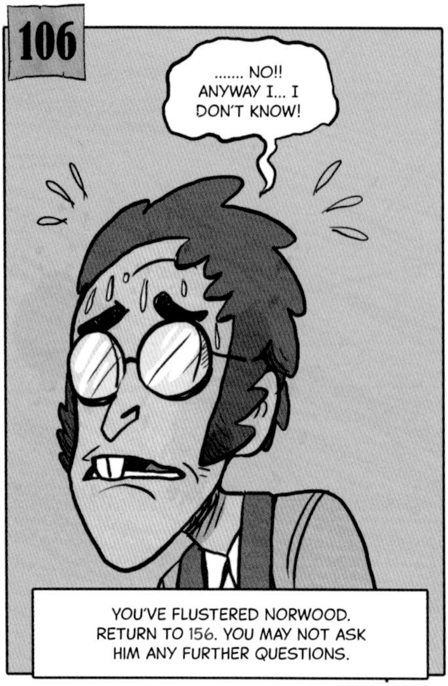
106
.... NO!! ANYWAY I... I DON'T KNOW!
YOU'VE FLUSTERED NORWOOD. RETURN TO 156. YOU MAY NOT ASK HIM ANY FURTHER QUESTIONS.

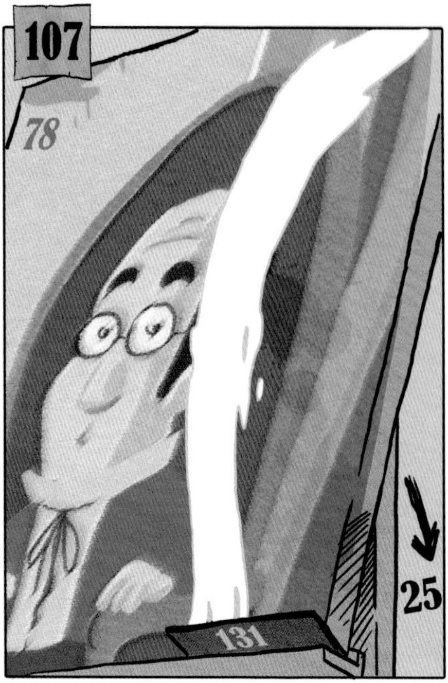
107
78
25
131

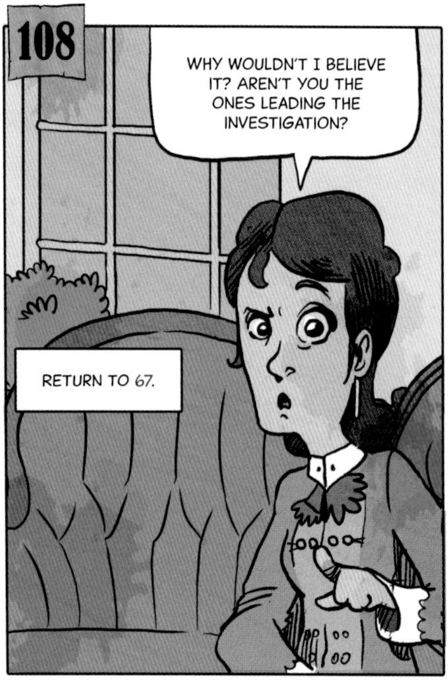
108
WHY WOULDN'T I BELIEVE IT? AREN'T YOU THE ONES LEADING THE INVESTIGATION?
RETURN TO 67.

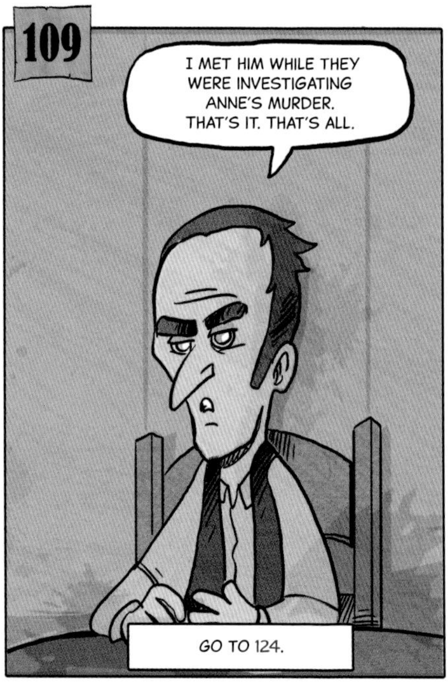
109
I MET HIM WHILE THEY WERE INVESTIGATING ANNE'S MURDER. THAT'S IT. THAT'S ALL.
GO TO 124.

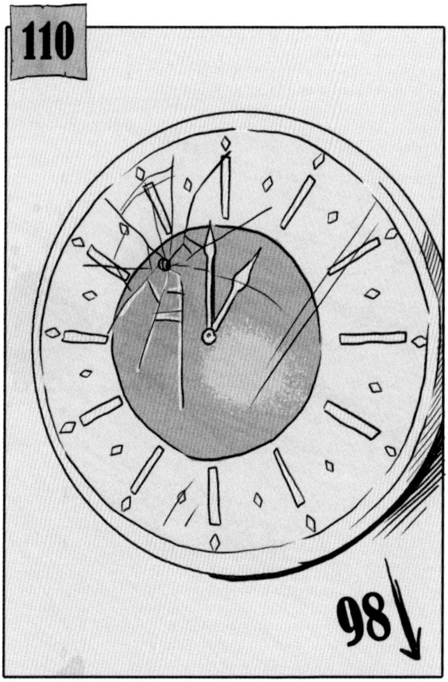
110
98

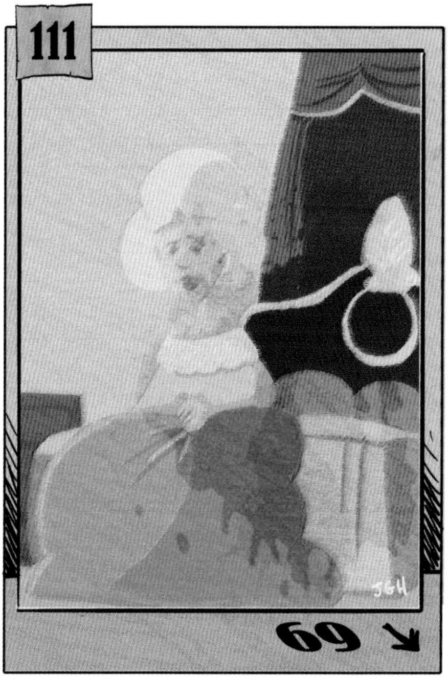
111
69

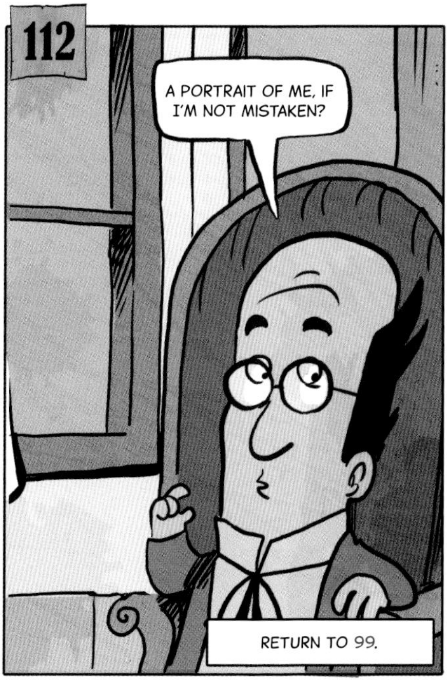
112
A PORTRAIT OF ME, IF I'M NOT MISTAKEN?
RETURN TO 99.

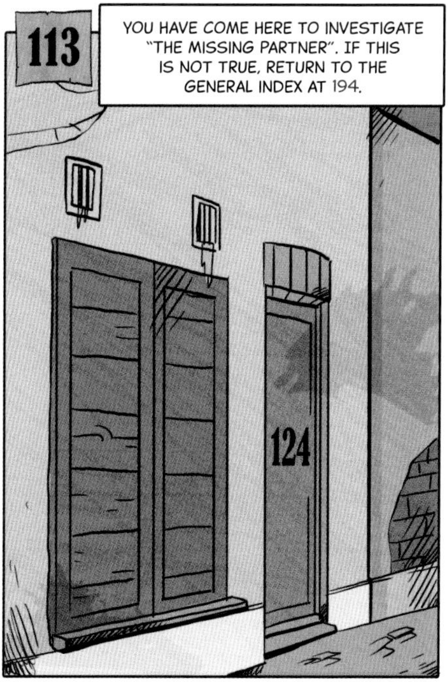
113
YOU HAVE COME HERE TO INVESTIGATE "THE MISSING PARTNER". IF THIS IS NOT TRUE, RETURN TO THE GENERAL INDEX AT 194.
124

114

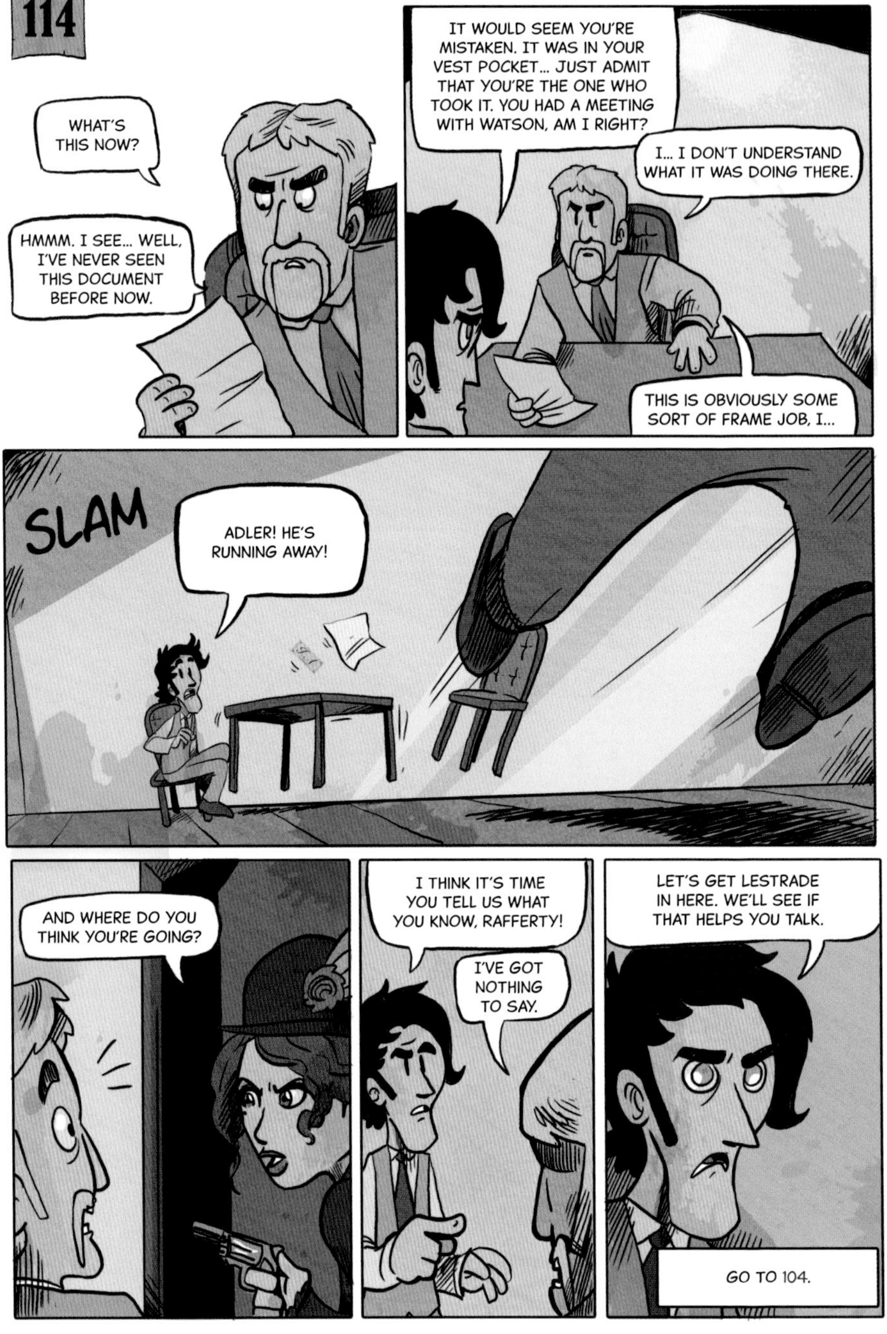

WHAT'S THIS NOW?
HMMM. I SEE... WELL, I'VE NEVER SEEN THIS DOCUMENT BEFORE NOW.
IT WOULD SEEM YOU'RE MISTAKEN. IT WAS IN YOUR VEST POCKET... JUST ADMIT THAT YOU'RE THE ONE WHO TOOK IT. YOU HAD A MEETING WITH WATSON, AM I RIGHT?
I... I DON'T UNDERSTAND WHAT IT WAS DOING THERE.
THIS IS OBVIOUSLY SOME SORT OF FRAME JOB, I...
SLAM
ADLER! HE'S RUNNING AWAY!
AND WHERE DO YOU THINK YOU'RE GOING?
I THINK IT'S TIME YOU TELL US WHAT YOU KNOW, RAFFERTY!
I'VE GOT NOTHING TO SAY.
LET'S GET LESTRADE IN HERE. WE'LL SEE IF THAT HELPS YOU TALK.
GO TO 104.

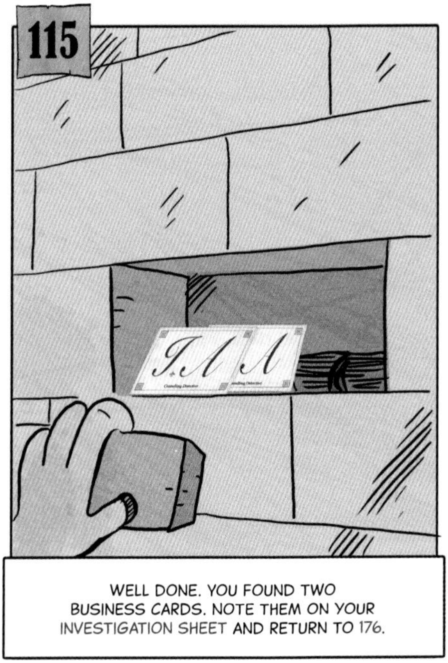
115
WELL DONE. YOU FOUND TWO BUSINESS CARDS. NOTE THEM ON YOUR INVESTIGATION SHEET AND RETURN TO 176.

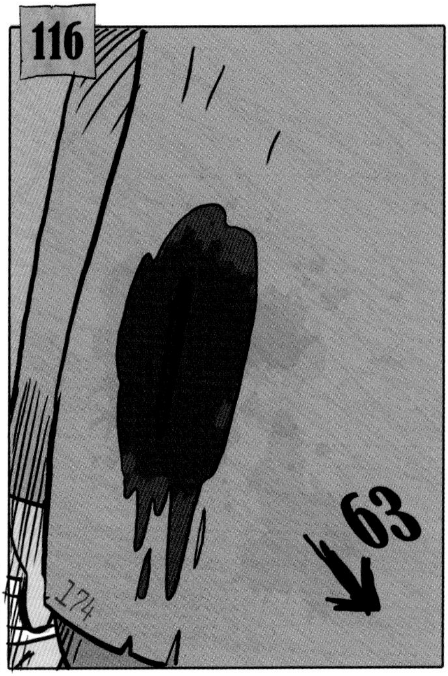
116
174
63

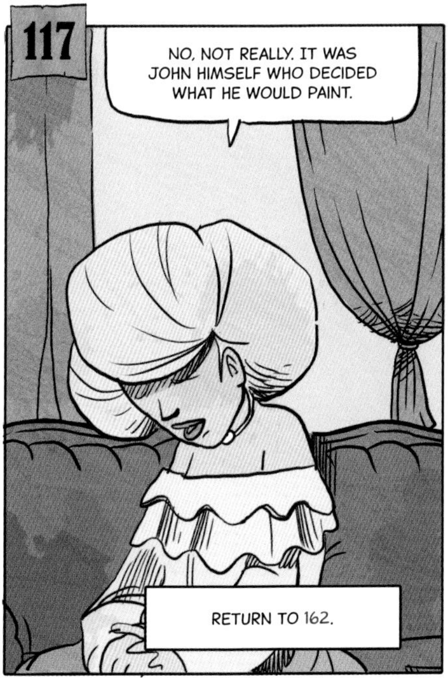
117
NO, NOT REALLY. IT WAS JOHN HIMSELF WHO DECIDED WHAT HE WOULD PAINT.
RETURN TO 162.

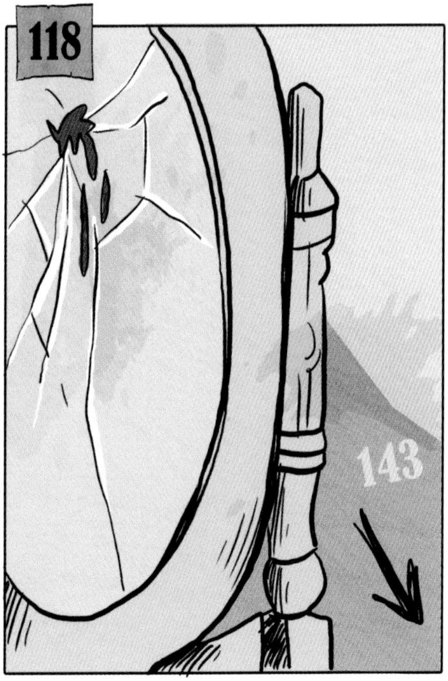
118
143

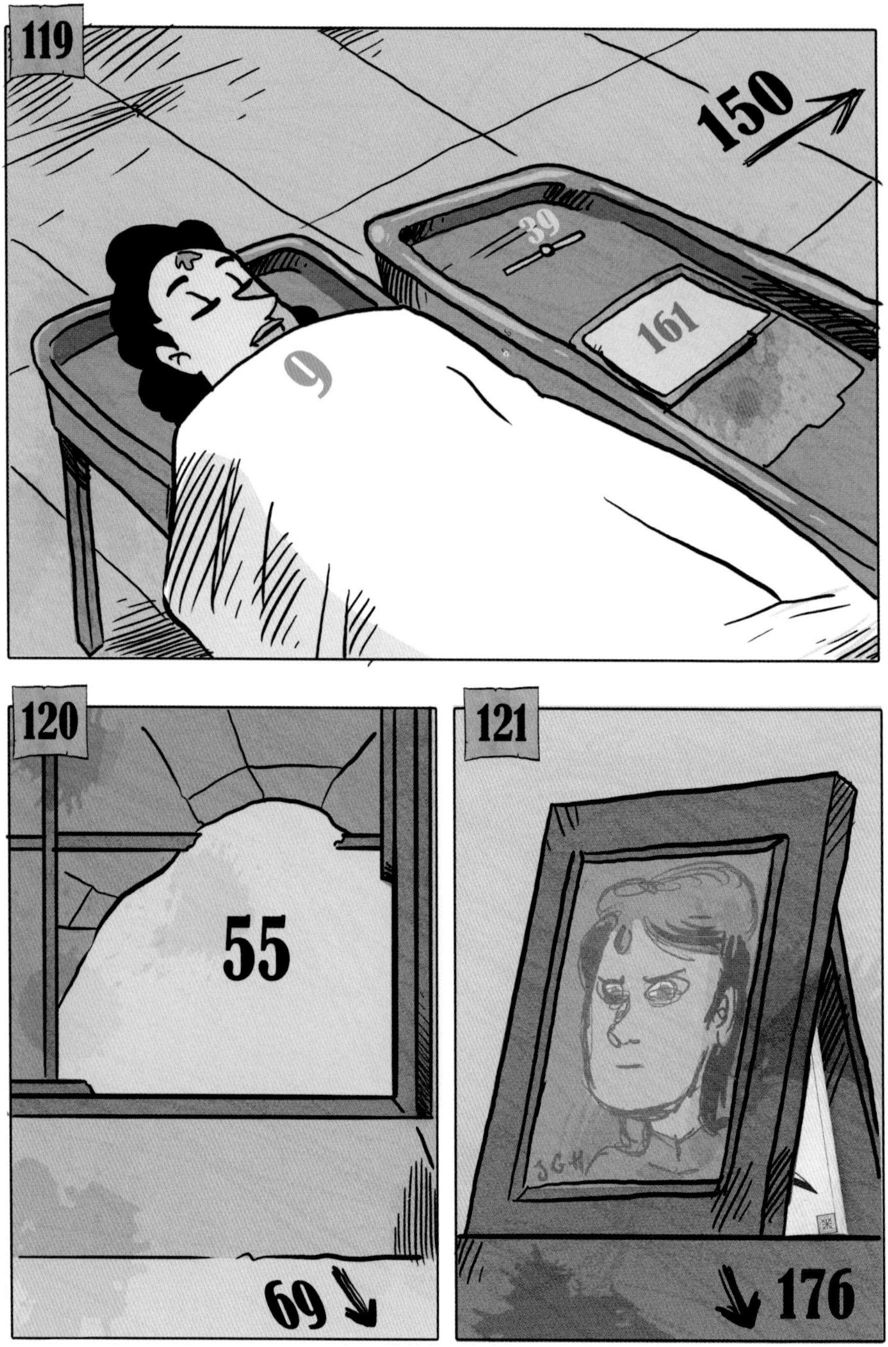
119
150
39
161
9
120
55
69
121
176

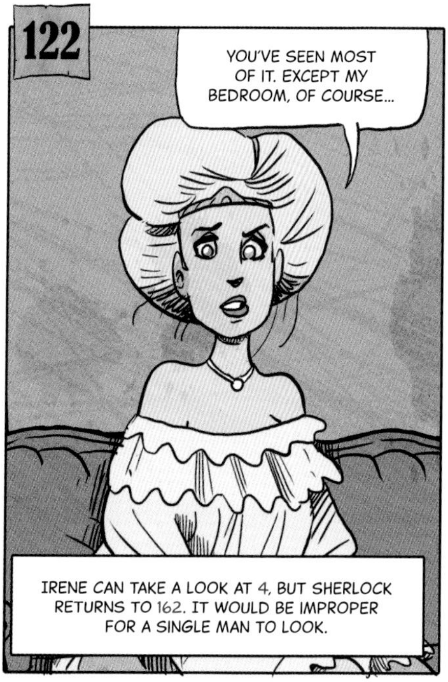
122
YOU'VE SEEN MOST OF IT. EXCEPT MY BEDROOM, OF COURSE...
IRENE CAN TAKE A LOOK AT 4, BUT SHERLOCK RETURNS TO 162. IT WOULD BE IMPROPER FOR A SINGLE MAN TO LOOK.

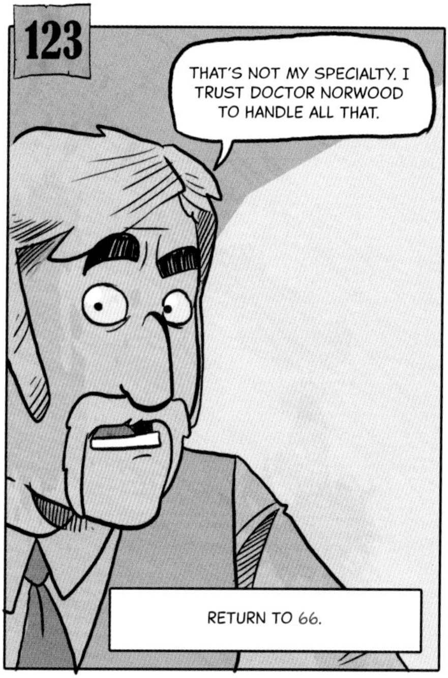
123
THAT'S NOT MY SPECIALTY. I TRUST DOCTOR NORWOOD TO HANDLE ALL THAT.
RETURN TO 66.

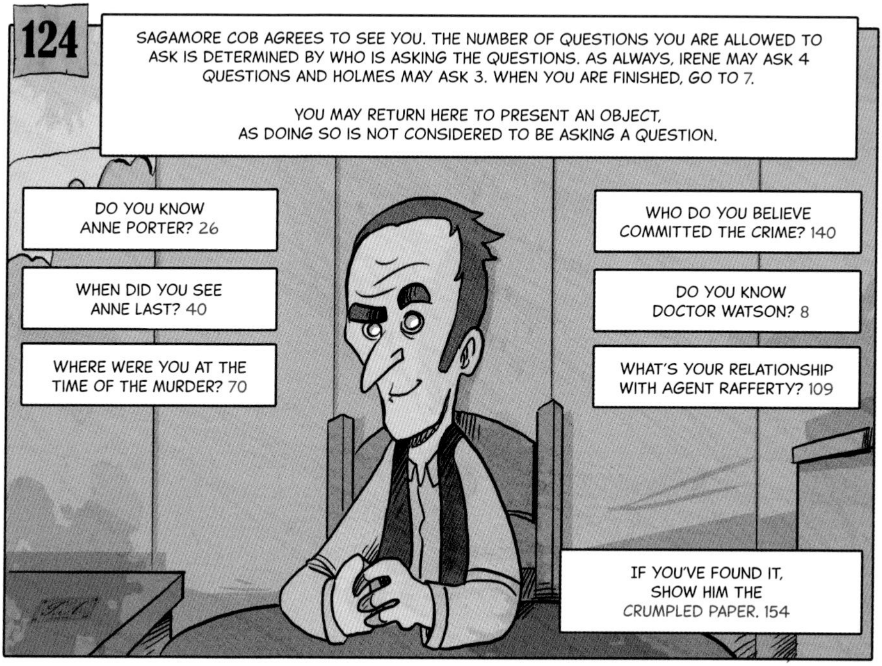
124
SAGAMORE COB AGREES TO SEE YOU. THE NUMBER OF QUESTIONS YOU ARE ALLOWED TO ASK IS DETERMINED BY WHO IS ASKING THE QUESTIONS. AS ALWAYS, IRENE MAY ASK 4 QUESTIONS AND HOLMES MAY ASK 3. WHEN YOU ARE FINISHED, GO TO 7.
YOU MAY RETURN HERE TO PRESENT AN OBJECT, AS DOING SO IS NOT CONSIDERED TO BE ASKING A QUESTION.
DO YOU KNOW ANNE PORTER? 26
WHEN DID YOU SEE ANNE LAST? 40
WHERE WERE YOU AT THE TIME OF THE MURDER? 70
WHO DO YOU BELIEVE COMMITTED THE CRIME? 140
DO YOU KNOW DOCTOR WATSON? 8
WHAT'S YOUR RELATIONSHIP WITH AGENT RAFFERTY? 109
IF YOU'VE FOUND IT, SHOW HIM THE CRUMPLED PAPER. 154

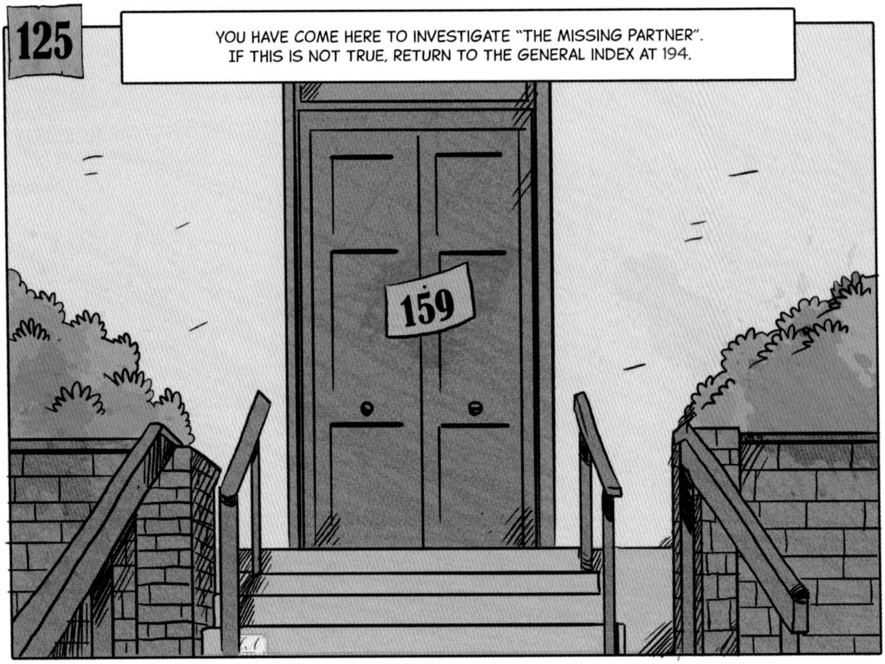
125
YOU HAVE COME HERE TO INVESTIGATE "THE MISSING PARTNER". IF THIS IS NOT TRUE, RETURN TO THE GENERAL INDEX AT 194.
159

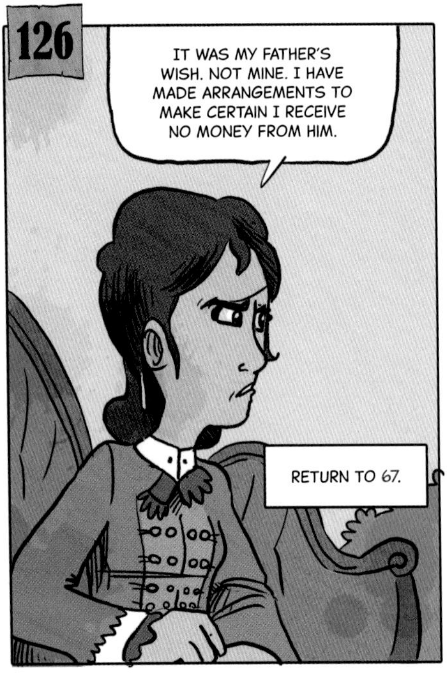
126
IT WAS MY FATHER'S WISH. NOT MINE. I HAVE MADE ARRANGEMENTS TO MAKE CERTAIN I RECEIVE NO MONEY FROM HIM.
RETURN TO 67.

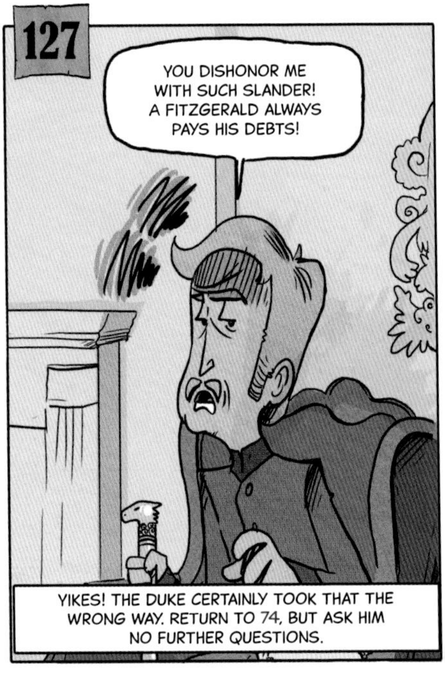
127
YOU DISHONOR ME WITH SUCH SLANDER! A FITZGERALD ALWAYS PAYS HIS DEBTS!
YIKES! THE DUKE CERTAINLY TOOK THAT THE WRONG WAY. RETURN TO 74, BUT ASK HIM NO FURTHER QUESTIONS.

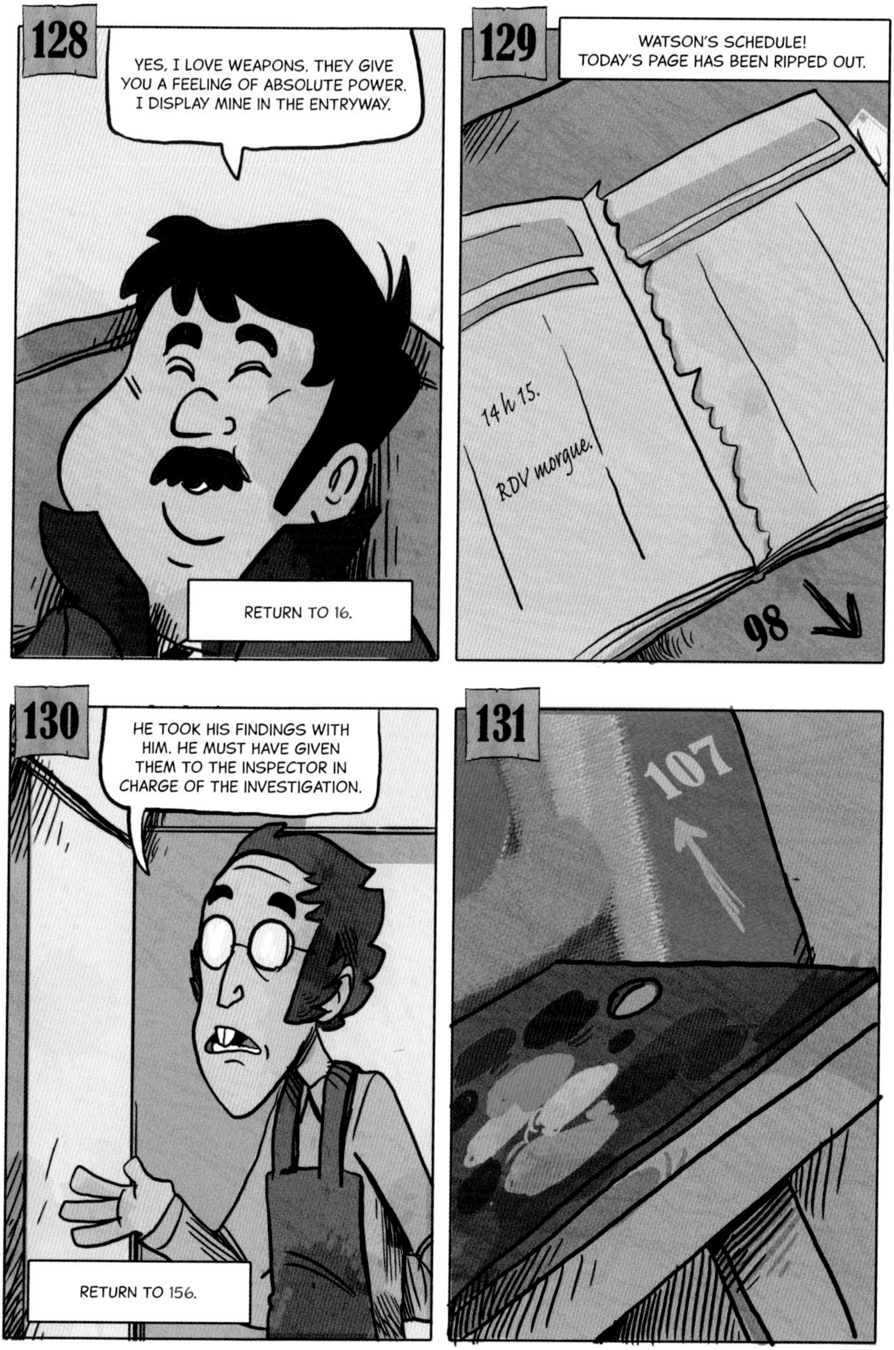
128
YES, I LOVE WEAPONS. THEY GIVE YOU A FEELING OF ABSOLUTE POWER. I DISPLAY MINE IN THE ENTRYWAY.
RETURN TO 16.
129
WATSON'S SCHEDULE! TODAY'S PAGE HAS BEEN RIPPED OUT.
14 h 15.
RDV morgue.
98
130
HE TOOK HIS FINDINGS WITH HIM. HE MUST HAVE GIVEN THEM TO THE INSPECTOR IN CHARGE OF THE INVESTIGATION.
RETURN TO 156.
131
107

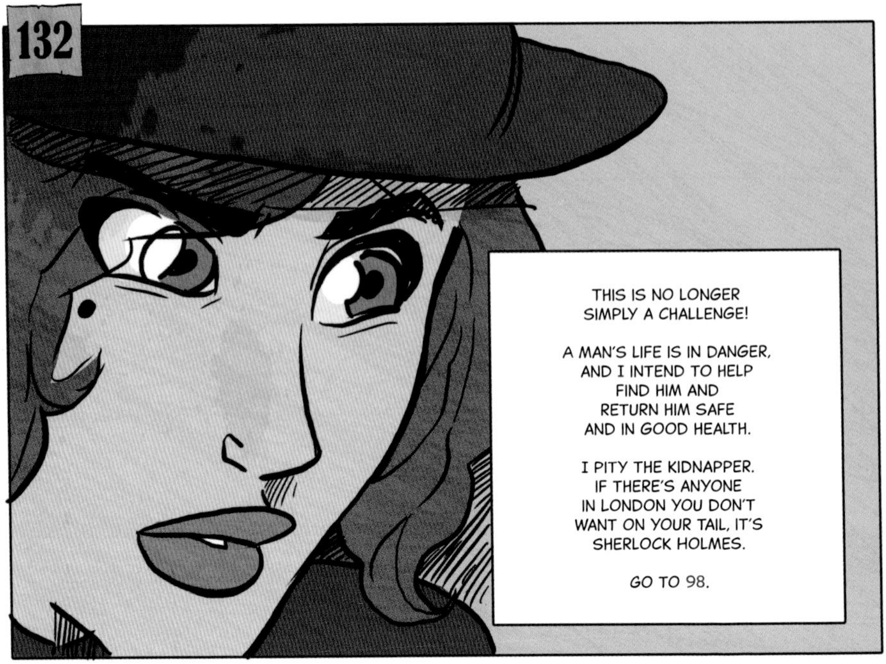
132
THIS IS NO LONGER SIMPLY A CHALLENGE!
A MAN'S LIFE IS IN DANGER, AND I INTEND TO HELP FIND HIM AND RETURN HIM SAFE AND IN GOOD HEALTH.
I PITY THE KIDNAPPER. IF THERE'S ANYONE IN LONDON YOU DON'T WANT ON YOUR TAIL, IT'S SHERLOCK HOLMES.
GO TO 98.

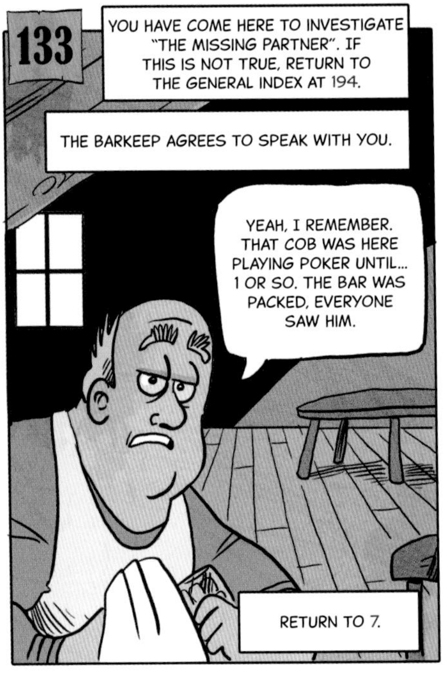
133
YOU HAVE COME HERE TO INVESTIGATE "THE MISSING PARTNER". IF THIS IS NOT TRUE, RETURN TO THE GENERAL INDEX AT 194.
THE BARKEEP AGREES TO SPEAK WITH YOU.
YEAH, I REMEMBER. THAT COB WAS HERE PLAYING POKER UNTIL... 1 OR SO. THE BAR WAS PACKED, EVERYONE SAW HIM.
RETURN TO 7.

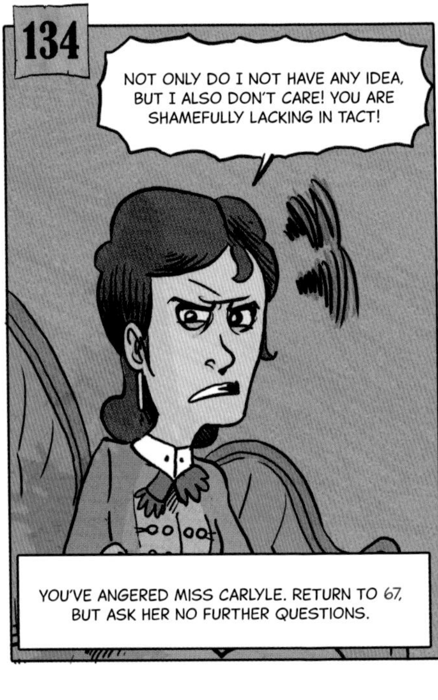
134
NOT ONLY DO I NOT HAVE ANY IDEA, BUT I ALSO DON'T CARE! YOU ARE SHAMEFULLY LACKING IN TACT!
YOU'VE ANGERED MISS CARLYLE. RETURN TO 67, BUT ASK HER NO FURTHER QUESTIONS.

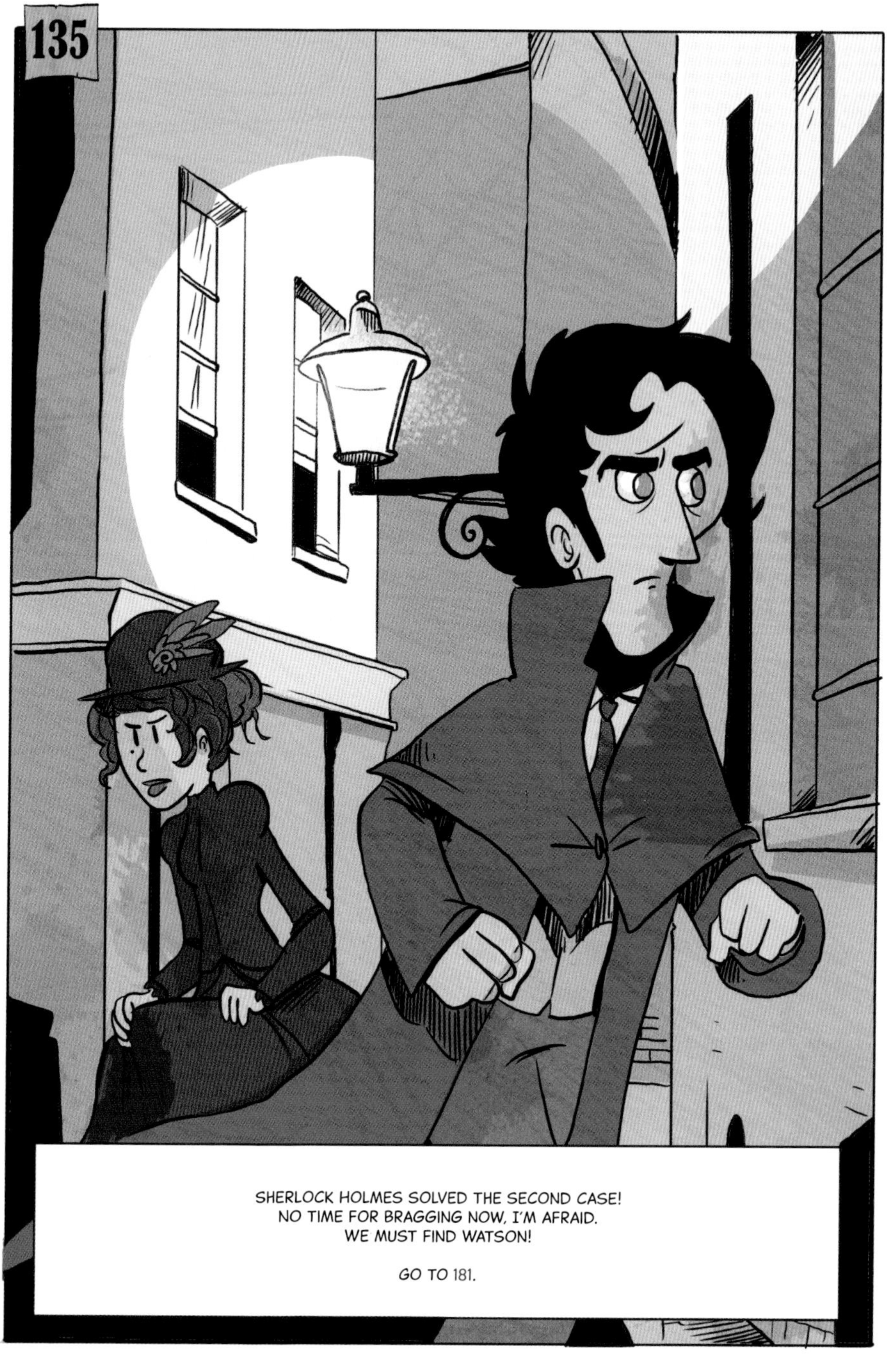
135
SHERLOCK HOLMES SOLVED THE SECOND CASE!
NO TIME FOR BRAGGING NOW, I'M AFRAID.
WE MUST FIND WATSON!
GO TO 181.

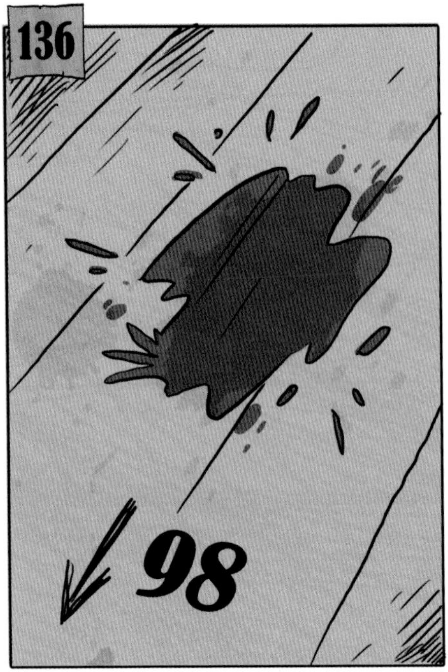
136
98

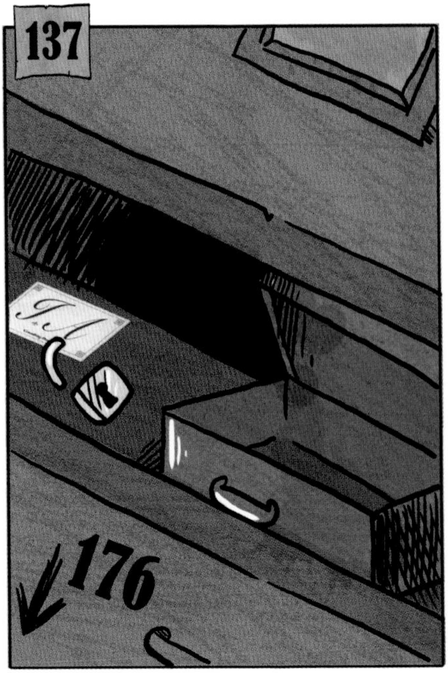
137
176

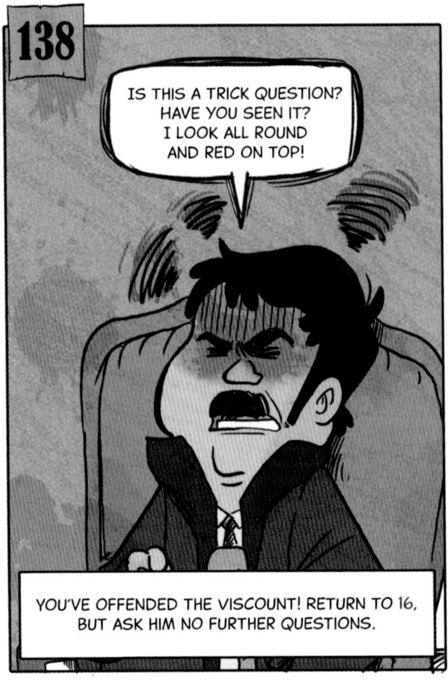
138
IS THIS A TRICK QUESTION? HAVE YOU SEEN IT? I LOOK ALL ROUND AND RED ON TOP!
YOU'VE OFFENDED THE VISCOUNT! RETURN TO 16, BUT ASK HIM NO FURTHER QUESTIONS.

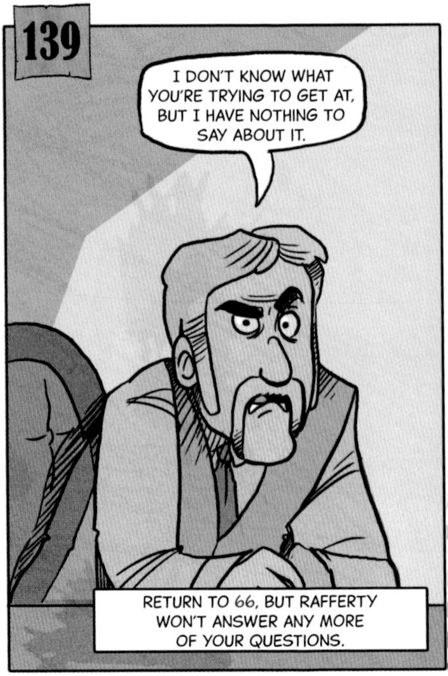
139
I DON'T KNOW WHAT YOU'RE TRYING TO GET AT, BUT I HAVE NOTHING TO SAY ABOUT IT.
RETURN TO 66, BUT RAFFERTY WON'T ANSWER ANY MORE OF YOUR QUESTIONS.

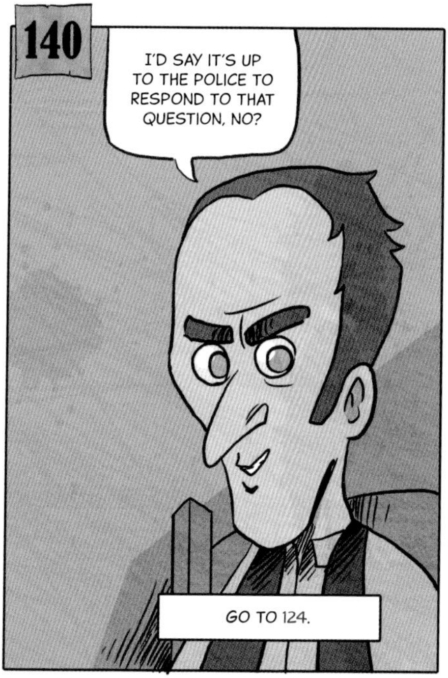
140
I'D SAY IT'S UP TO THE POLICE TO RESPOND TO THAT QUESTION, NO?
GO TO 124.

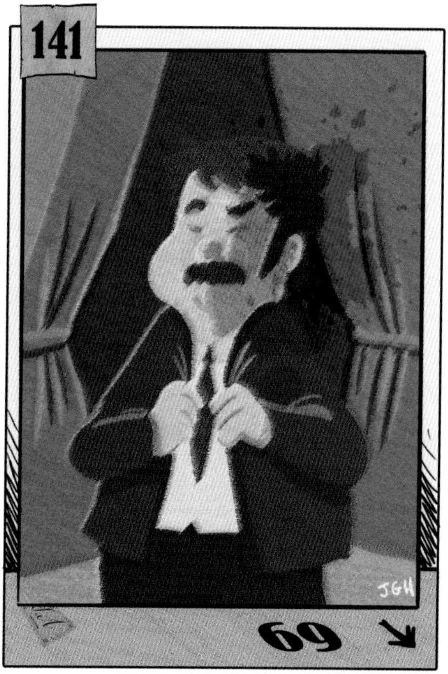
141
69

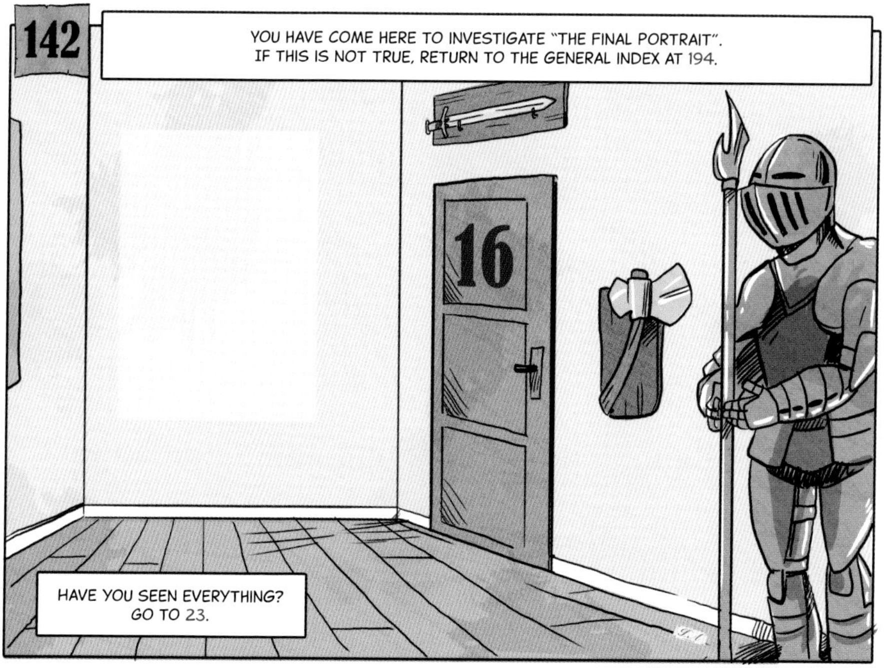
142
YOU HAVE COME HERE TO INVESTIGATE "THE FINAL PORTRAIT". IF THIS IS NOT TRUE, RETURN TO THE GENERAL INDEX AT 194.
16
HAVE YOU SEEN EVERYTHING? GO TO 23.

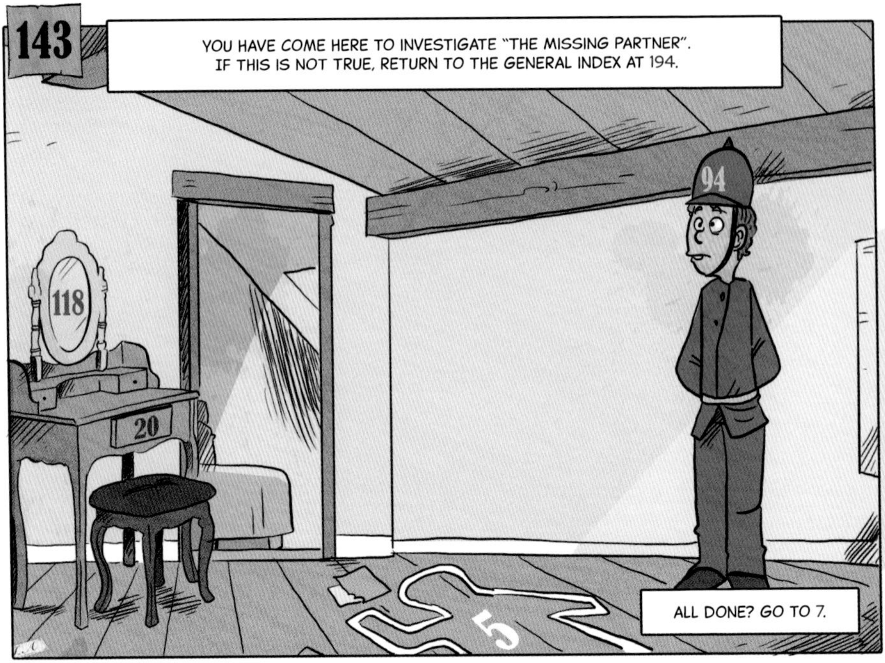
143
YOU HAVE COME HERE TO INVESTIGATE "THE MISSING PARTNER".
IF THIS IS NOT TRUE, RETURN TO THE GENERAL INDEX AT 194.
118
20
94
5
ALL DONE? GO TO 7.

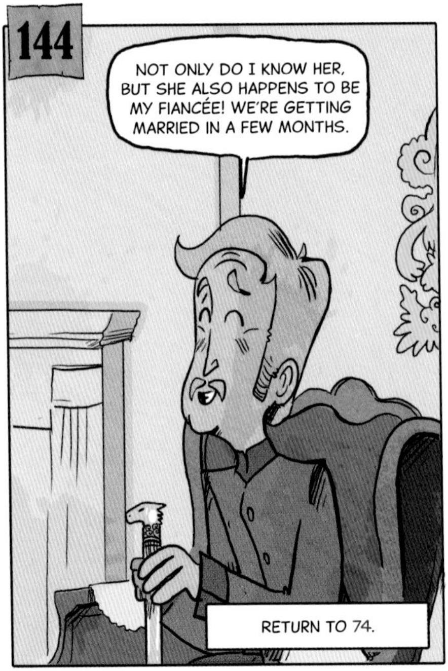
144
NOT ONLY DO I KNOW HER, BUT SHE ALSO HAPPENS TO BE MY FIANCÉE! WE'RE GETTING MARRIED IN A FEW MONTHS.
RETURN TO 74.

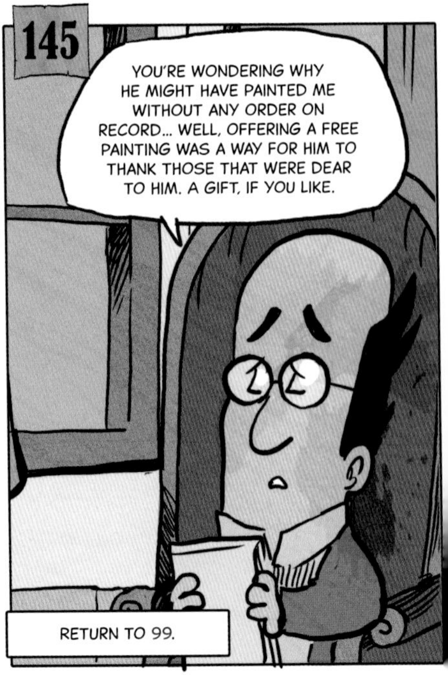
145
YOU'RE WONDERING WHY HE MIGHT HAVE PAINTED ME WITHOUT ANY ORDER ON RECORD... WELL, OFFERING A FREE PAINTING WAS A WAY FOR HIM TO THANK THOSE THAT WERE DEAR TO HIM. A GIFT, IF YOU LIKE.
RETURN TO 99.

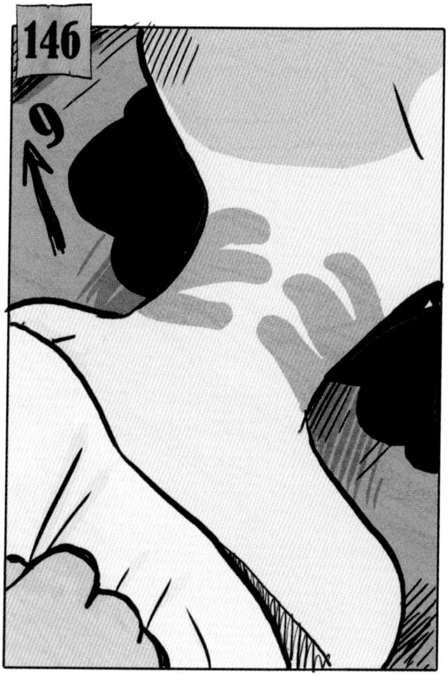
146
9

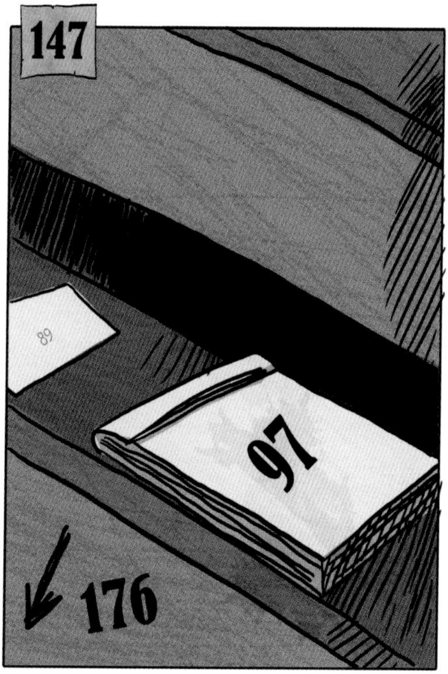
147
89
97
176

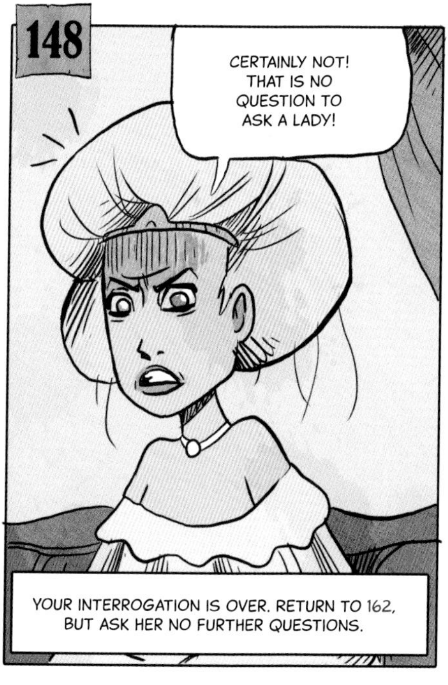
148
CERTAINLY NOT! THAT IS NO QUESTION TO ASK A LADY!
YOUR INTERROGATION IS OVER. RETURN TO 162, BUT ASK HER NO FURTHER QUESTIONS.

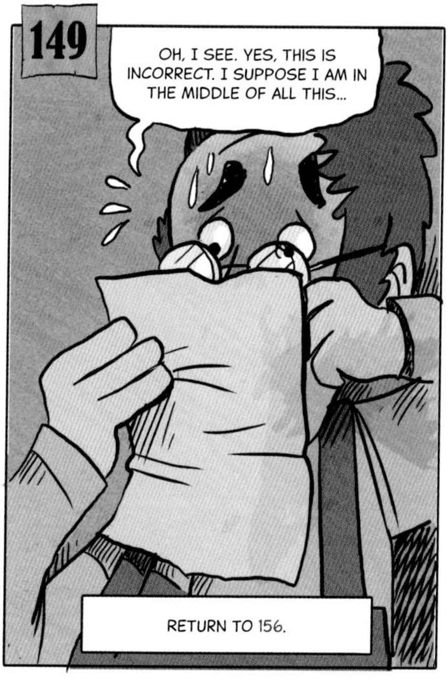
149
OH, I SEE. YES, THIS IS INCORRECT. I SUPPOSE I AM IN THE MIDDLE OF ALL THIS...
RETURN TO 156.

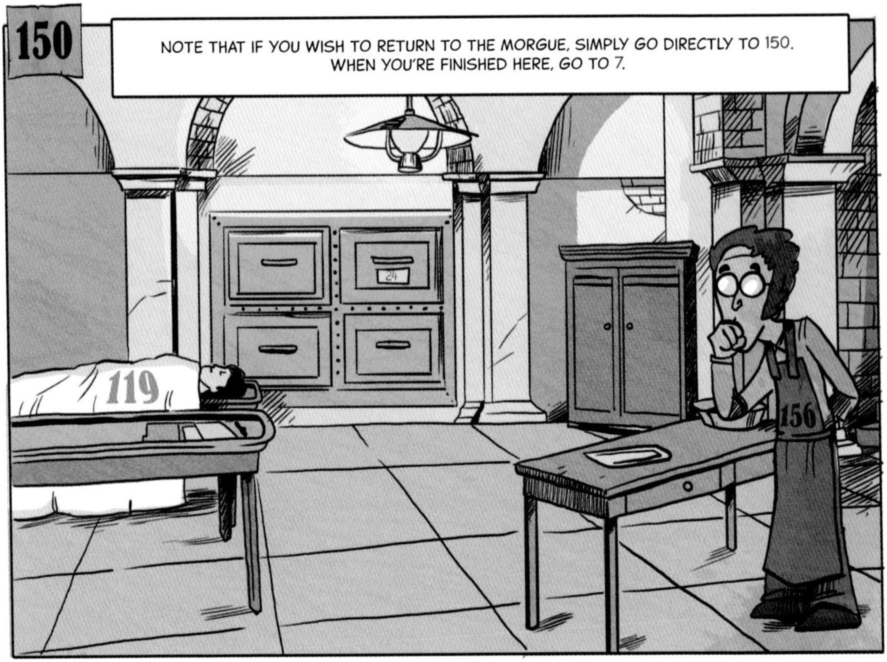
150
NOTE THAT IF YOU WISH TO RETURN TO THE MORGUE, SIMPLY GO DIRECTLY TO 150. WHEN YOU'RE FINISHED HERE, GO TO 7.
24
119
156

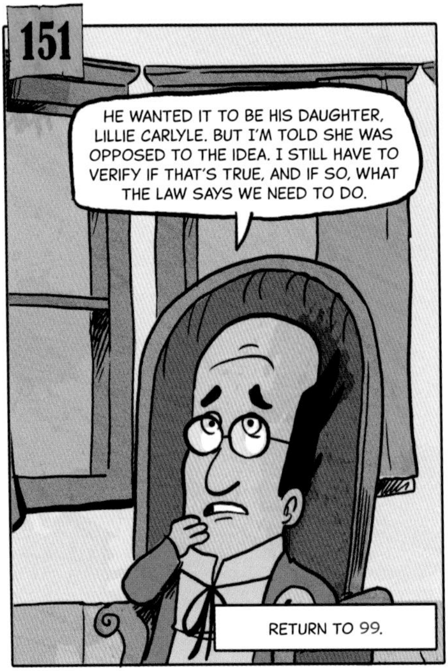
151
HE WANTED IT TO BE HIS DAUGHTER, LILLIE CARLYLE. BUT I'M TOLD SHE WAS OPPOSED TO THE IDEA. I STILL HAVE TO VERIFY IF THAT'S TRUE, AND IF SO, WHAT THE LAW SAYS WE NEED TO DO.
RETURN TO 99.

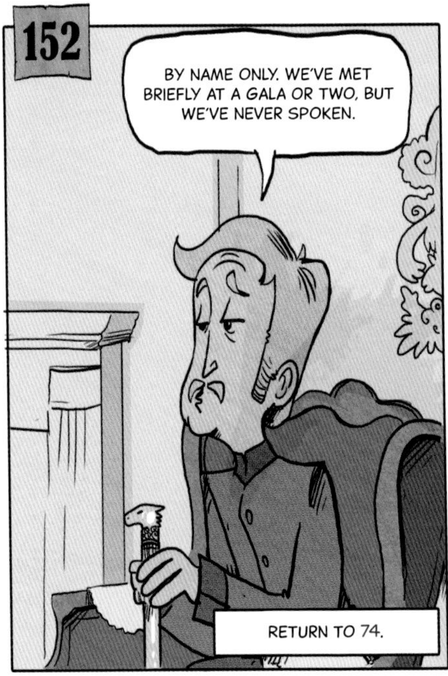
152
BY NAME ONLY. WE'VE MET BRIEFLY AT A GALA OR TWO, BUT WE'VE NEVER SPOKEN.
RETURN TO 74.

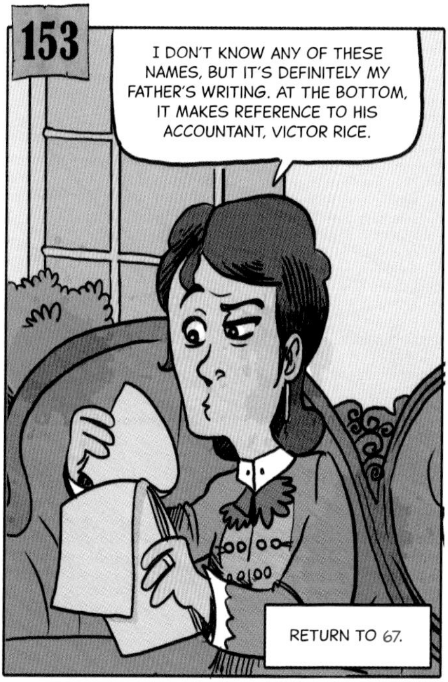
153
I DON'T KNOW ANY OF THESE NAMES, BUT IT'S DEFINITELY MY FATHER'S WRITING. AT THE BOTTOM, IT MAKES REFERENCE TO HIS ACCOUNTANT, VICTOR RICE.
RETURN TO 67.

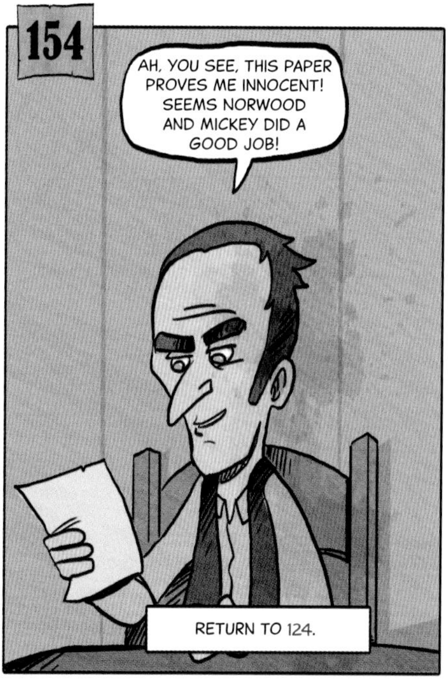
154
AH, YOU SEE, THIS PAPER PROVES ME INNOCENT! SEEMS NORWOOD AND MICKEY DID A GOOD JOB!
RETURN TO 124.

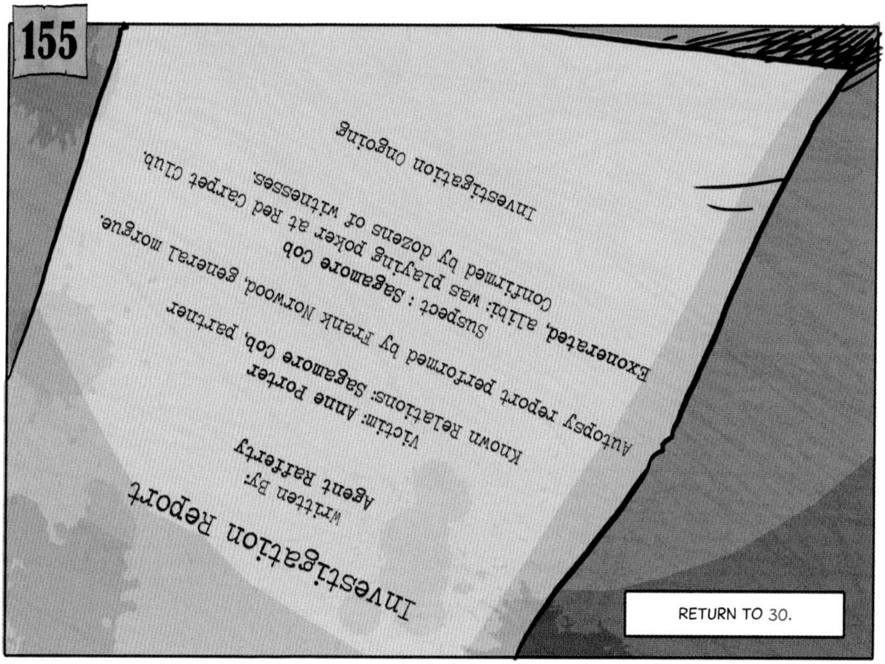
155
Investigation Report
Written By:
Agent Rafferty
Victim: Anne Porter
Known Relations: Sagamore Cob, partner
Autopsy report performed by Frank Norwood, general morgue.
Suspect : Sagamore Cob
Exonerated, alibi: was playing poker at Red Carpet Club.
Confirmed by dozens of witnesses.
Investigation Ongoing
RETURN TO 30.

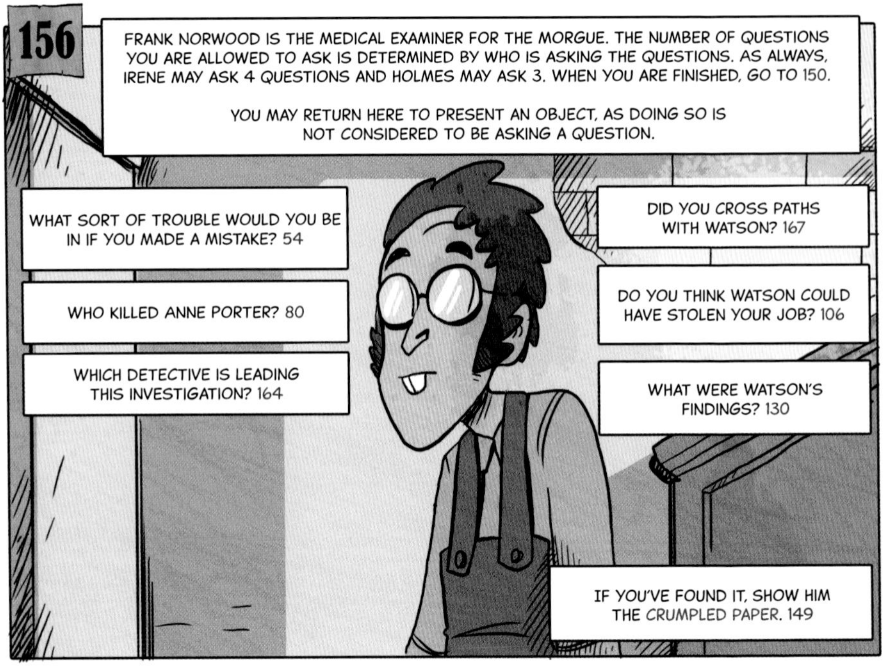
156
FRANK NORWOOD IS THE MEDICAL EXAMINER FOR THE MORGUE. THE NUMBER OF QUESTIONS YOU ARE ALLOWED TO ASK IS DETERMINED BY WHO IS ASKING THE QUESTIONS. AS ALWAYS, IRENE MAY ASK 4 QUESTIONS AND HOLMES MAY ASK 3. WHEN YOU ARE FINISHED, GO TO 150.
YOU MAY RETURN HERE TO PRESENT AN OBJECT, AS DOING SO IS NOT CONSIDERED TO BE ASKING A QUESTION.
WHAT SORT OF TROUBLE WOULD YOU BE IN IF YOU MADE A MISTAKE? 54
WHO KILLED ANNE PORTER? 80
WHICH DETECTIVE IS LEADING THIS INVESTIGATION? 164
DID YOU CROSS PATHS WITH WATSON? 167
DO YOU THINK WATSON COULD HAVE STOLEN YOUR JOB? 106
WHAT WERE WATSON'S FINDINGS? 130
IF YOU'VE FOUND IT, SHOW HIM THE CRUMPLED PAPER. 149

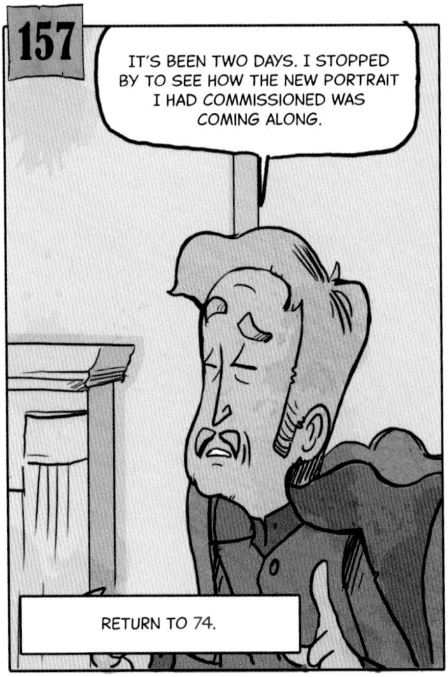
157
IT'S BEEN TWO DAYS. I STOPPED BY TO SEE HOW THE NEW PORTRAIT I HAD COMMISSIONED WAS COMING ALONG.
RETURN TO 74.

158

The result you're looking for is
Five hundred and twenty-two.

One Player:

If you succeeded with Holmes
go to 87, otherwise go to 57.

If you succeeded with Adler,
go to 57, otherwise go to 87.

Two Players:

Only Holmes succeeded: 87
Only Adler succeeded: 57
Both succeeded: 36
Neither succeeded: 77

159

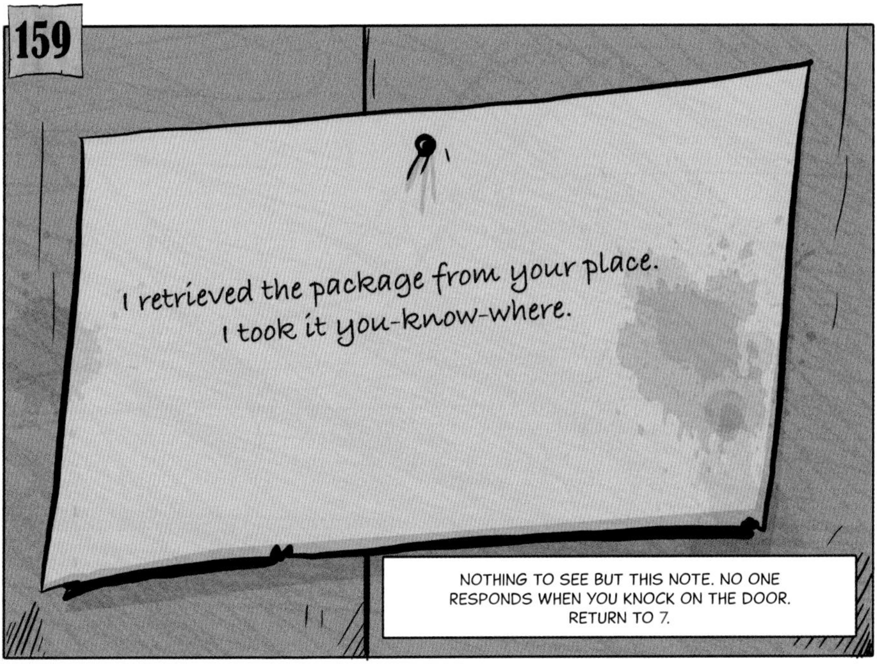
I retrieved the package from your place.
I took it you-know-where.
NOTHING TO SEE BUT THIS NOTE. NO ONE RESPONDS WHEN YOU KNOCK ON THE DOOR. RETURN TO 7.

160

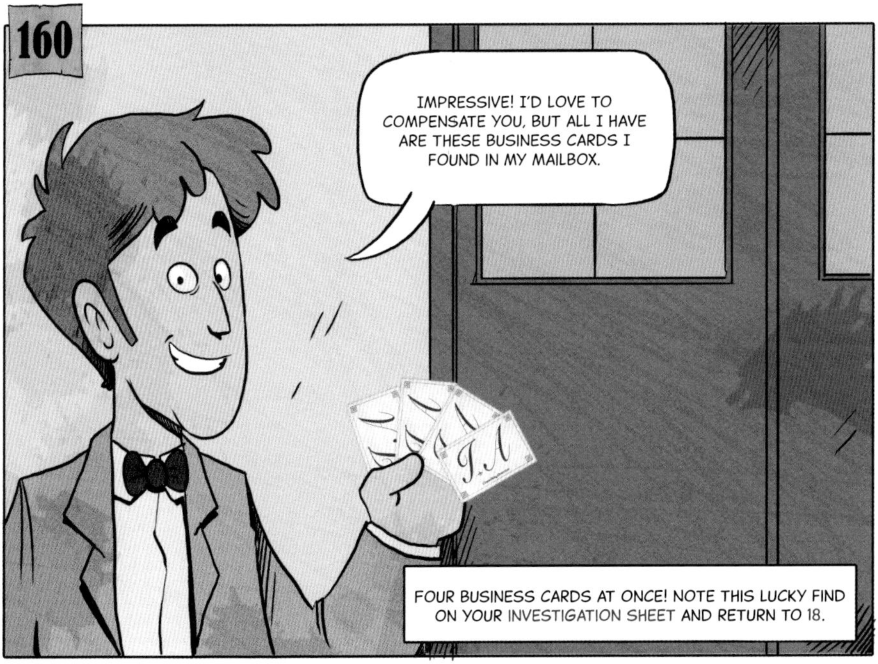
IMPRESSIVE! I'D LOVE TO COMPENSATE YOU, BUT ALL I HAVE ARE THESE BUSINESS CARDS I FOUND IN MY MAILBOX.
FOUR BUSINESS CARDS AT ONCE! NOTE THIS LUCKY FIND ON YOUR INVESTIGATION SHEET AND RETURN TO 18.

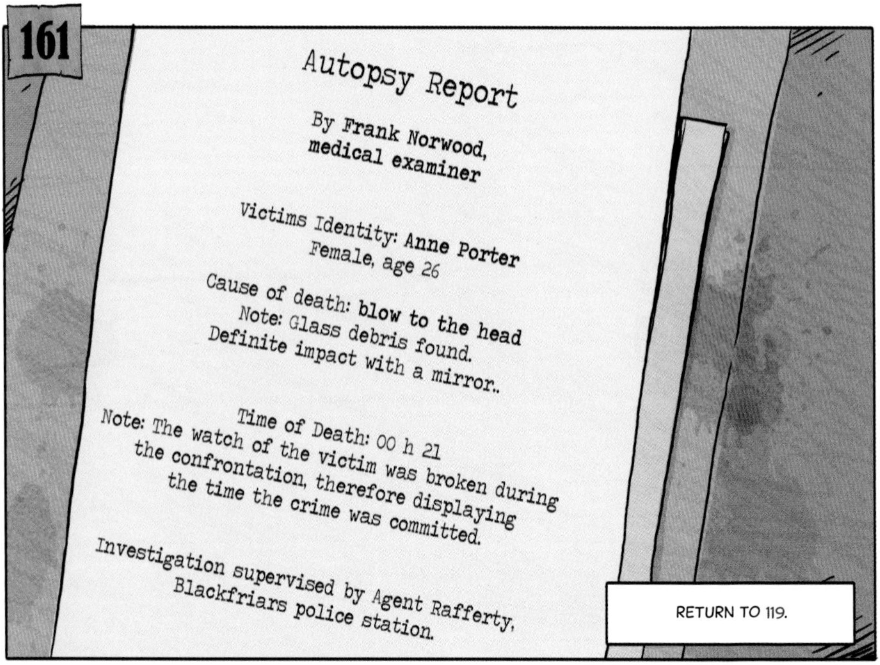
161
Autopsy Report
By Frank Norwood, medical examiner
Victims Identity: Anne Porter
Female, age 26
Cause of death: blow to the head
Note: Glass debris found.
Definite impact with a mirror..
Time of Death: 00 h 21
Note: The watch of the victim was broken during the confrontation, therefore displaying the time the crime was committed.
Investigation supervised by Agent Rafferty, Blackfriars police station.
RETURN TO 119.

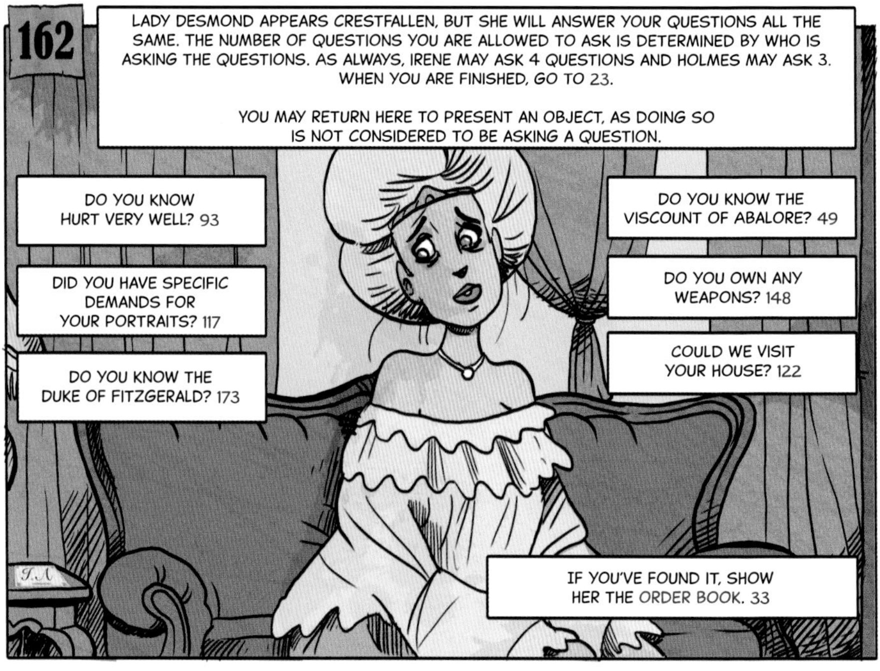
162
LADY DESMOND APPEARS CRESTFALLEN, BUT SHE WILL ANSWER YOUR QUESTIONS ALL THE SAME. THE NUMBER OF QUESTIONS YOU ARE ALLOWED TO ASK IS DETERMINED BY WHO IS ASKING THE QUESTIONS. AS ALWAYS, IRENE MAY ASK 4 QUESTIONS AND HOLMES MAY ASK 3. WHEN YOU ARE FINISHED, GO TO 23.
YOU MAY RETURN HERE TO PRESENT AN OBJECT, AS DOING SO IS NOT CONSIDERED TO BE ASKING A QUESTION.
DO YOU KNOW HURT VERY WELL? 93
DID YOU HAVE SPECIFIC DEMANDS FOR YOUR PORTRAITS? 117
DO YOU KNOW THE DUKE OF FITZGERALD? 173
DO YOU KNOW THE VISCOUNT OF ABALORE? 49
DO YOU OWN ANY WEAPONS? 148
COULD WE VISIT YOUR HOUSE? 122
IF YOU'VE FOUND IT, SHOW HER THE ORDER BOOK. 33

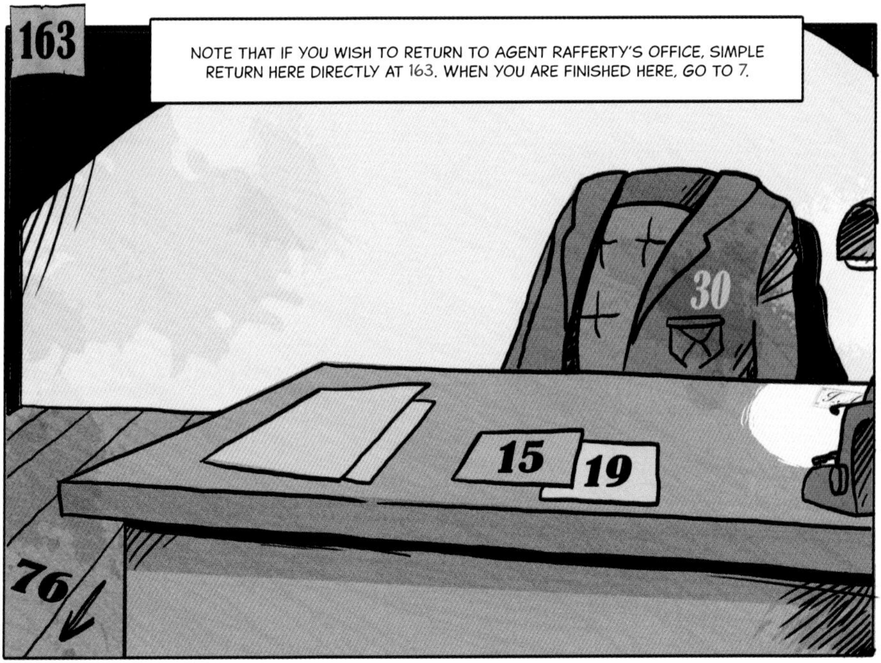
163
NOTE THAT IF YOU WISH TO RETURN TO AGENT RAFFERTY'S OFFICE, SIMPLE RETURN HERE DIRECTLY AT 163. WHEN YOU ARE FINISHED HERE, GO TO 7.
30
15
19
76

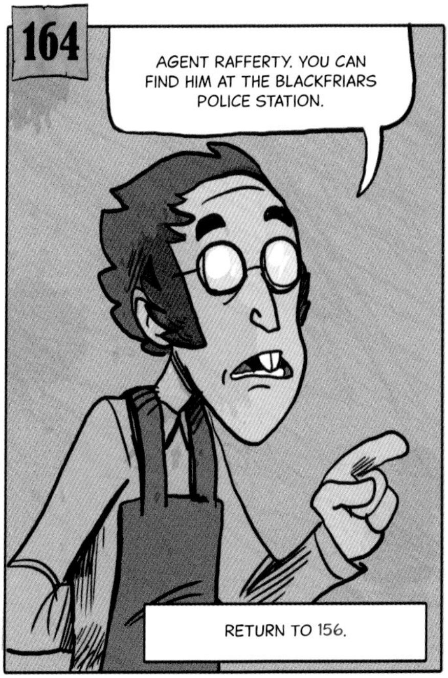
164
AGENT RAFFERTY. YOU CAN FIND HIM AT THE BLACKFRIARS POLICE STATION.
RETURN TO 156.

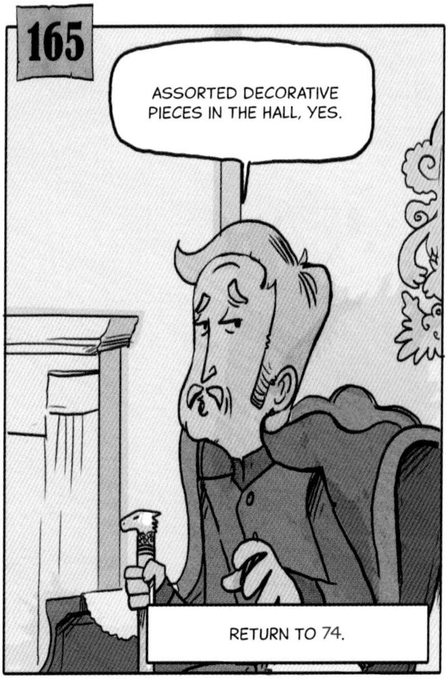
165
ASSORTED DECORATIVE PIECES IN THE HALL, YES.
RETURN TO 74.

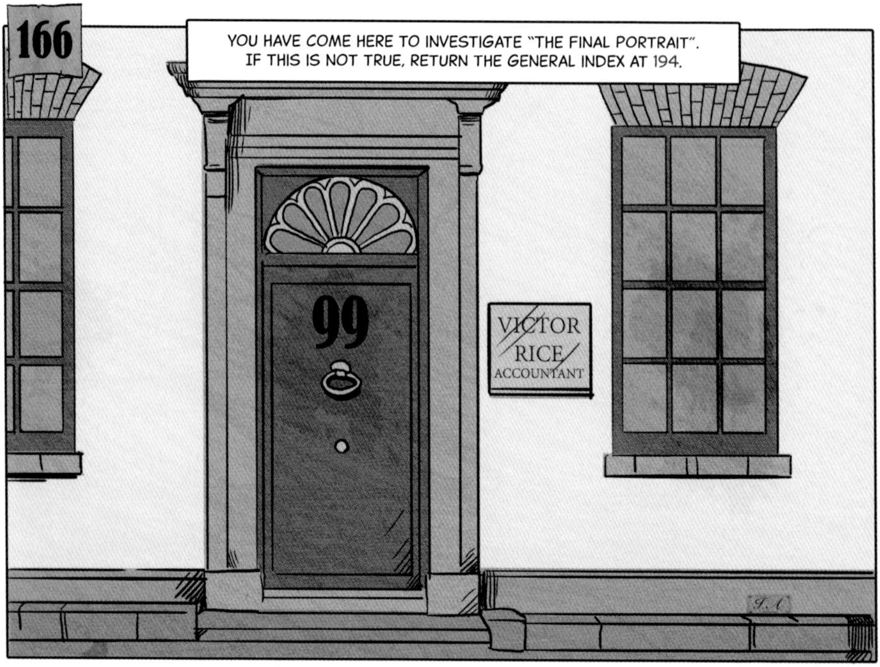
166
YOU HAVE COME HERE TO INVESTIGATE "THE FINAL PORTRAIT". IF THIS IS NOT TRUE, RETURN THE GENERAL INDEX AT 194.
99
VICTOR RICE ACCOUNTANT

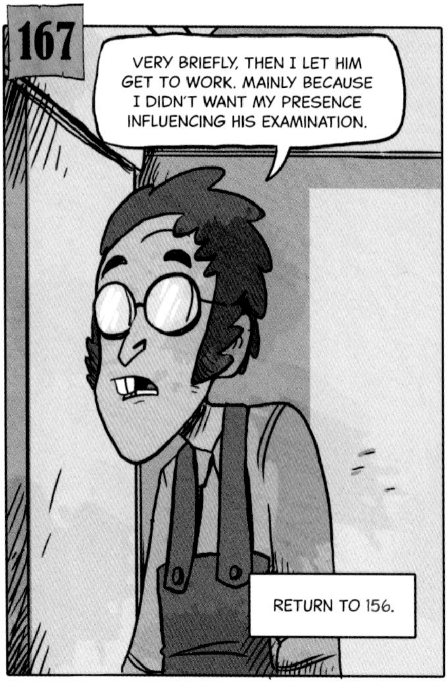
167
VERY BRIEFLY, THEN I LET HIM GET TO WORK. MAINLY BECAUSE I DIDN'T WANT MY PRESENCE INFLUENCING HIS EXAMINATION.
RETURN TO 156.

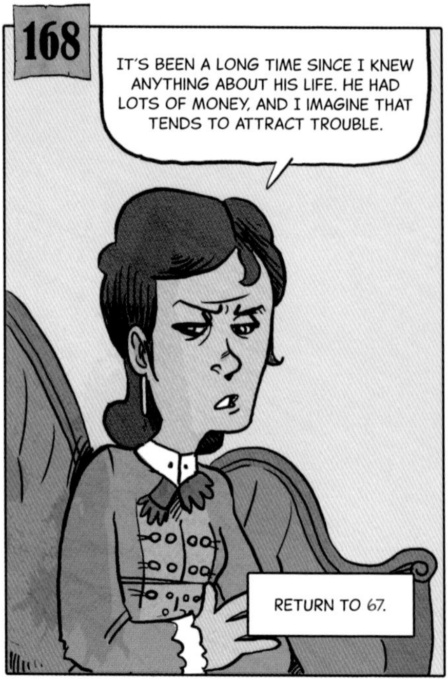
168
IT'S BEEN A LONG TIME SINCE I KNEW ANYTHING ABOUT HIS LIFE. HE HAD LOTS OF MONEY, AND I IMAGINE THAT TENDS TO ATTRACT TROUBLE.
RETURN TO 67.

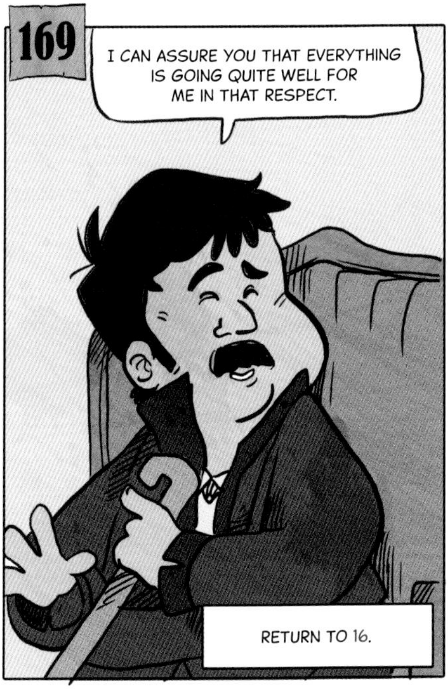
169
I CAN ASSURE YOU THAT EVERYTHING IS GOING QUITE WELL FOR ME IN THAT RESPECT.
RETURN TO 16.

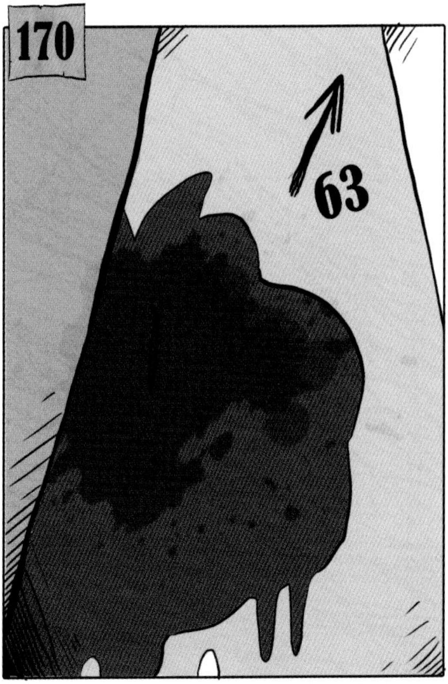
170
63

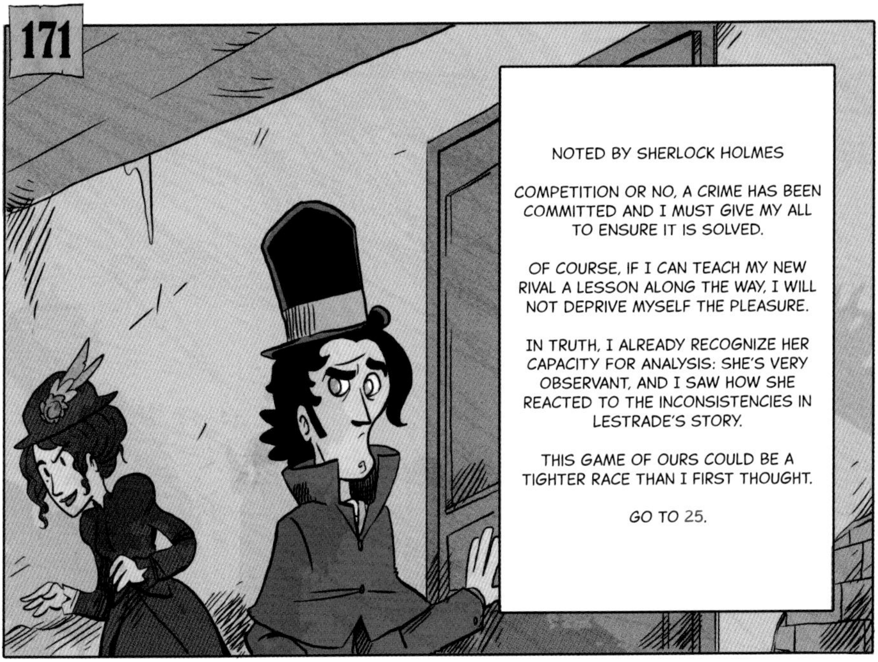
171
NOTED BY SHERLOCK HOLMES
COMPETITION OR NO, A CRIME HAS BEEN COMMITTED AND I MUST GIVE MY ALL TO ENSURE IT IS SOLVED.
OF COURSE, IF I CAN TEACH MY NEW RIVAL A LESSON ALONG THE WAY, I WILL NOT DEPRIVE MYSELF THE PLEASURE.
IN TRUTH, I ALREADY RECOGNIZE HER CAPACITY FOR ANALYSIS: SHE'S VERY OBSERVANT, AND I SAW HOW SHE REACTED TO THE INCONSISTENCIES IN LESTRADE'S STORY.
THIS GAME OF OURS COULD BE A TIGHTER RACE THAN I FIRST THOUGHT.
GO TO 25.

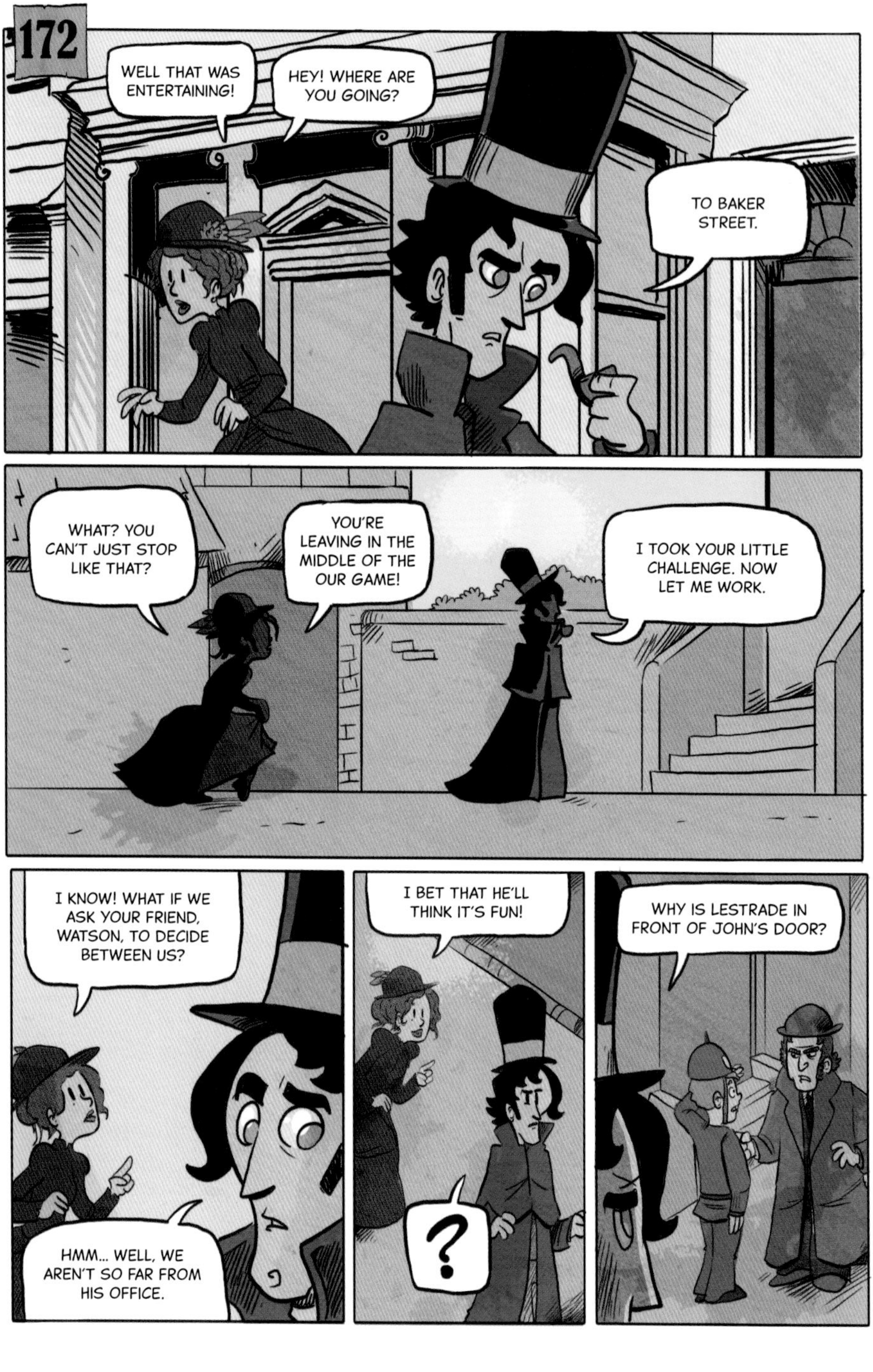
172
WELL THAT WAS ENTERTAINING!
HEY! WHERE ARE YOU GOING?
TO BAKER STREET.
WHAT? YOU CAN'T JUST STOP LIKE THAT?
YOU'RE LEAVING IN THE MIDDLE OF THE OUR GAME!
I TOOK YOUR LITTLE CHALLENGE. NOW LET ME WORK.
I KNOW! WHAT IF WE ASK YOUR FRIEND, WATSON, TO DECIDE BETWEEN US?
HMM... WELL, WE AREN'T SO FAR FROM HIS OFFICE.
I BET THAT HE'LL THINK IT'S FUN!
?
WHY IS LESTRADE IN FRONT OF JOHN'S DOOR?

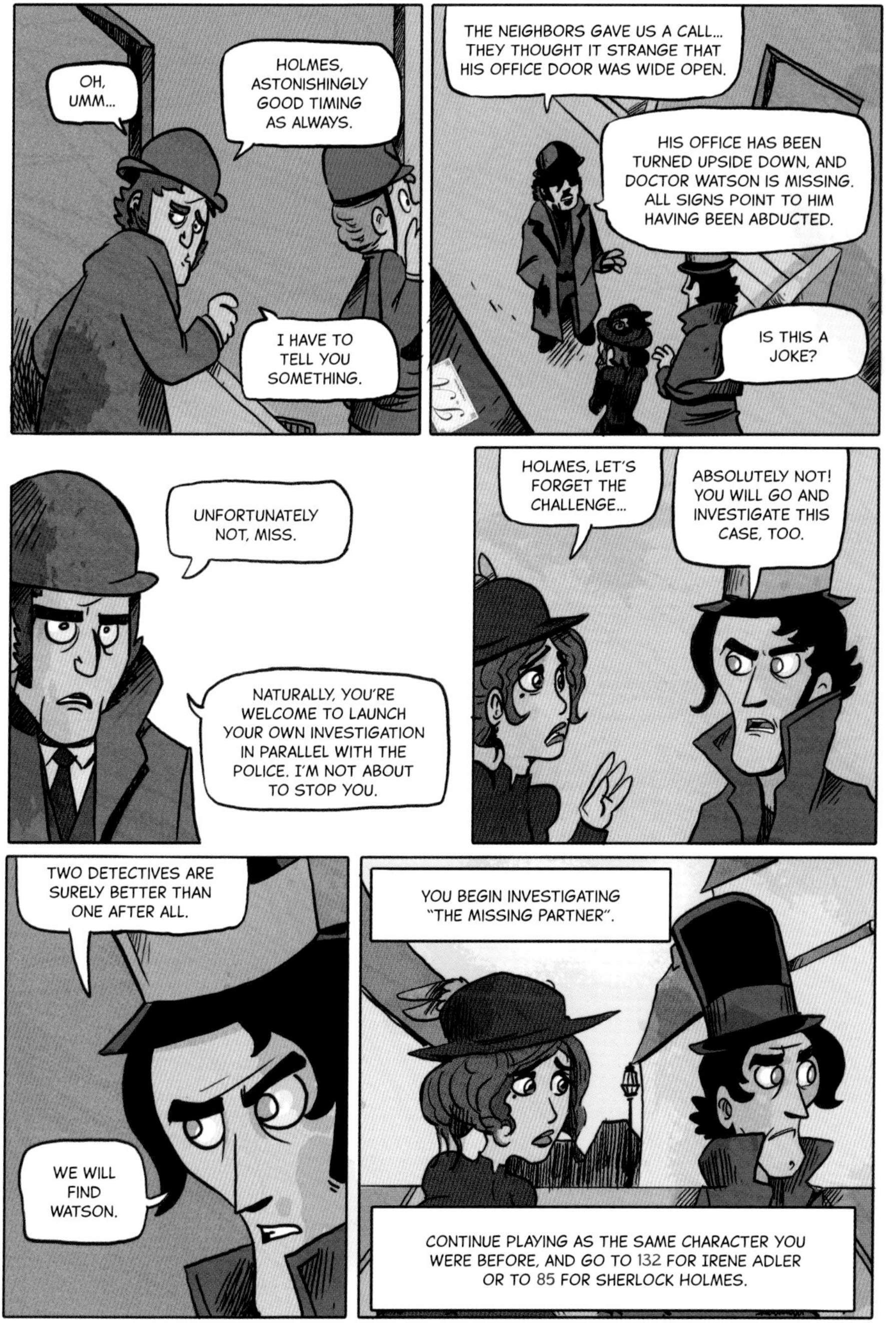
OH, UMM...
HOLMES, ASTONISHINGLY GOOD TIMING AS ALWAYS.
I HAVE TO TELL YOU SOMETHING.
THE NEIGHBORS GAVE US A CALL... THEY THOUGHT IT STRANGE THAT HIS OFFICE DOOR WAS WIDE OPEN.
HIS OFFICE HAS BEEN TURNED UPSIDE DOWN, AND DOCTOR WATSON IS MISSING. ALL SIGNS POINT TO HIM HAVING BEEN ABDUCTED.
IS THIS A JOKE?
UNFORTUNATELY NOT, MISS.
NATURALLY, YOU'RE WELCOME TO LAUNCH YOUR OWN INVESTIGATION IN PARALLEL WITH THE POLICE. I'M NOT ABOUT TO STOP YOU.
HOLMES, LET'S FORGET THE CHALLENGE...
ABSOLUTELY NOT! YOU WILL GO AND INVESTIGATE THIS CASE, TOO.
TWO DETECTIVES ARE SURELY BETTER THAN ONE AFTER ALL.
WE WILL FIND WATSON.
YOU BEGIN INVESTIGATING "THE MISSING PARTNER".
CONTINUE PLAYING AS THE SAME CHARACTER YOU WERE BEFORE, AND GO TO 132 FOR IRENE ADLER OR TO 85 FOR SHERLOCK HOLMES.

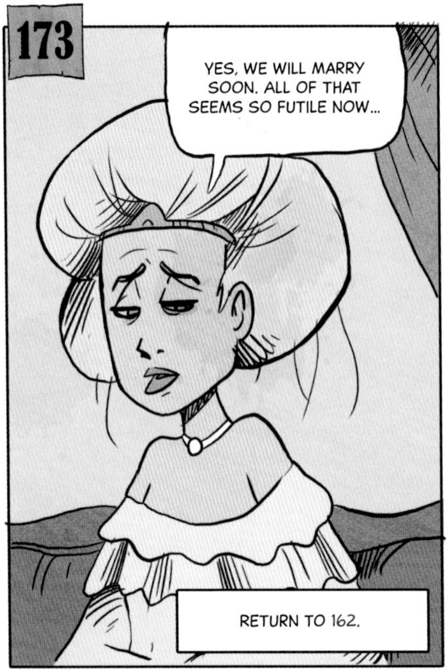
173
YES, WE WILL MARRY SOON. ALL OF THAT SEEMS SO FUTILE NOW...
RETURN TO 162.

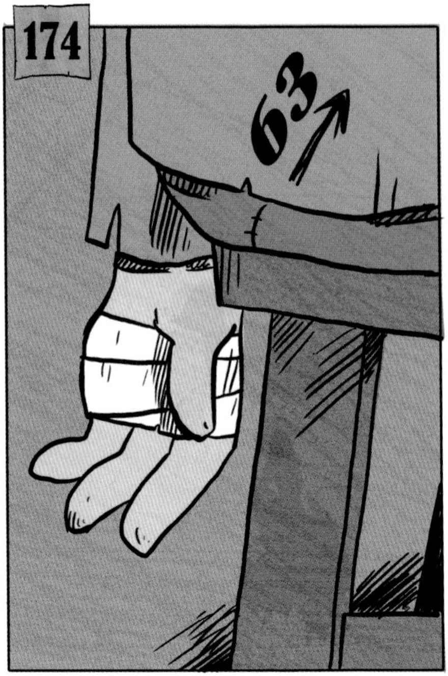
174
63

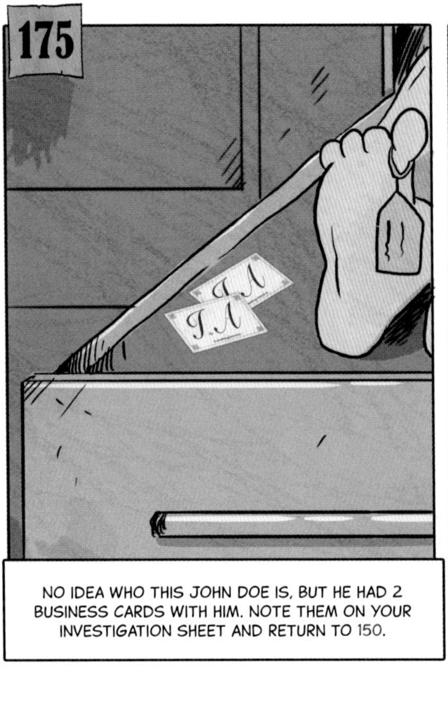
175
NO IDEA WHO THIS JOHN DOE IS, BUT HE HAD 2 BUSINESS CARDS WITH HIM. NOTE THEM ON YOUR INVESTIGATION SHEET AND RETURN TO 150.

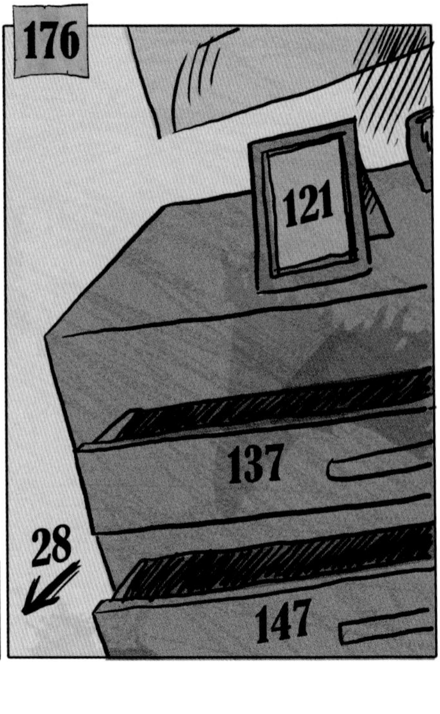
176
121
137
28
147

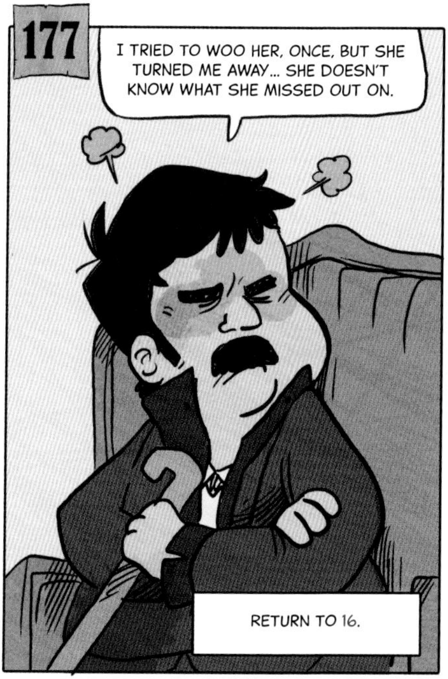
177
I TRIED TO WOO HER, ONCE, BUT SHE TURNED ME AWAY... SHE DOESN'T KNOW WHAT SHE MISSED OUT ON.
RETURN TO 16.

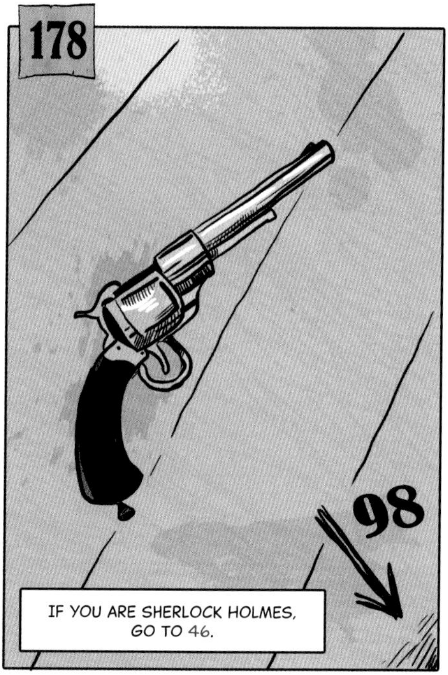
178
98
IF YOU ARE SHERLOCK HOLMES, GO TO 46.

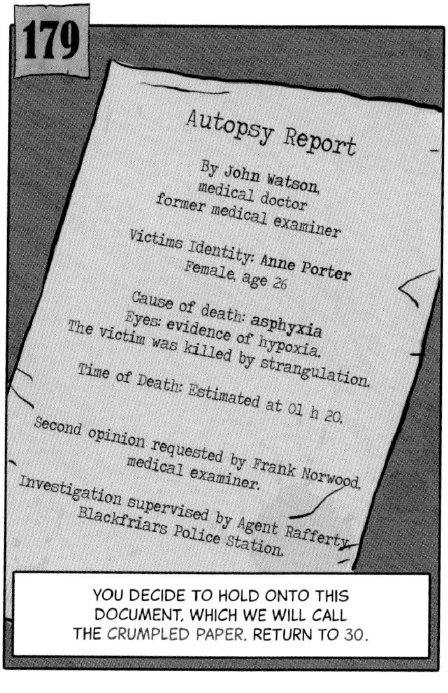
179
Autopsy Report
By John Watson,
medical doctor
former medical examiner
Victims Identity: Anne Porter
Female, age 26
Cause of death: asphyxia
Eyes: evidence of hypoxia.
The victim was killed by strangulation.
Time of Death: Estimated at 01 h 20.
Second opinion requested by Frank Norwood,
medical examiner.
Investigation supervised by Agent Rafferty,
Blackfriars Police Station.
YOU DECIDE TO HOLD ONTO THIS DOCUMENT, WHICH WE WILL CALL THE CRUMPLED PAPER. RETURN TO 30.

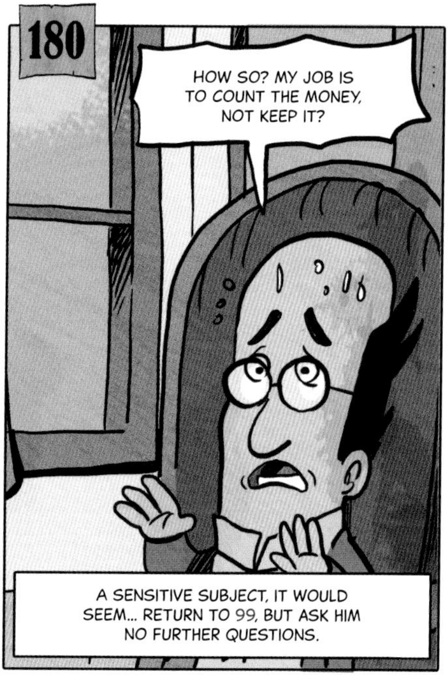
180
HOW SO? MY JOB IS TO COUNT THE MONEY, NOT KEEP IT?
A SENSITIVE SUBJECT, IT WOULD SEEM... RETURN TO 99, BUT ASK HIM NO FURTHER QUESTIONS.

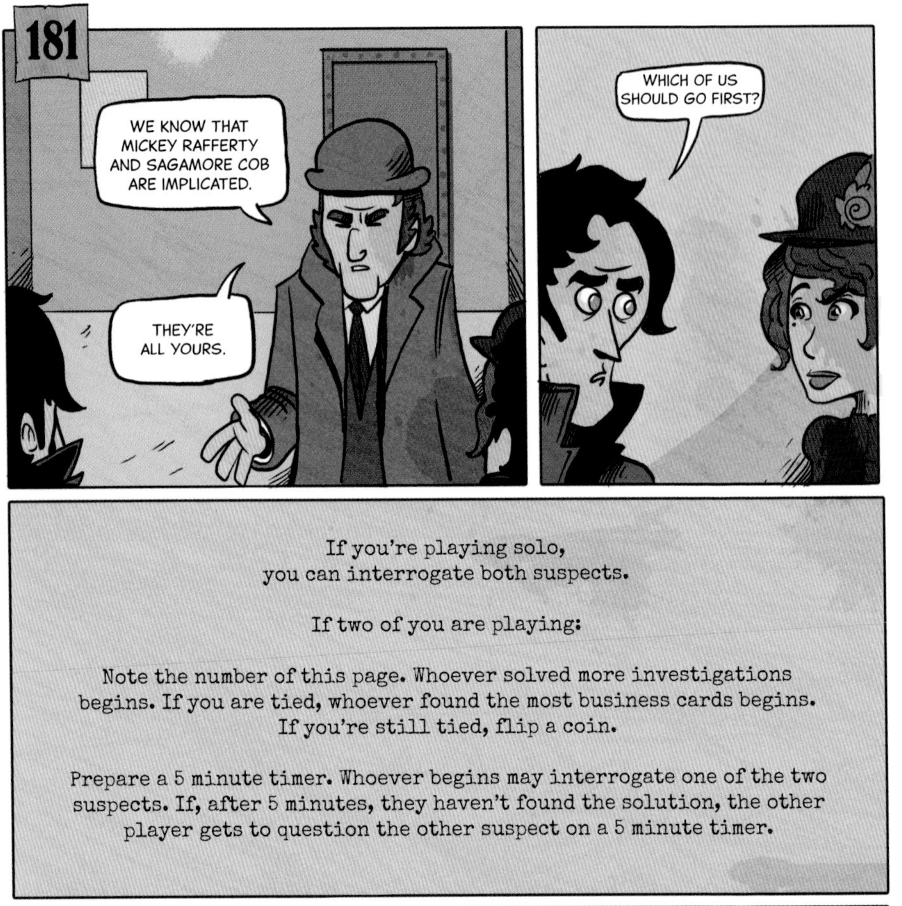
181
WE KNOW THAT MICKEY RAFFERTY AND SAGAMORE COB ARE IMPLICATED.
THEY'RE ALL YOURS.
WHICH OF US SHOULD GO FIRST?

If you're playing solo,
you can interrogate both suspects.

If two of you are playing:

Note the number of this page. Whoever solved more investigations begins. If you are tied, whoever found the most business cards begins. If you're still tied, flip a coin.

Prepare a 5 minute timer. Whoever begins may interrogate one of the two suspects. If, after 5 minutes, they haven't found the solution, the other player gets to question the other suspect on a 5 minute timer.

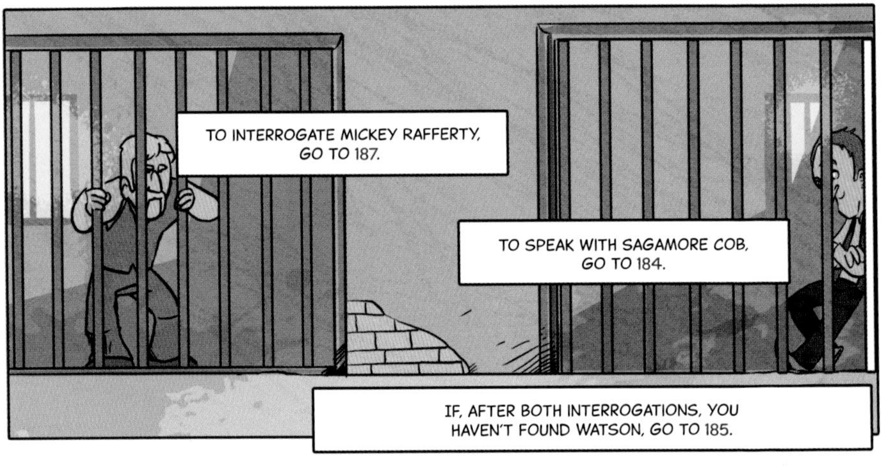
TO INTERROGATE MICKEY RAFFERTY, GO TO 187.
TO SPEAK WITH SAGAMORE COB, GO TO 184.
IF, AFTER BOTH INTERROGATIONS, YOU HAVEN'T FOUND WATSON, GO TO 185.

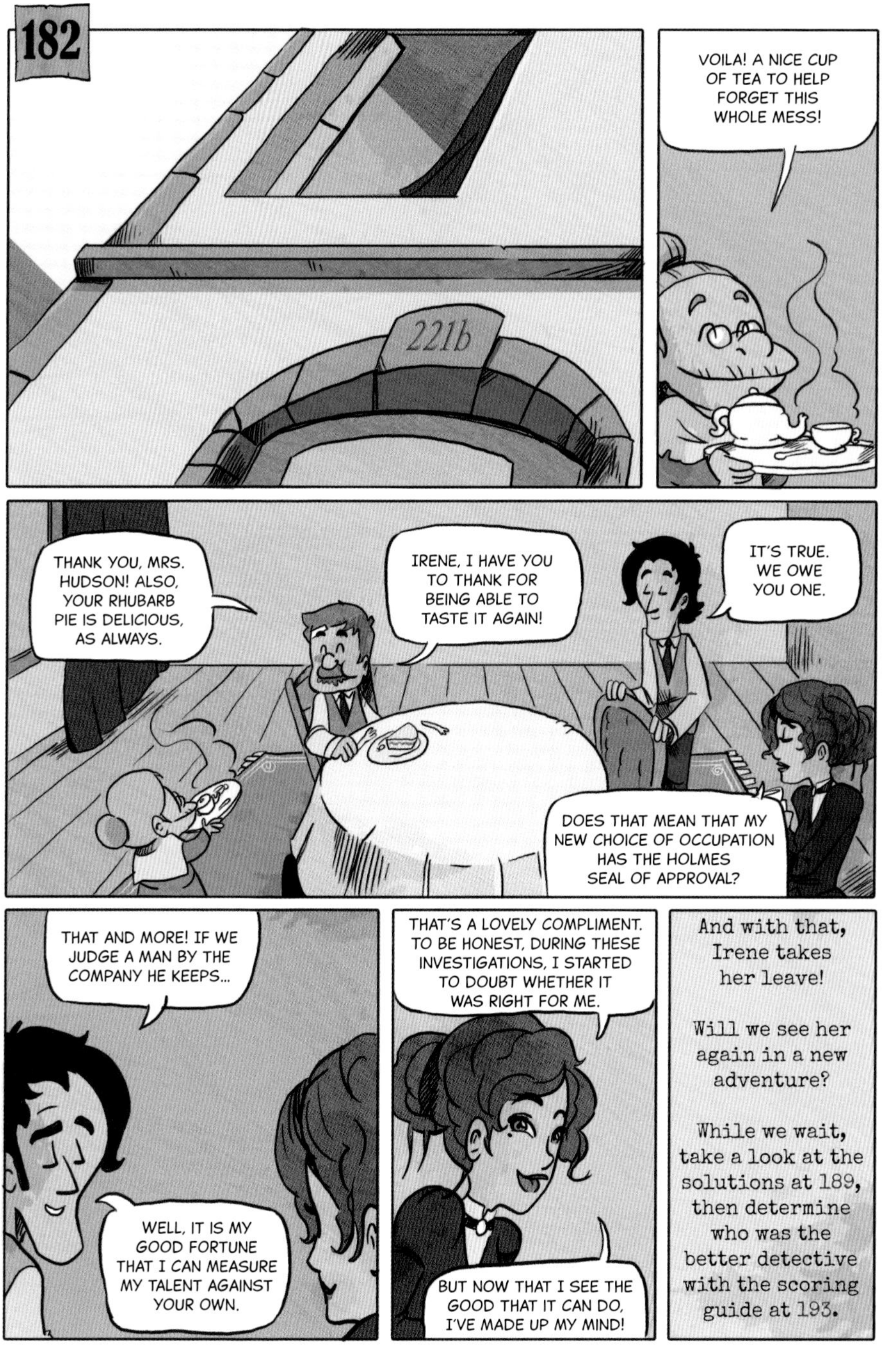
182
221b
VOILA! A NICE CUP OF TEA TO HELP FORGET THIS WHOLE MESS!
THANK YOU, MRS. HUDSON! ALSO, YOUR RHUBARB PIE IS DELICIOUS, AS ALWAYS.
IRENE, I HAVE YOU TO THANK FOR BEING ABLE TO TASTE IT AGAIN!
IT'S TRUE. WE OWE YOU ONE.
DOES THAT MEAN THAT MY NEW CHOICE OF OCCUPATION HAS THE HOLMES SEAL OF APPROVAL?
THAT AND MORE! IF WE JUDGE A MAN BY THE COMPANY HE KEEPS...
WELL, IT IS MY GOOD FORTUNE THAT I CAN MEASURE MY TALENT AGAINST YOUR OWN.
THAT'S A LOVELY COMPLIMENT. TO BE HONEST, DURING THESE INVESTIGATIONS, I STARTED TO DOUBT WHETHER IT WAS RIGHT FOR ME.
BUT NOW THAT I SEE THE GOOD THAT IT CAN DO, I'VE MADE UP MY MIND!
And with that, Irene takes her leave!
Will we see her again in a new adventure?
While we wait, take a look at the solutions at 189, then determine who was the better detective with the scoring guide at 193.

183
HEY YOU! GOT TIME FOR A PUZZLE?
HERE'S MY CHALLENGE: YOU MUST PASS THROUGH EACH DOOR OF MY HOUSE ONCE AND ONLY ONCE.
YOU START AT A AND MUST FINISH AT B.
HERE'S A HINT: YOU CAN ALSO TRAVEL AROUND THE OUTSIDE OF THE BUILDING.

+ 3
x 11
- 4
+ 2
A
- 5
÷ 2
x 2
- 6
- 2
x 3
B
x 10
- 7
÷ 2

Every time you pass through a door, apply the corresponding mathematical operation.

Once you arrive at B, the number you have calculated is the number of the frame you will visit.

Several routes are possible, but only one will give you a result that corresponds to an existing frame number.

If you are unable to find the correct number, return to 18.

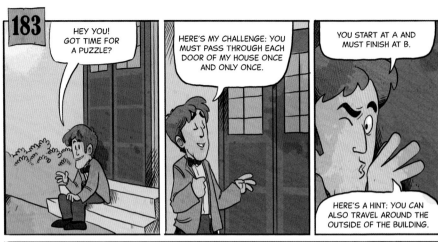

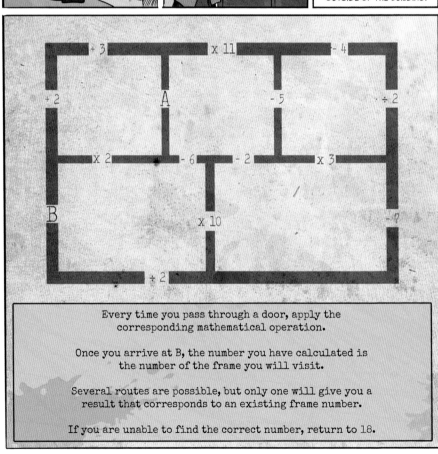

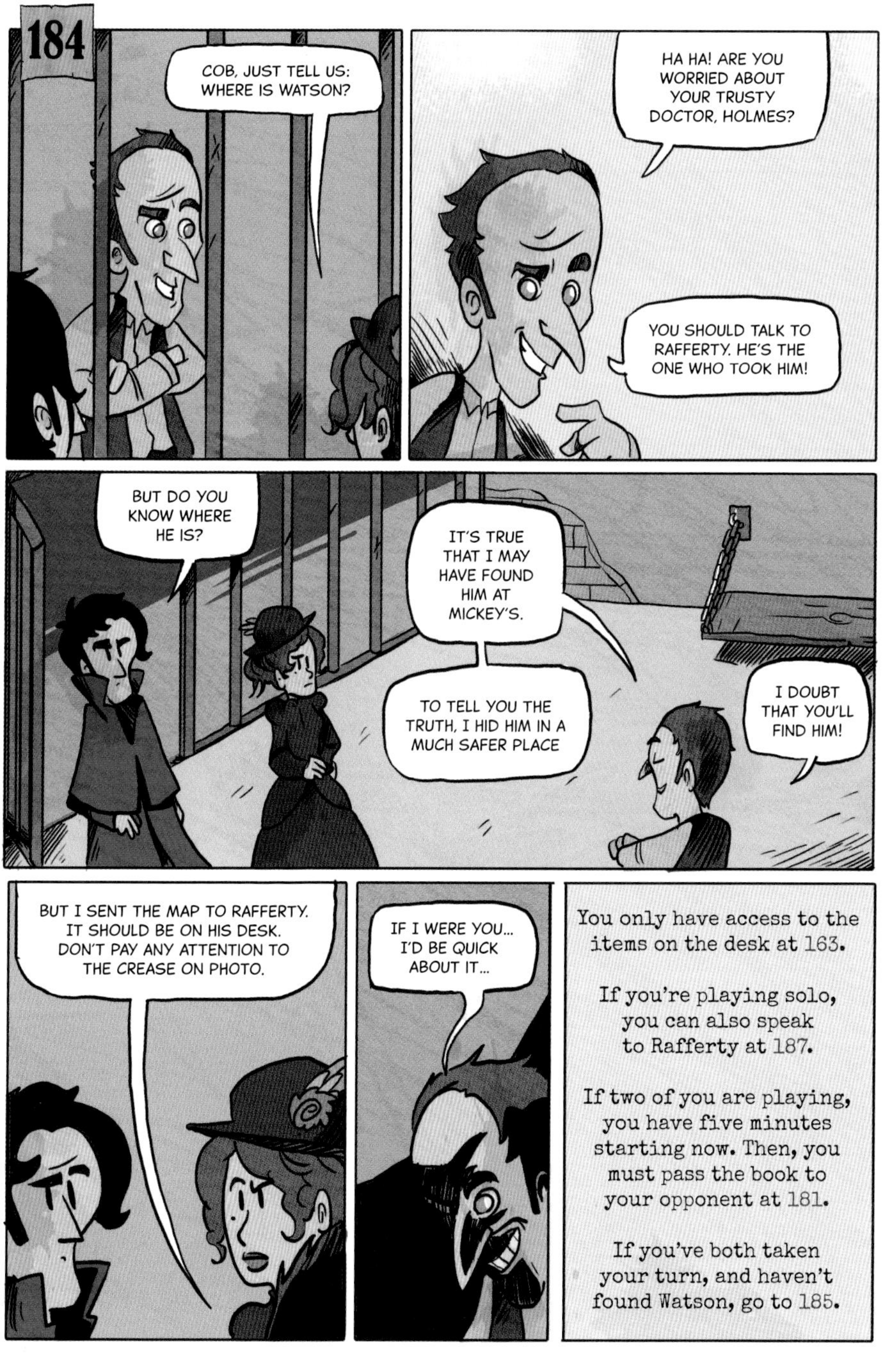
184
COB, JUST TELL US: WHERE IS WATSON?
HA HA! ARE YOU WORRIED ABOUT YOUR TRUSTY DOCTOR, HOLMES?
YOU SHOULD TALK TO RAFFERTY. HE'S THE ONE WHO TOOK HIM!
BUT DO YOU KNOW WHERE HE IS?
IT'S TRUE THAT I MAY HAVE FOUND HIM AT MICKEY'S.
TO TELL YOU THE TRUTH, I HID HIM IN A MUCH SAFER PLACE
I DOUBT THAT YOU'LL FIND HIM!
BUT I SENT THE MAP TO RAFFERTY. IT SHOULD BE ON HIS DESK. DON'T PAY ANY ATTENTION TO THE CREASE ON PHOTO.
IF I WERE YOU... I'D BE QUICK ABOUT IT...
You only have access to the items on the desk at 163.
If you're playing solo, you can also speak to Rafferty at 187.
If two of you are playing, you have five minutes starting now. Then, you must pass the book to your opponent at 181.
If you've both taken your turn, and haven't found Watson, go to 185.

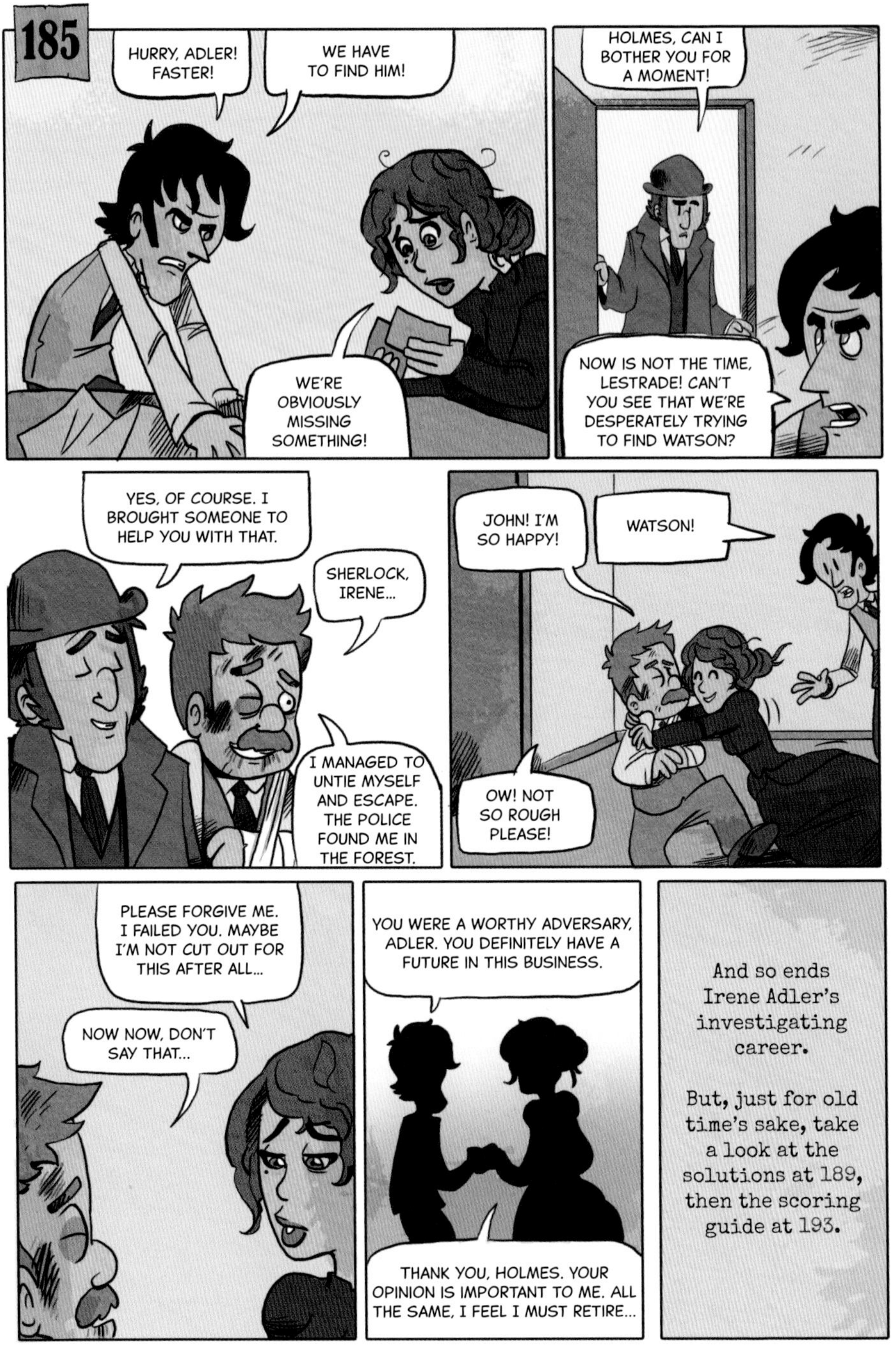
185
HURRY, ADLER! FASTER!
WE HAVE TO FIND HIM!
WE'RE OBVIOUSLY MISSING SOMETHING!
HOLMES, CAN I BOTHER YOU FOR A MOMENT!
NOW IS NOT THE TIME, LESTRADE! CAN'T YOU SEE THAT WE'RE DESPERATELY TRYING TO FIND WATSON?
YES, OF COURSE. I BROUGHT SOMEONE TO HELP YOU WITH THAT.
SHERLOCK, IRENE...
I MANAGED TO UNTIE MYSELF AND ESCAPE. THE POLICE FOUND ME IN THE FOREST.
JOHN! I'M SO HAPPY!
WATSON!
OW! NOT SO ROUGH PLEASE!
PLEASE FORGIVE ME. I FAILED YOU. MAYBE I'M NOT CUT OUT FOR THIS AFTER ALL...
NOW NOW, DON'T SAY THAT...
YOU WERE A WORTHY ADVERSARY, ADLER. YOU DEFINITELY HAVE A FUTURE IN THIS BUSINESS.
THANK YOU, HOLMES. YOUR OPINION IS IMPORTANT TO ME. ALL THE SAME, I FEEL I MUST RETIRE...
And so ends Irene Adler's investigating career.
But, just for old time's sake, take a look at the solutions at 189, then the scoring guide at 193.

OH NO, HE'S BACK!

BLOM
BLOM
BLOM

VLAM

JOHN! YOU'RE SAFE AND SOUND!

SHERLOCK! IRENE! WHAT A RELIEF!

NOTHING TO SAY FOR YOURSELF WATSON?

I TRULY THOUGHT I'D NEVER SEE YOU AGAIN, MY DEAR FRIEND!

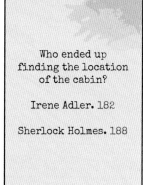

Who ended up finding the location of the cabin?

Irene Adler. 182

Sherlock Holmes. 188

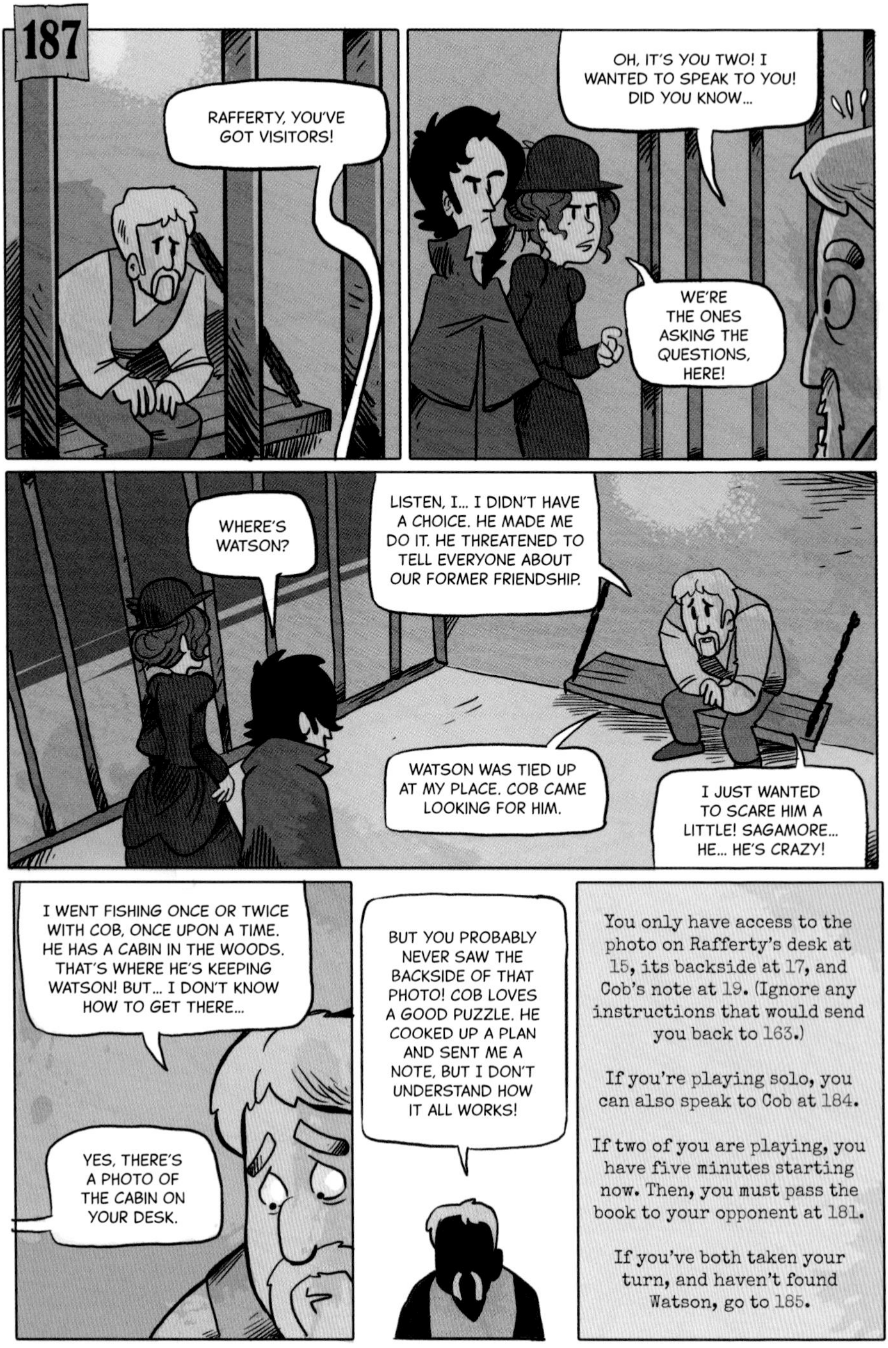
187
RAFFERTY, YOU'VE GOT VISITORS!
OH, IT'S YOU TWO! I WANTED TO SPEAK TO YOU! DID YOU KNOW...
WE'RE THE ONES ASKING THE QUESTIONS, HERE!
WHERE'S WATSON?
LISTEN, I... I DIDN'T HAVE A CHOICE. HE MADE ME DO IT. HE THREATENED TO TELL EVERYONE ABOUT OUR FORMER FRIENDSHIP.
WATSON WAS TIED UP AT MY PLACE. COB CAME LOOKING FOR HIM.
I JUST WANTED TO SCARE HIM A LITTLE! SAGAMORE... HE... HE'S CRAZY!
I WENT FISHING ONCE OR TWICE WITH COB, ONCE UPON A TIME. HE HAS A CABIN IN THE WOODS. THAT'S WHERE HE'S KEEPING WATSON! BUT... I DON'T KNOW HOW TO GET THERE...
YES, THERE'S A PHOTO OF THE CABIN ON YOUR DESK.
BUT YOU PROBABLY NEVER SAW THE BACKSIDE OF THAT PHOTO! COB LOVES A GOOD PUZZLE. HE COOKED UP A PLAN AND SENT ME A NOTE, BUT I DON'T UNDERSTAND HOW IT ALL WORKS!
You only have access to the photo on Rafferty's desk at 15, its backside at 17, and Cob's note at 19. (Ignore any instructions that would send you back to 163.)
If you're playing solo, you can also speak to Cob at 184.
If two of you are playing, you have five minutes starting now. Then, you must pass the book to your opponent at 181.
If you've both taken your turn, and haven't found Watson, go to 185.

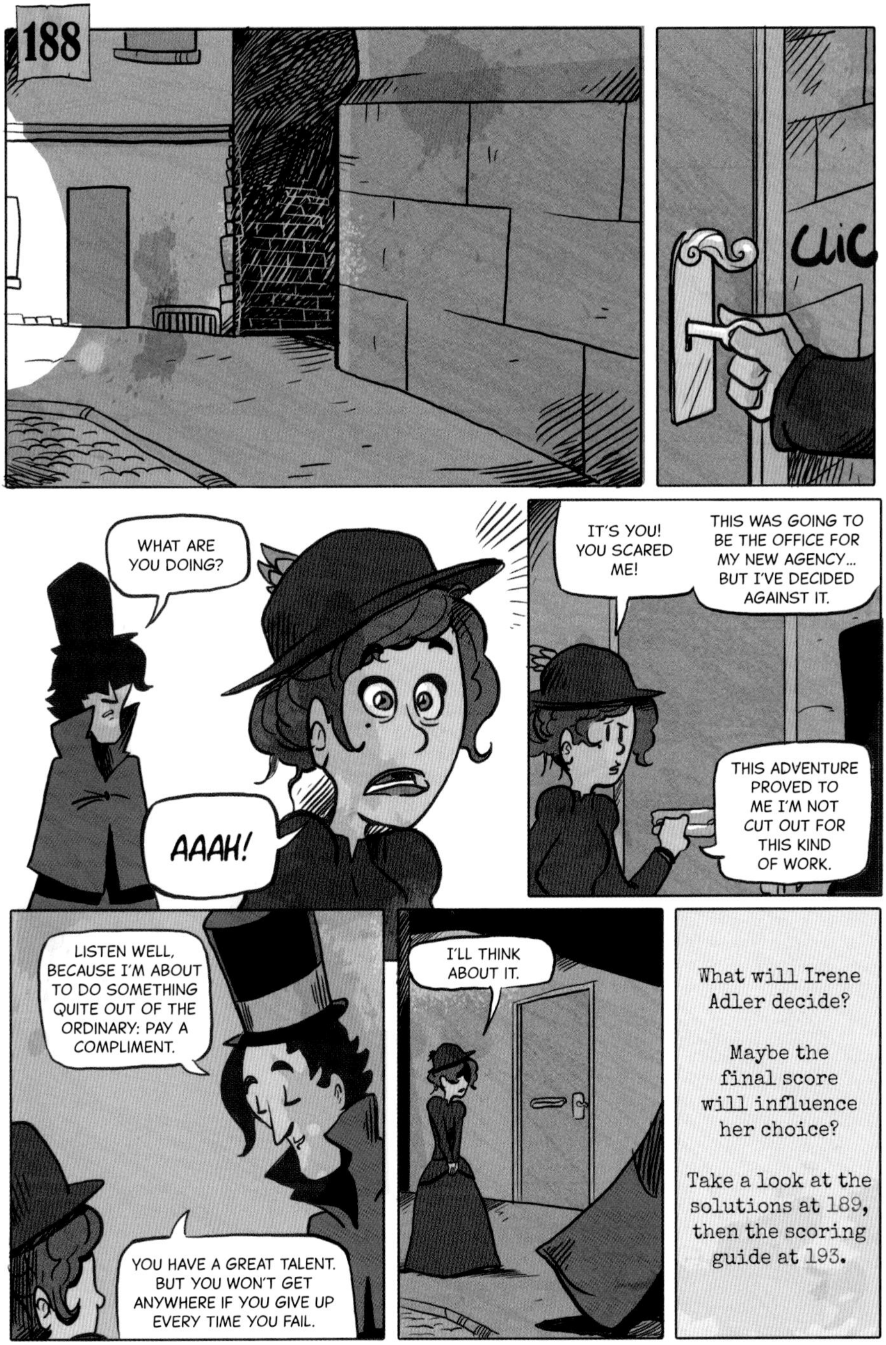
188
CLIC
WHAT ARE YOU DOING?
AAAH!
IT'S YOU! YOU SCARED ME!
THIS WAS GOING TO BE THE OFFICE FOR MY NEW AGENCY... BUT I'VE DECIDED AGAINST IT.
THIS ADVENTURE PROVED TO ME I'M NOT CUT OUT FOR THIS KIND OF WORK.
LISTEN WELL, BECAUSE I'M ABOUT TO DO SOMETHING QUITE OUT OF THE ORDINARY: PAY A COMPLIMENT.
YOU HAVE A GREAT TALENT. BUT YOU WON'T GET ANYWHERE IF YOU GIVE UP EVERY TIME YOU FAIL.
I'LL THINK ABOUT IT.
What will Irene Adler decide?
Maybe the final score will influence her choice?
Take a look at the solutions at 189, then the scoring guide at 193.

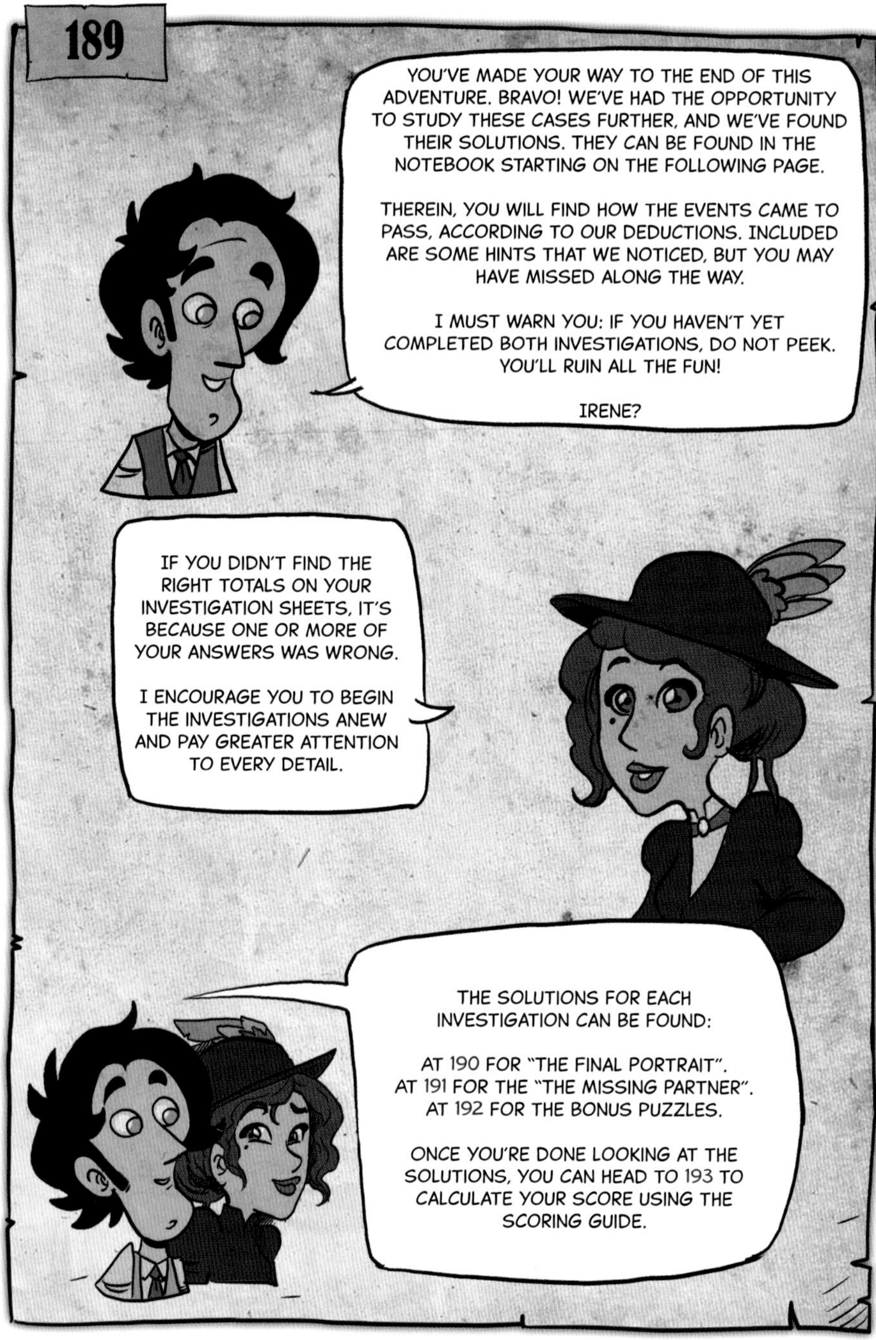
189
YOU'VE MADE YOUR WAY TO THE END OF THIS ADVENTURE. BRAVO! WE'VE HAD THE OPPORTUNITY TO STUDY THESE CASES FURTHER, AND WE'VE FOUND THEIR SOLUTIONS. THEY CAN BE FOUND IN THE NOTEBOOK STARTING ON THE FOLLOWING PAGE.
THEREIN, YOU WILL FIND HOW THE EVENTS CAME TO PASS, ACCORDING TO OUR DEDUCTIONS. INCLUDED ARE SOME HINTS THAT WE NOTICED, BUT YOU MAY HAVE MISSED ALONG THE WAY.
I MUST WARN YOU: IF YOU HAVEN'T YET COMPLETED BOTH INVESTIGATIONS, DO NOT PEEK. YOU'LL RUIN ALL THE FUN!
IRENE?
IF YOU DIDN'T FIND THE RIGHT TOTALS ON YOUR INVESTIGATION SHEETS, IT'S BECAUSE ONE OR MORE OF YOUR ANSWERS WAS WRONG.
I ENCOURAGE YOU TO BEGIN THE INVESTIGATIONS ANEW AND PAY GREATER ATTENTION TO EVERY DETAIL.
THE SOLUTIONS FOR EACH INVESTIGATION CAN BE FOUND:
AT 190 FOR "THE FINAL PORTRAIT".
AT 191 FOR THE "THE MISSING PARTNER".
AT 192 FOR THE BONUS PUZZLES.
ONCE YOU'RE DONE LOOKING AT THE SOLUTIONS, YOU CAN HEAD TO 193 TO CALCULATE YOUR SCORE USING THE SCORING GUIDE.

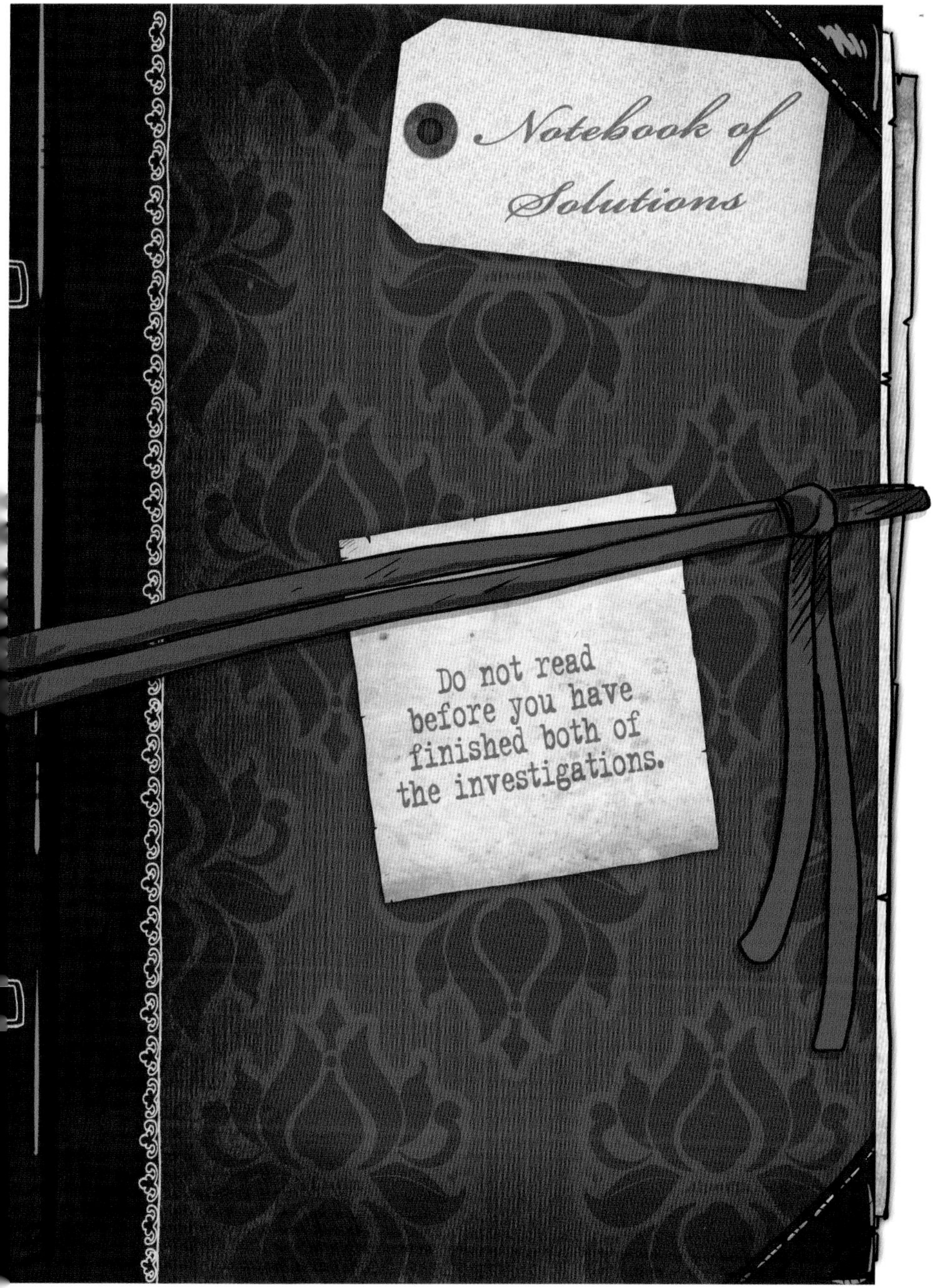
Notebook of Solutions
Do not read before you have finished both of the investigations.

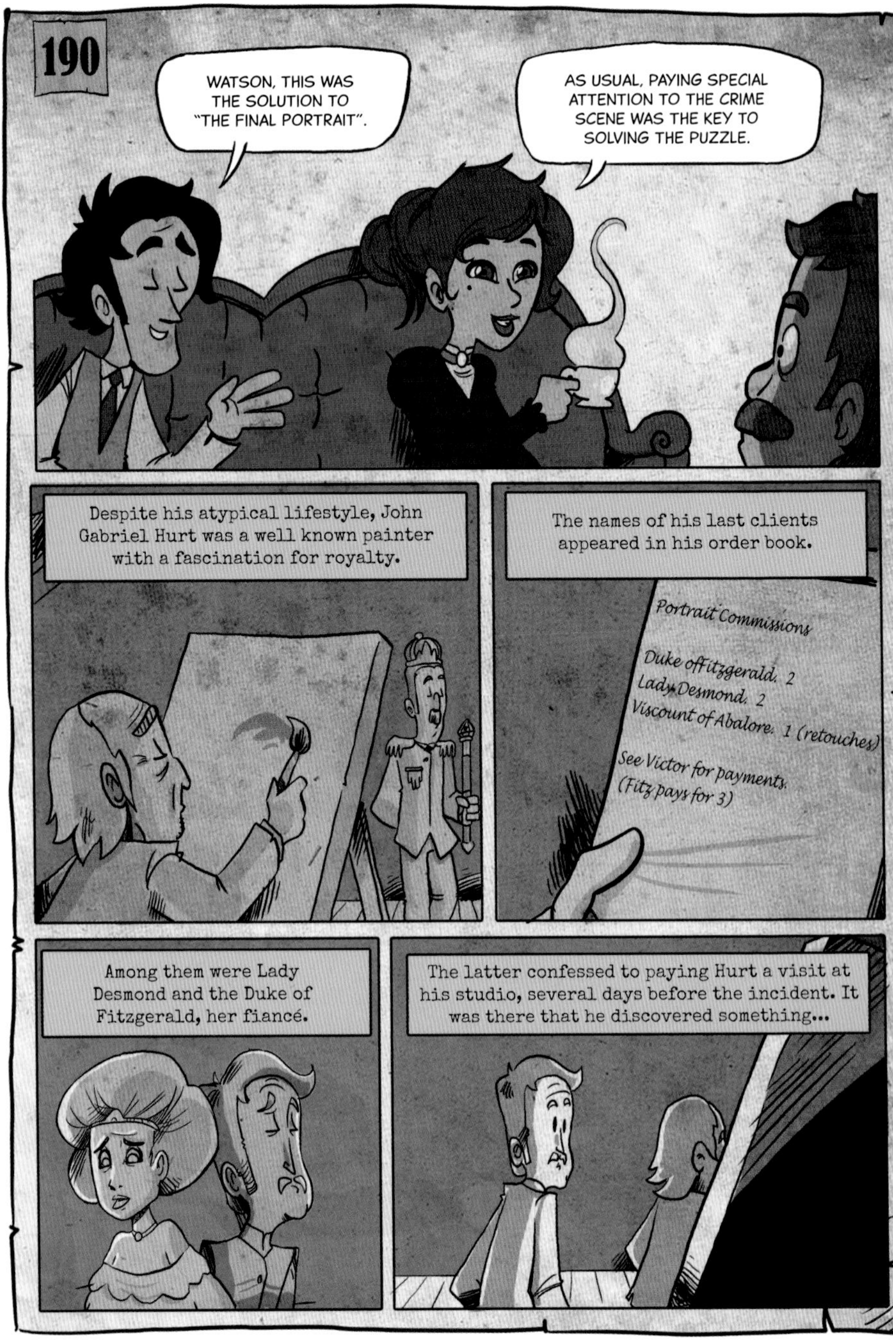
190
WATSON, THIS WAS THE SOLUTION TO "THE FINAL PORTRAIT".
AS USUAL, PAYING SPECIAL ATTENTION TO THE CRIME SCENE WAS THE KEY TO SOLVING THE PUZZLE.
Despite his atypical lifestyle, John Gabriel Hurt was a well known painter with a fascination for royalty.
The names of his last clients appeared in his order book.
Portrait Commissions
Duke of Fitzgerald. 2
Lady Desmond. 2
Viscount of Abalore. 1 (retouches)
See Victor for payments.
(Fitz pays for 3)
Among them were Lady Desmond and the Duke of Fitzgerald, her fiancé.
The latter confessed to paying Hurt a visit at his studio, several days before the incident. It was there that he discovered something...

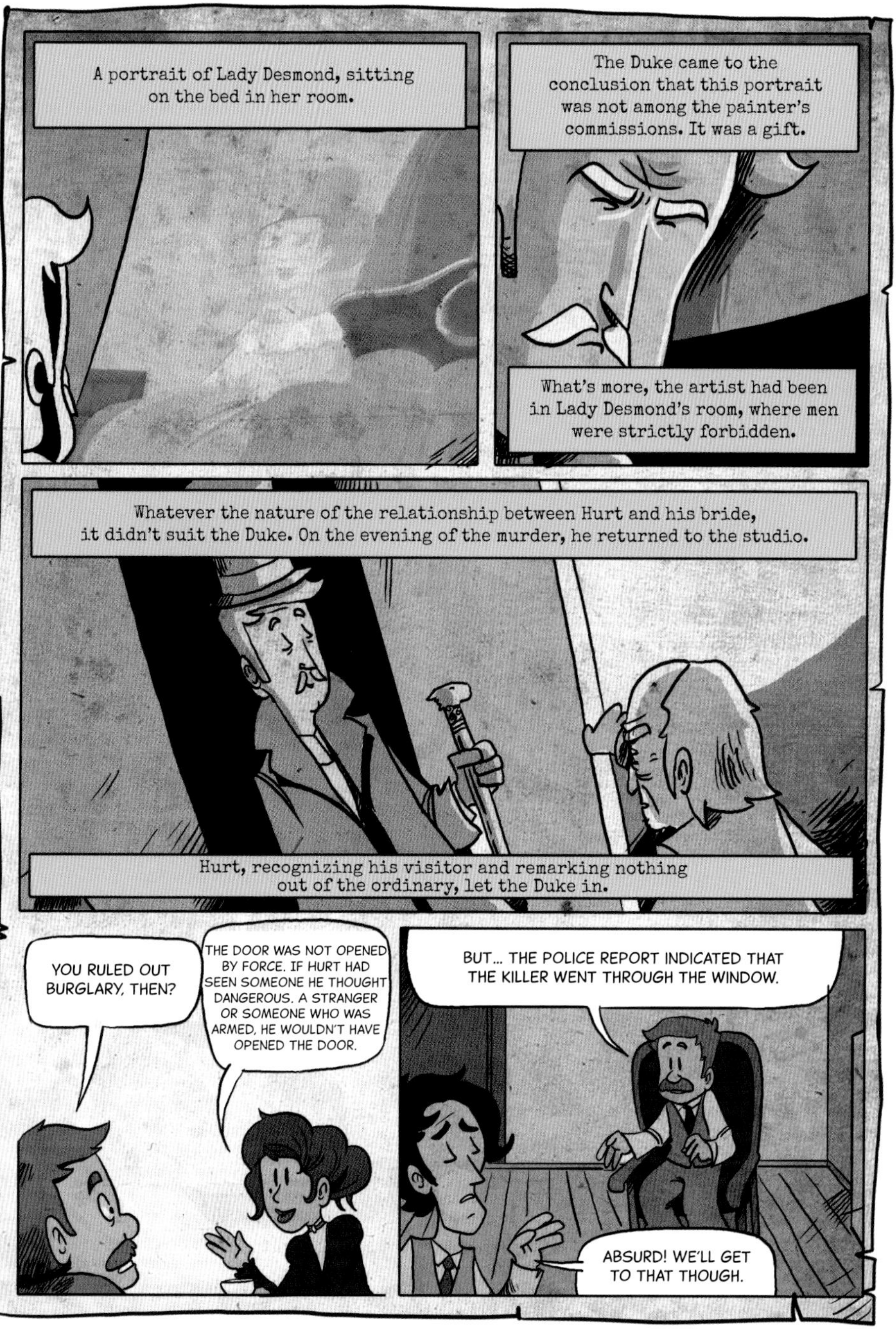

A portrait of Lady Desmond, sitting on the bed in her room.
The Duke came to the conclusion that this portrait was not among the painter's commissions. It was a gift.
What's more, the artist had been in Lady Desmond's room, where men were strictly forbidden.
Whatever the nature of the relationship between Hurt and his bride, it didn't suit the Duke. On the evening of the murder, he returned to the studio.
Hurt, recognizing his visitor and remarking nothing out of the ordinary, let the Duke in.
YOU RULED OUT BURGLARY, THEN?
THE DOOR WAS NOT OPENED BY FORCE. IF HURT HAD SEEN SOMEONE HE THOUGHT DANGEROUS, A STRANGER OR SOMEONE WHO WAS ARMED, HE WOULDN'T HAVE OPENED THE DOOR.
BUT... THE POLICE REPORT INDICATED THAT THE KILLER WENT THROUGH THE WINDOW.
ABSURD! WE'LL GET TO THAT THOUGH.

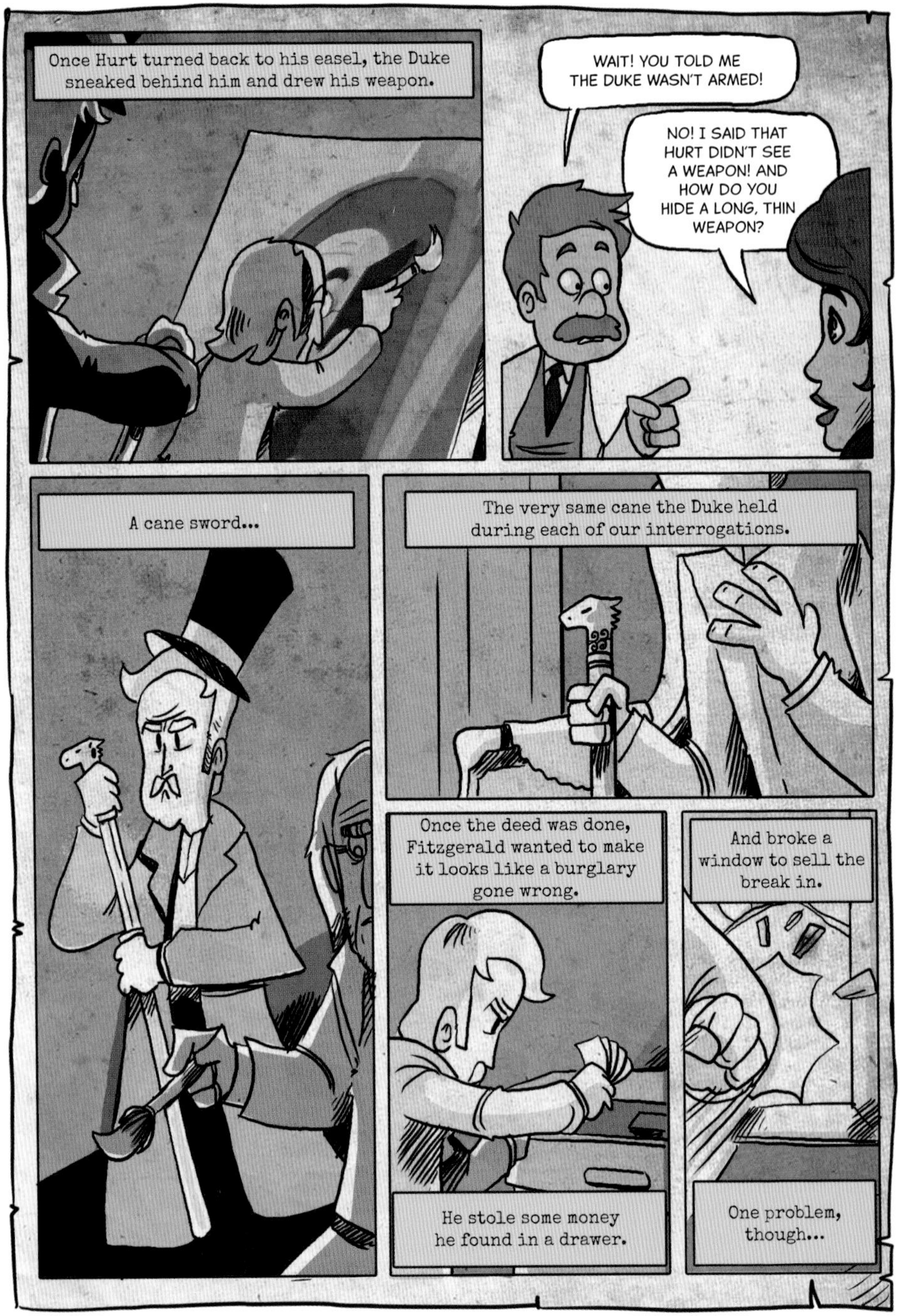

Once Hurt turned back to his easel, the Duke sneaked behind him and drew his weapon.
WAIT! YOU TOLD ME THE DUKE WASN'T ARMED!
NO! I SAID THAT HURT DIDN'T SEE A WEAPON! AND HOW DO YOU HIDE A LONG, THIN WEAPON?
A cane sword...
The very same cane the Duke held during each of our interrogations.
Once the deed was done, Fitzgerald wanted to make it looks like a burglary gone wrong.
He stole some money he found in a drawer.
And broke a window to sell the break in.
One problem, though...

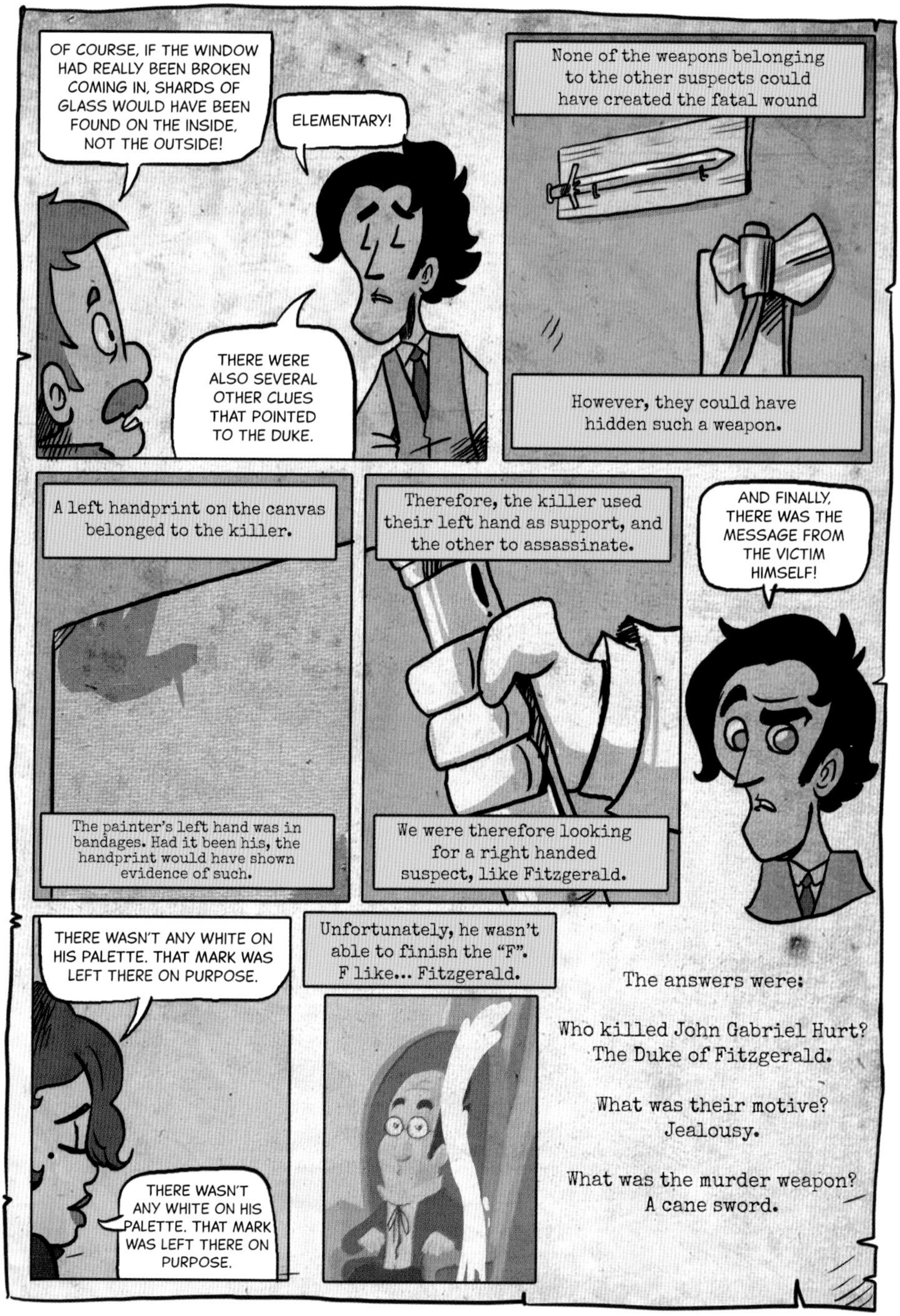
OF COURSE, IF THE WINDOW HAD REALLY BEEN BROKEN COMING IN, SHARDS OF GLASS WOULD HAVE BEEN FOUND ON THE INSIDE, NOT THE OUTSIDE!
ELEMENTARY!
THERE WERE ALSO SEVERAL OTHER CLUES THAT POINTED TO THE DUKE.
None of the weapons belonging to the other suspects could have created the fatal wound
However, they could have hidden such a weapon.
A left handprint on the canvas belonged to the killer.
The painter's left hand was in bandages. Had it been his, the handprint would have shown evidence of such.
Therefore, the killer used their left hand as support, and the other to assassinate.
We were therefore looking for a right handed suspect, like Fitzgerald.
AND FINALLY, THERE WAS THE MESSAGE FROM THE VICTIM HIMSELF!
THERE WASN'T ANY WHITE ON HIS PALETTE. THAT MARK WAS LEFT THERE ON PURPOSE.
THERE WASN'T ANY WHITE ON HIS PALETTE. THAT MARK WAS LEFT THERE ON PURPOSE.
Unfortunately, he wasn't able to finish the "F". F like... Fitzgerald.
The answers were:
Who killed John Gabriel Hurt? The Duke of Fitzgerald.
What was their motive? Jealousy.
What was the murder weapon? A cane sword.

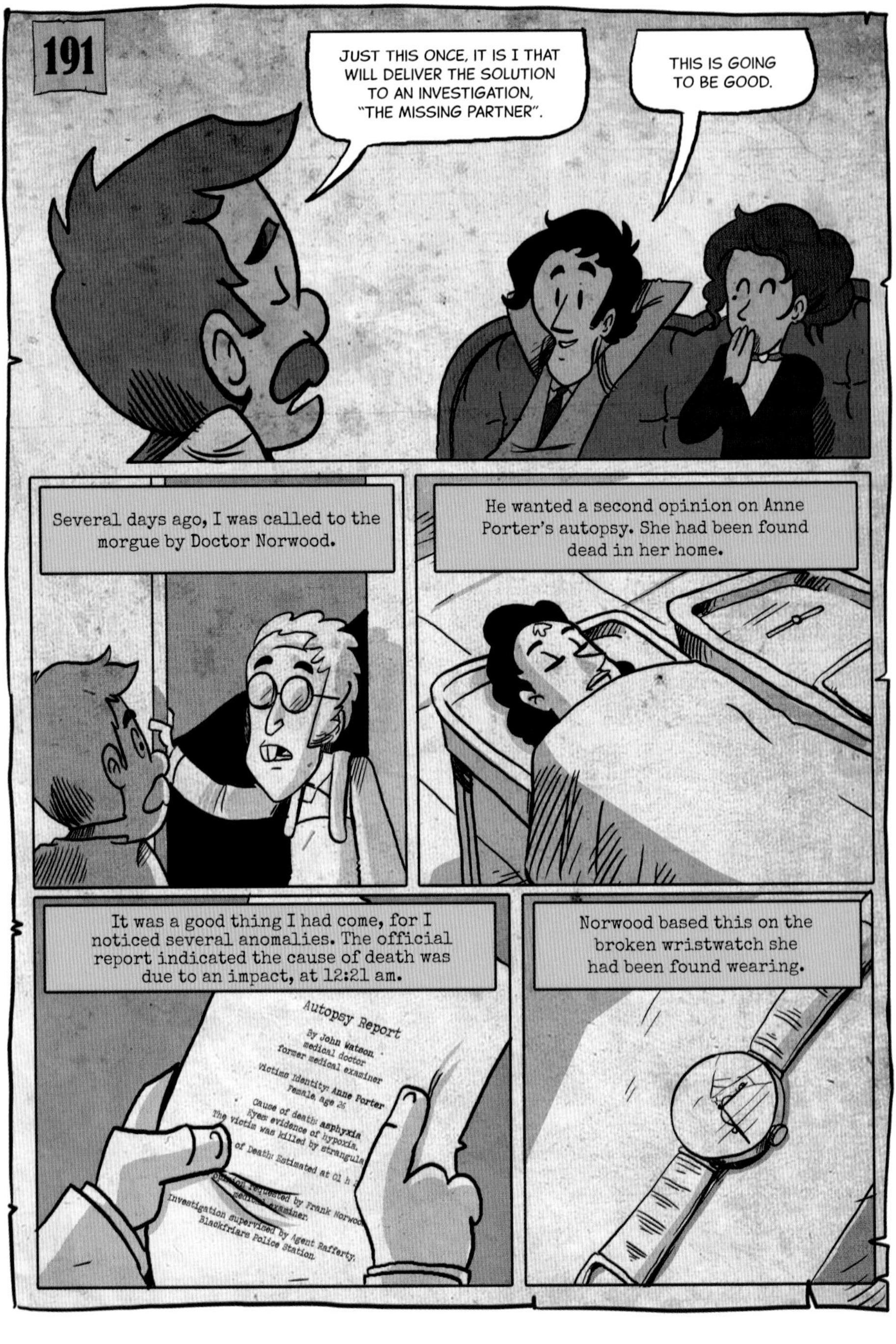
191
JUST THIS ONCE, IT IS I THAT WILL DELIVER THE SOLUTION TO AN INVESTIGATION, "THE MISSING PARTNER".
THIS IS GOING TO BE GOOD.
Several days ago, I was called to the morgue by Doctor Norwood.
He wanted a second opinion on Anne Porter's autopsy. She had been found dead in her home.
It was a good thing I had come, for I noticed several anomalies. The official report indicated the cause of death was due to an impact, at 12:21 am.
Autopsy Report
By John Watson,
medical doctor
former medical examiner
Victims Identity: Anne Porter
Female, age 26
Cause of death: asphyxia
Eyes: evidence of hypoxia.
The victim was killed by strangula
of Death: Estimated at 01 h
requested by Frank Norwoo
examiner.
Investigation supervised by Agent Rafferty,
Blackfriars Police Station.
Norwood based this on the broken wristwatch she had been found wearing.

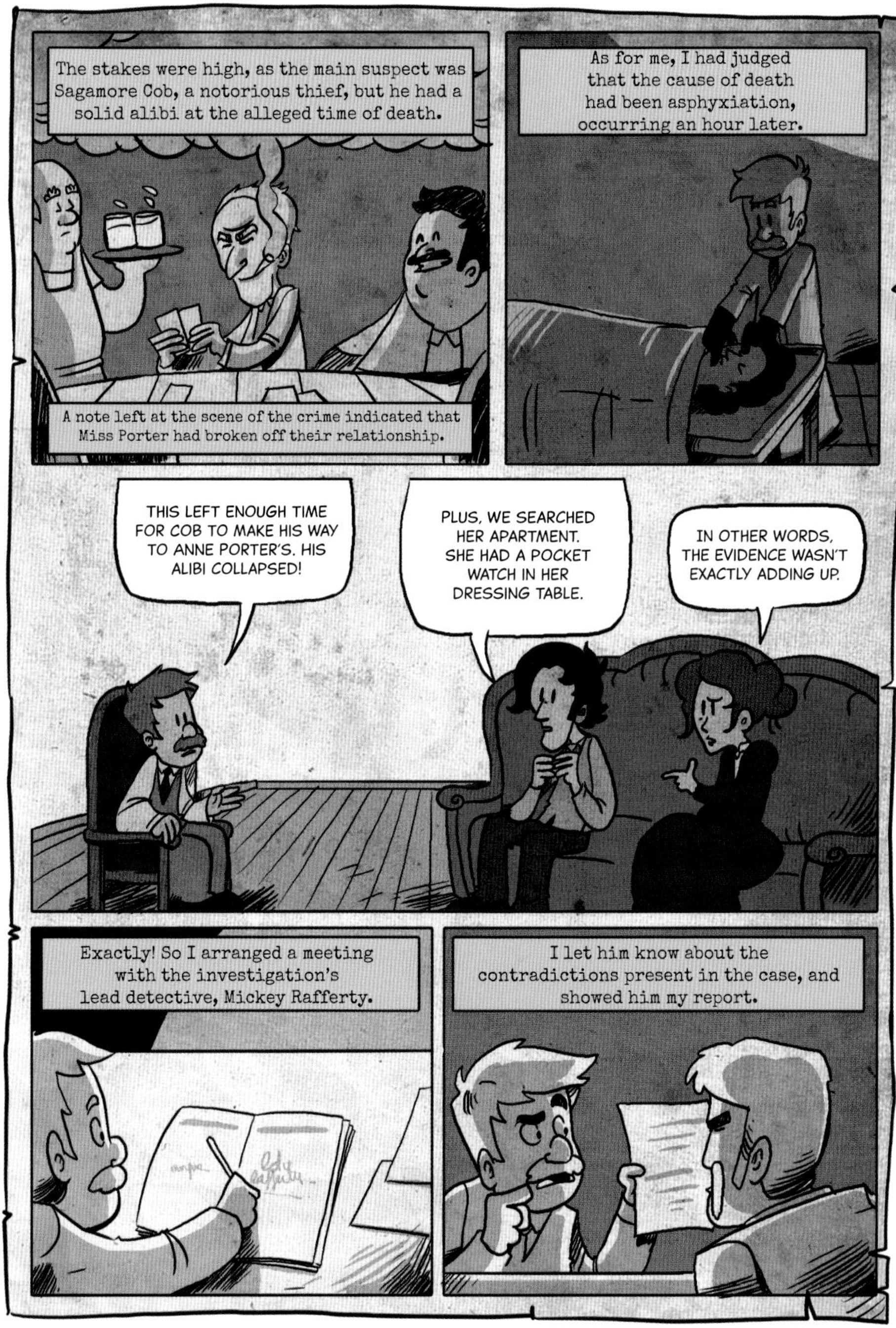
The stakes were high, as the main suspect was Sagamore Cob, a notorious thief, but he had a solid alibi at the alleged time of death.
A note left at the scene of the crime indicated that Miss Porter had broken off their relationship.
As for me, I had judged that the cause of death had been asphyxiation, occurring an hour later.
THIS LEFT ENOUGH TIME FOR COB TO MAKE HIS WAY TO ANNE PORTER'S. HIS ALIBI COLLAPSED!
PLUS, WE SEARCHED HER APARTMENT. SHE HAD A POCKET WATCH IN HER DRESSING TABLE.
IN OTHER WORDS, THE EVIDENCE WASN'T EXACTLY ADDING UP.
Exactly! So I arranged a meeting with the investigation's lead detective, Mickey Rafferty.
I let him know about the contradictions present in the case, and showed him my report.

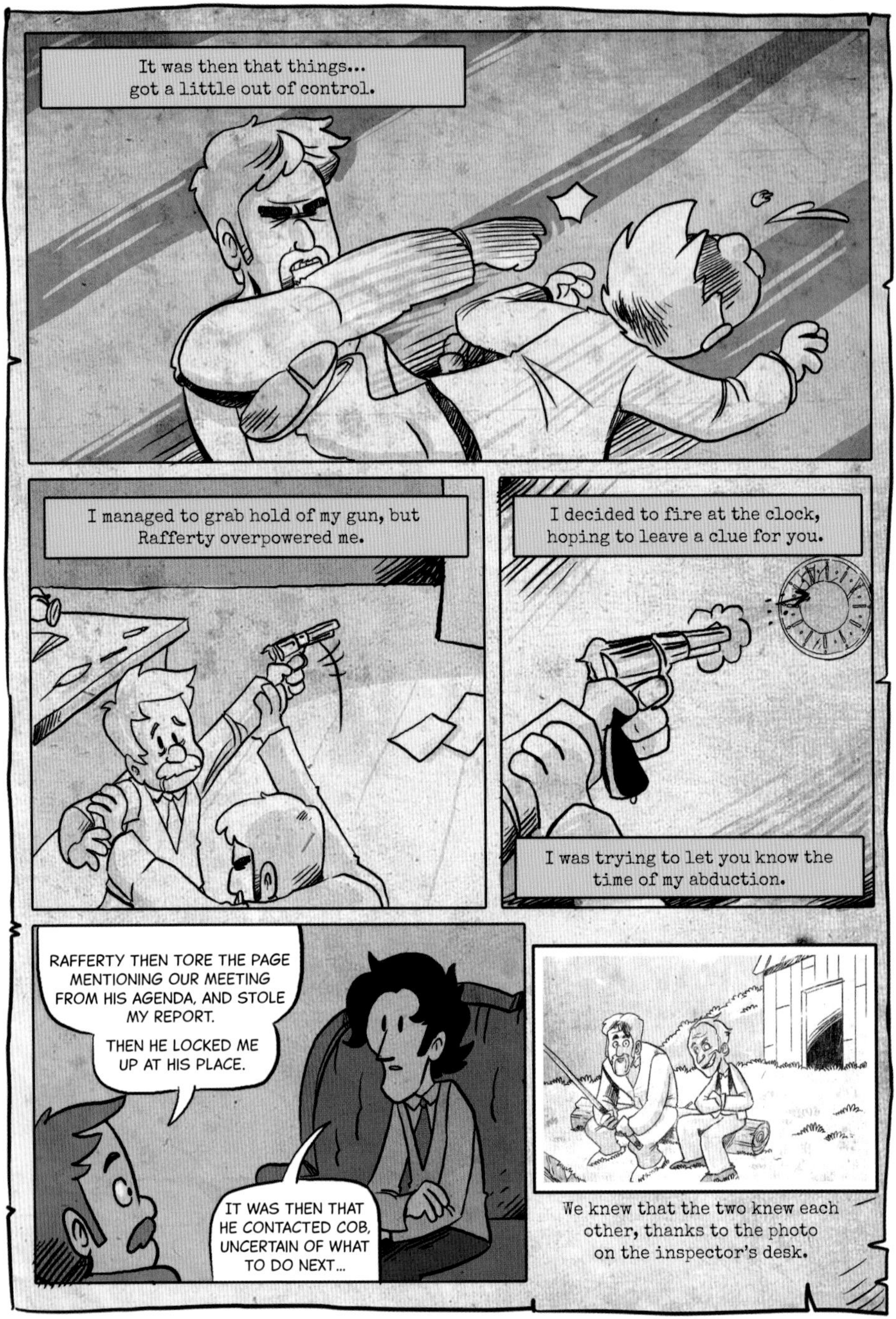

It was then that things...
got a little out of control.
I managed to grab hold of my gun, but Rafferty overpowered me.
I decided to fire at the clock, hoping to leave a clue for you.
I was trying to let you know the time of my abduction.
RAFFERTY THEN TORE THE PAGE MENTIONING OUR MEETING FROM HIS AGENDA, AND STOLE MY REPORT.
THEN HE LOCKED ME UP AT HIS PLACE.
IT WAS THEN THAT HE CONTACTED COB, UNCERTAIN OF WHAT TO DO NEXT...
We knew that the two knew each other, thanks to the photo on the inspector's desk.

SO RAFFERTY WAS TRYING TO PROTECT COB.

WE LEARNED LATER THAT THE *CROOK* WAS MAKING HIM SING. BUT YES, THAT'S IT.

Then Cob came looking for me.

As we left, he left a note for his "friend".

I retrieved the package from your place. I took it you-know-where.

By comparing the writing on the notes left at Anne Porter's place and on Rafferty's desk, it was clear that Cob was the one detaining me.

Should you be unable to mov... go way b...

I am deeply wounded by your decision.

S.C.

...eved the package fr... ... I took it you-know-where.

HE TIED ME UP IN HIS FISHING CABIN IN THE WOODS, WHERE I THOUGHT I WOULD SPEND MY LAST DAYS.

BUT HERE YOU ARE, SAFE AND SOUND, LIKE ALWAYS.

Who abducted Doctor Watson?
Mickey Rafferty.

What was their motive?
To keep him quiet.

Who was actually detaining him?
Sagamore Cob.

192

24. The morgue puzzle

1 2 3
4 5 6
7 8 9

"Press then twice down".
To be able to move down twice means the first number would have to be on the first row.
So 1,2,3.

There are three presses, so it must be a 3 digit number. Starting on the 3 is impossible, as you wouldn't be able go right after the second digit. Therefore, the answer has to be either 175 or 286. Seeing as frame 286 doesn't exist, the solution must be 175.

86. Watson's puzzle

Holmes will surely adore this one.
ABCDEFGHI
JKLMNOPQ
RSTUVWXYZ

If you complete the unfinished letters, you end up drawing the answer: the number 102.

89. The painter's puzzle

Victor,
I hid some money,
just in case.
Just solve the equation:
DIX - 394.
J.G.H.

DIX is a Roman numeral equal to 509.
And 509 - 394 is 115,
Which is the answer to the riddle.

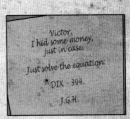

183. The doors puzzle

A
B

A + 3 + 2 x 2 - 6 x 11 - 4 ÷ 2
- 7 x 3 - 5 - 2 x 10 ÷ 2 B

The total is 160.

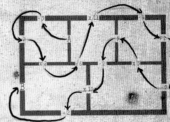

15, 17 and 19. The final puzzle.

These frames are positioned in this book the same as they are on Rafferty's desk.

When you fold the photo along the visible crease, the back of the photo and the frame beneath display the puzzle's solution: frame 101.

Scoring

Score 3 points per correct solution (correct sum)
Score 2 points per case where you discovered the
correct guilty party but one or more of the other
answers are incorrect
Score 1 point if you found Cob's cabin.

The Business Cards:
If you found
- between 10 and 19, score 1 point.
- between 20 and 29, score 2 points.
- 30 or more found, score 3 points.

What's your score?

This gives you a maximum score of 10.

If you played solo, a score of at least 7/10 gets you the
title of "London's Greatest Detective".

If you played with two players, compare your scores.
Whoever has the highest score earns the title of
"London's Greatest Detective".

194

The general index. Adler and Holmes can both use this index. It's simple: just go to the frame corresponding to the person or location you are interested in investigating.

General Index

To get the most out of your adventure, we recommend that you do not visit these frames "randomly". Wait until these names appear during your investigation before consulting the index and "discovering" them.

Need a drink?

THE RED CARPET BAR

Beers - Liqueurs - Absinthe

133

As a reminder, go here if you're lost.

THE CONTACTS OF IRENE ADLER

Irene Adler may consult two of her contacts during each investigation.

To do so, simply affix the number of the contact you wish to speak with to the number of the case you wish to ask about.

Use a '1' for the first case, "The Final Portrait".

Use a '2' for the second case, "The Missing Partner".

For example, to speak to Godfrey Norton about the first case, go to 21. To consult him regarding the second case, go to 22.

Your contacts are well informed on the details of your cases. If they speak of a person or place you aren't yet familiar with, it would be wise to research that lead.

Godfrey Norton 2

Godfrey is Irene Adler's husband. He is also a brilliant lawyer with a thorough understanding of both legal texts and the court system.

Wilhelm von Ormstein 4

Wilhelm von Ormstein is the King of Belgrave, and is currently visiting London. Although he and Irene have had their disputes, they've finally reconciled their differences. He is excellent counsel on subjects concerning royalty.

Olivia Norwood 6

Olivia Norwood is the head of cleaning and maintenance at Scotland Yard. For the right price, she'll listen to conversations through closed doors or rummage through files for you.

Candice Albani 8

Candice Albani is the prop master at London's Royal Opera House. Irene made her acquaintance while she was performing as a contralto at La Scala in Milan. Candice's specialty is in weapons and how they work.